Praise for *Building Recommendation Systems in Python and JAX*

Bryan and Hector have created something special here, introducing concepts that take most people years to learn within the RecSys domain and then providing clear code examples that put them into practice. I wish I had this book when I started out on my RecSys journey.

—*Even Oldridge, Director of Engineering,
Recommender Systems, NVIDIA*

This is a book I've been waiting for, making recommendation systems accessible using JAX. The only other thing you need is your laptop.

—*Shaked Zychlinski, former Head of
Recommendations at Lightricks*

Bryan and Hector have distilled decades of recommendation system advancements into a concise, yet practical guide. Bridging the gap between theory and application, this book is packed with easy-to-understand Python and JAX examples. This is an indispensable guide for RecSys practitioners at all levels, from novices to experts.

—*Eugene Yan, Applied Scientist, Amazon*

This book takes a holistic approach to building recommender systems, synthesizing math, code, systems design, and business application. It covers all the nuances that practitioners need to consider to implement real-world solutions. The intuitive examples using publicly available datasets enables the reader to turn abstract concepts into concrete learnings.

—*Eric Colson, AI Advisor, Former Chief Algorithms Officer at
Stitch Fix, Former VP of Data Science and Engineering at Netflix*

Recommender systems are among the most impactful ML systems ever deployed. This book brilliantly navigates the balance between principled modeling, clear code examples, and architectural best practices. A must read for practitioners aspiring to build real-world systems, not just train models.

—Jacopo Tagliabue, Co-founder of Bauplan, Adjunct Professor of ML Systems at NYU, Co-creator of RecList and evalRS

For years I've found there is a tremendous gap between recommendation systems as described in texts and as practiced in the field. Yee and Bischof's excellent *Building Recommendation Systems in Python and JAX* closes this gap and will make readers finally feel initiated into this vital area of data science.

—Will Kurt, AI Engineer and author of Bayesian Statistics the Fun Way *and* Get Programming with Haskell

This book is an essential resource for anyone interested in the information retrieval (IR) space. The authors take special care to do the incredibly important and nuanced work of preparing the reader to solve problems in this space. With this book as a reference, you will be able to think through how to set up the IR problem, think through the practical steps to take, and then get building.

—Eric Schles, Research Scientist, Johns Hopkins University

Building Recommendation Systems in Python and JAX
Hands-on Production Systems at Scale

Bryan Bischof and Hector Yee

Beijing · Boston · Farnham · Sebastopol · Tokyo

Building Recommendation Systems in Python and JAX

by Bryan Bischof and Hector Yee

Published by O'Reilly Media, Inc., 1005 Gravenstein Highway North, Sebastopol, CA 95472.

O'Reilly books may be purchased for educational, business, or sales promotional use. Online editions are also available for most titles (*http://oreilly.com*). For more information, contact our corporate/institutional sales department: 800-998-9938 or *corporate@oreilly.com*.

Acquisitions Editor: Nicole Butterfield	**Indexer:** Judith McConville
Development Editor: Jill Leonard	**Interior Designer:** David Futato
Production Editor: Aleeya Rahman	**Cover Designer:** Karen Montgomery
Copyeditor: Sharon Wilkey	**Illustrator:** Kate Dullea
Proofreader: Piper Editorial Consulting, LLC	

December 2023:   First Edition

Revision History for the First Edition

2023-12-04:   First Release

See *http://oreilly.com/catalog/errata.csp?isbn=9781492097990* for release details.

978-1-492-09799-0

[LSI]

Table of Contents

Part I.   Warming Up

Part II. Retrieval

Part III.   Ranking

Part IV.   Serving

Part V. The Future of Recs

Preface

How did you come to find this book? Did you see an ad for it on a website? Maybe a friend or mentor suggested it; or perhaps you saw a post on social media that referenced it. Could it be that you found it sitting on a shelf in a bookstore—a bookstore that your trusty maps app led you to? However you came to find it, you've almost certainly come to this book via a recommendation system.

Implementing and designing systems that provide suggestions to users is among the most popular and most essential applications of machine learning (ML) to any business. Whether you want to help your users find the best clothing to match their tastes, the most appealing items to buy from an online store, videos to enrich and entertain them, maximally engaging content to surface from their networks, or the news highlights they need to know on that day, recommendation systems provide the way.

Modern recommendation system designs are as diverse as the domains they serve. These systems consist of the computer software architectures to implement and execute product goals, in addition to the algorithmic components of ranking. Methods for ranking recommendations can come from traditional statistical learning algorithms, linear-algebraic inspirations, geometric considerations, and, of course, gradient-based methods. Just as the algorithmic methods are diverse, so too are the modeling and evaluation considerations for recommending: personalized ranking, search recommendations, sequence modeling, and the scoring for all of these are now need-to-know for the ML engineer working with recommendation systems.

 The abbreviation RecSys is often used by practitioners to describe the field of recommendation systems. Therefore, in this book, we use RecSys when referring to the field, and recommendation system when referring to what we build.

If you're an ML practitioner, you are probably aware of recommendation systems, and you may know one or two of the simplest modeling approaches and be able to speak intelligently about the relevant data structures and model architectures; however, RecSys frequently falls outside the core curriculum of data science and ML. Many senior data scientists with years of experience in the industry know little about actually building a recommendation system and may feel intimidated when the topic comes up. Despite drawing on similar foundations and skills as other ML problems, RecSys has a vibrant community with a fast-moving focus that can make it easy to relegate building recommendation systems to *other* data scientists who have already invested the time, or are willing to stay on top of the latest information.

The reason this book exists, is to break through those perceived barriers. Understanding recommendation systems at a practical level is not only useful for business cases requiring content to be served to users, but the underlying ideas of RecSys often bridge gaps between an incredibly diverse set of other types of ML. Take, for example, an article recommendation system that may utilize natural language processing (NLP) to find representations of the articles, sequential modeling to promote longer engagement, and contextual components to allow user queries to guide results. If you're approaching the field from a purely academic interest, no matter what aspects of mathematics you're interested in, sooner or later, there appears a link or application in RecSys!

Finally, if connections to other fields, applications of nearly all of mathematics, or the obvious business utility *aren't* enough to get you interested in RecSys, the stunning cutting-edge technology might: RecSys is at and beyond the forefront of ML at all times. One benefit of having obvious revenue impact is that companies and practitioners need to always be pushing the boundaries of what is possible and how they go about it. The most advanced deep learning architectures and best code infrastructures are brought to bear on this field. That's hardly a surprise when you consider that at the heart of four of the five letters in FAANG—which stands for Meta (formerly Facebook), Apple, Amazon, Netflix, and Google—lies one or many recommendation systems.[1]

As a practitioner, you'll need to understand how to do the following:

- Take your data and business problem and frame it as a RecSys problem
- Identify the essential data to get started building a RecSys

---

[1] Some may quibble that Apple also has core recommendation systems at the heart of its company. While it's certainly true that the App Store forms a crucial strategic product for the company, we remain conservative in our four-out-of-five assessment and say that recommendation systems are not Apple's primary revenue-generating capability.

- Determine the appropriate models for your RecSys problem and how should you evaluate them.

- Implement, train, test, and deploy the aforementioned models

- Track metrics to ensure that your system is working as planned

- Incrementally improve your system as you learn more about your users, products, and business case

This book illustrates the core concepts and examples necessary to complete these steps, whatever the industry or scale. We'll guide you through the math, ideas, and implementation details for building recommendation systems—whether it's your first or your fiftieth. We'll show you how to build these systems with Python and JAX.

If you're not yet familiar, JAX is a Python framework from Google that seeks to make autodifferentiation and functional programming paradigms first-class objects. Additionally, it uses a NumPy API style especially convenient for ML practitioners from a variety of backgrounds.

We will show code examples and architecture models that capture the essential concepts necessary and provide the way to scale these systems to production applications.

Conventions Used in This Book

The following typographical conventions are used in this book:

Italic
    Indicates new terms, URLs, email addresses, filenames, and file extensions.

`Constant width`
    Used for program listings, as well as within paragraphs to refer to program elements such as variable or function names, databases, data types, environment variables, statements, and keywords.

`Constant width bold`
    Shows commands or other text that should be typed literally by the user.

`Constant width italic`
    Shows text that should be replaced with user-supplied values or by values determined by context.

 This element signifies a tip or suggestion.

This element signifies a general note.

 This element indicates a warning or caution.

Using Code Examples

The included code snippets reference notebooks that will run on moderate-size and, in most cases, free resources. To facilitate easy experimentation and exploration we provide the code via Google Colab notebooks.

Supplemental material (code examples, exercises, etc.) is available for download at ESRecsys on GitHub (*https://github.com/BBischof/ESRecsys/*).

If you have a technical question or a problem using the code examples, please send email to *bookquestions@oreilly.com*.

This book is here to help you get your job done. In general, if example code is offered with this book, you may use it in your programs and documentation. You do not need to contact us for permission unless you're reproducing a significant portion of the code. For example, writing a program that uses several chunks of code from this book does not require permission. Selling or distributing examples from O'Reilly books does require permission. Answering a question by citing this book and quoting example code does not require permission. Incorporating a significant amount of example code from this book into your product's documentation does require permission.

We appreciate, but generally do not require, attribution. An attribution usually includes the title, author, publisher, and ISBN. For example: "*Building Recommendation Systems in Python and JAX* by Bryan Bischof and Hector Yee. Copyright 2024 Bryan Bischof and Resonant Intelligence LLC, 978-1-492-09799-0."

If you feel your use of code examples falls outside fair use or the permission given above, feel free to contact us at *permissions@oreilly.com*.

O'Reilly Online Learning

 For more than 40 years, *O'Reilly Media* has provided technology and business training, knowledge, and insight to help companies succeed.

Our unique network of experts and innovators share their knowledge and expertise through books, articles, and our online learning platform. O'Reilly's online learning platform gives you on-demand access to live training courses, in-depth learning paths, interactive coding environments, and a vast collection of text and video from O'Reilly and 200+ other publishers. For more information, visit *http://oreilly.com*.

How to Contact Us

Please address comments and questions concerning this book to the publisher:

O'Reilly Media, Inc.
1005 Gravenstein Highway North
Sebastopol, CA 95472
800-889-8969 (in the United States or Canada)
707-829-7019 (international or local)
707-829-0104 (fax)
support@oreilly.com
https://www.oreilly.com/about/contact.html

We have a web page for this book, where we list errata, examples, and any additional information. You can access this page at *https://oreil.ly/build_rec_sys_python_jax*.

For news and information about our books and courses, visit *https://oreilly.com*.

Find us on LinkedIn: *https://linkedin.com/company/oreilly-media*

Follow us on Twitter: *https://twitter.com/oreillymedia*

Watch us on YouTube: *https://youtube.com/oreillymedia*

Acknowledgments

Hector would like to thank his husband, Donald, for his loving support during the writing of this book and for the snacks his sister Serena sends all the time. He would also like to dedicate this book to his relatives who have passed. A big thank you goes to the Google reviewers Ed Chi, Courtney Hohne, Sally Goldman, Richa Nigam, Mingliang Jiang, and Anselm Levskaya. Thanks to Bryan Hughes for reviewing the Wikipedia code.

Bryan would like to thank his colleagues from Stitch Fix, where he learned many of the key ideas in this book—in particular, Ian Horn's patient guidance on transfer learning, Dr. Molly Davies's mentorship on experimentation and effect estimates, Mark Weiss's deep partnership on understanding the relationship between availability and recommendations, Dr. Reza Sohrabi's introduction to transformers, Dr. Xi Chen's encouragement on GNNs for recs, and Dr. Leland McInnes for his careful advice on dimension reduction and approximate nearest neighbors. Bryan benefitted a lot from conversations with Dr. Natalia Gardiol, Dr. Daniel Fleischman, Dr. Andrew Ho, Jason Liu, Dr. Dan Marthaler, Dr. Chris Moody, Oz Raza, Dr. Anna Schneider, Ujjwal Sarin, Agnieszka Szefer, Dr. Daniel Tasse, Diyang Tang, Zach Winston, and others he has almost certainly forgotten. Outside of his incredible Stitch Fix colleagues, he especially wants to thank Dr. Eric Bunch, Dr. Lee Goerl, Dr. Will Chernoff, Leo Rosenberg, and Janu Verma for collaboration over the years. Dr. Brian Amadio as an excellent colleague and originally suggested that he write this book. Dr. Even Oldridge for encouraging him to actually try it. Eugene Yan and Karl Higley—neither of whom he's met but has been significantly inspired by. He'd like to thank Dr. Zhongzhu Lin and Dr. Alexander Rosenberg, who both had formative impacts on his career. Cianna Salvatora, who assisted in early literature review, and Valentina Besprozvannykh, who greatly assisted in reading early draft notes and providing guidance.

Both authors thank Tobias Zwingmann, Ted Dunning, Vicki Boykis, Eric Schles, Shaked Zychlinski, and Will Kurt, who spend much time giving careful technical feedback on book manuscripts—without which this book would have been incomprehensible. Rebecca Novack, who harangued us into signing up for this project. And Jill Leonard, who removed nearly 100 erroneous instances of the word *utilize* from the manuscript, and who offered an incredible amount of patient partnership on the book text.

## PART I

Warming Up

How do we get all the data in the right place to train a recommendation system, and for real-time inference?

So, you've decided to dive into the world of recommendation systems! Are you hoping to suggest just the right thing based on users' quirky preferences across a vast sea of choices? If so, you've set quite the challenge for yourself! On the surface, these systems might seem straightforward: if User A and User B have similar tastes, then maybe what A likes, B will too. But, as with all things that seem simple, there's a depth that's waiting to be explored.

How do we capture the essence of a user's history and feed it into a model? Where do we stash this model so it's ready to serve up suggestions on the fly? And how do we make sure it doesn't suggest something that steps out of bounds or goes against the business rulebook? Collaborative filtering is our starting point, a guiding light. But there's an entire universe beyond it that makes these systems tick, and together, we're going to navigate it.

## CHAPTER 1

Introduction

Recommendation systems are integral to the development of the internet that we know today and are a central function of emerging technology companies. Beyond the search ranking that opened the web's breadth to everyone, the new and exciting movies all your friends are watching, or the most relevant ads that companies pay top dollar to show you lie more applications of recommendation systems every year. The addictive For You page from TikTok, the Discover Weekly playlist by Spotify, board suggestions on Pinterest, and Apple's App Store are all hot technologies enabled by the recommendation systems. These days, sequential transformer models, multimodal representations, and graph neural nets are among the brightest areas of R&D in machine learning (ML)—all being put to use in recommendation systems.

Ubiquity of any technology often prompts questions of how the technology works, why it has become so common, and if we can get in on the action. For recommendation systems, the *how* is quite complicated. We'll need to understand the geometry of taste, and how only a little bit of interaction from a user can provide us a *GPS signal* in that abstract space. You'll see how to quickly gather a great set of candidates and how to refine them to a cohesive set of recommendations. Finally, you'll learn how to evaluate your recommender, build the endpoint that serves inference, and log about its behavior.

We will formulate variants of the core problem to be solved by recommendation systems but, ultimately, the motivating problem framing is as follows:

> Given a collection of things that may be recommended, choose an ordered few for the current context and user that best match according to a certain objective.

Key Components of a Recommendation System

As we increase complexity and sophistication, let's keep in mind the components of our system. We will use *string diagrams* to keep track of our components, but in the literature these diagrams are presented in a variety of ways.

We will identify and build on three core components of recommendation systems: the collector, ranker, and server.

Collector

The collector's role is to know what is in the collection of things that may be recommended, and the necessary features or attributes of those things. Note that this collection is often a subset based on context or state.

Ranker

The ranker's role is to take the collection provided by the collector and order some or all of its elements, according to a model for the context and user.

Server

The server's role is to take the ordered subset provided by the ranker, ensure that the necessary data schema is satisfied—including essential business logic—and return the requested number of recommendations.

Take, for example, a hospitality scenario with a waiter:

> When you sit down at your table, you look at the menu, unsure of what you should order. You ask the waiter, "What do you think I should order for dessert?"
>
> The waiter checks their notes and says, "We're out of the key lime pie, but people really like our banana cream pie. If you like pomegranate, we make pom ice cream from scratch; and it's hard to go wrong with the donut a la mode—it's our most popular dessert."

In this short exchange, the waiter first serves as a collector: identifying the desserts on the menu, accommodating current inventory conditions, and preparing to talk about the characteristics of the desserts by checking their notes.

Next, the waiter serves as a ranker; they mention items high scoring in popularity (banana cream pie and donut a la mode) as well as a contextually high match item based on the patron's features (if they like pomegranate).

Finally, the waiter serves the recommendations verbally, including both explanatory features of their algorithm and multiple choices.

While this seems a bit cartoonish, remember to ground discussions of recommendation systems in real-world applications. One of the advantages of working in RecSys is that inspiration is always nearby.

Simplest Possible Recommenders

We've established the components of a recommender, but to really make this practical, we need to see this in action. While much of the book is dedicated to practical recommendation systems, first we'll start with a toy and scaffold from there.

The Trivial Recommender

The absolute simplest recommender is not very interesting but can still be demonstrated in the framework. It's called *the trivial recommender* (*TR*) because it contains virtually no logic:

```
def get_trivial_recs() -> Optional[List[str]]:
    item_id = random.randint(0, MAX_ITEM_INDEX)

    if get_availability(item_id):
        return [item_id]
    return None
```

Notice that this recommender may return either a specific item_id or None. Also observe that this recommender takes no arguments, and MAX_ITEM_INDEX is referencing a variable out of scope. Software principles ignored, let's think about the three components:

Collector

A random item_id is generated. The TR collects by checking the availability of item_id. We could argue that having access to item_id is also part of the collector's responsibility. Conditional upon the availability, the collection of recommendable things is either [item_id] or None (*recall that None is a collection in the set-theoretic sense*).

Ranker

The TR ranks with a no-op; i.e., the ranking of 1 or 0 objects in a collection is the identity function on that collection, so we merely do nothing and move on to the next step.

Server

The TR serves recommendations by its return statements. The only schema that's been specified in this example is that the return type is Optional [List[str]].

This recommender, which is not interesting or useful, provides a skeleton that we will add to as we develop further.

Most-Popular-Item Recommender

The *most-popular-item recommender* (MPIR) is the simplest recommender that contains any utility. You probably won't want to build applications around it, but it's useful in tandem with other components in addition to providing a basis for further development.

An MPIR works just as it says; it returns the most popular items:

```
def get_item_popularities() -> Optional[Dict[str, int]]:
    ...
        # Dict of pairs: (item-identifier, count times item chosen)
        return item_choice_counts
    return None

def get_most_popular_recs(max_num_recs: int) -> Optional[List[str]]:
    items_popularity_dict = get_item_popularities()
    if items_popularity_dict:
        sorted_items = sorted(
            items_popularity_dict.items(),
            key=lambda item: item[1]),
            reverse=True,
        )
        return [i[0] for i in sorted_items][:max_num_recs]
    return None
```

Here we assume that `get_item_popularities` has knowledge of all available items and the number of times they've been chosen.

This recommender attempts to return the k most popular items available. While simple, this is a useful recommender that serves as a great place to start when building a recommendation system. Additionally, we will see this example return over and over, because other recommenders use this core and iteratively improve the internal components.

Let's look at the three components of our system again:

Collector

The MPIR first makes a call to `get_item_popularities` that—via database or memory access—knows which items are available and how many times they've been selected. For convenience, we assume that the items are returned as a dictionary, with keys given by the string that identifies the item, and values indicating the number of times that item has been chosen. We implicitly assume here that items not appearing in this list are not available.

Ranker

> Here we see our first simple ranker: ranking by sorting on values. Because the collector has organized our data such that the values of the dictionary are the counts, we use the Python built-in sorting function `sorted`. Note that we use `key` to indicate that we wish to sort by the second element of the tuples—in this case, equivalent to sorting by values—and we send the `reverse` flag to make our sort descending.

Server

> Finally, we need to satisfy our API schema, which is again provided via the return type hint: `Optional[List[str]]`. This wants the return type to be the nullable list of item-identifier strings that we're recommending, so we use a list comprehension to grab the first element of the tuples. But wait! Our function has this `max_num_recs` field—what might that be doing there? Of course, this is suggesting that our API schema is looking for no greater than `max_num_recs` in the response. We handle this via the slice operator, but note that our return is between 0 and `max_num_recs` results.

Consider the possibilities at your fingertips equipped with the MPIR; recommending customers' favorite item in each top-level category could make for a simple but useful first stab at recommendations for ecommerce. The most popular video of the day may make for a good home-page experience on your video site.

A Gentle Introduction to JAX

Since this book has *JAX* in the title, we will provide a gentle introduction to JAX here. Its official documentation can be found on the JAX website (*https://jax.readthe docs.io/en/latest/*).

JAX is a framework for writing mathematical code in Python that is just-in-time (JIT) compiled. JIT compilation allows the same code to run on CPUs, GPUs, and TPUs. This makes it easy to write performant code that takes advantage of the parallel-processing power of vector processors.

Additionally, one of the design philosophies of JAX is to support tensors and gradients as core concepts, making it an ideal tool for ML systems that utilize gradient-based learning on tensor-shaped data. The easiest way to play with JAX is probably via Google Colab (*https://colab.research.google.com/*), which is a hosted Python notebook on the web.

Basic Types, Initialization, and Immutability

Let's start by learning about JAX types. We'll construct a small, three-dimensional vector in JAX and point out some differences between JAX and NumPy:

```
import jax.numpy as jnp
import numpy as np

x = jnp.array([1.0, 2.0, 3.0], dtype=jnp.float32)

print(x)
[1. 2. 3.]

print(x.shape)
(3,)

print(x[0])
1.0

x[0] = 4.0
TypeError: '<class 'jaxlib.xla_extension.ArrayImpl'>'
object does not support item assignment. JAX arrays are immutable.
```

JAX's interface is mostly similar to that of NumPy. We import JAX's version of NumPy as jnp to distinguish it from NumPy (np) by convention so that we know which version of a mathematical function we want to use. This is because sometimes we might want to run code on a vector processor like a GPU or TPU that we can use JAX for, or we might prefer to run some code on a CPU in NumPy.

The first point to notice is that JAX arrays have types. The typical float type is float32, which uses 32 bits to represent a floating-point number. Other types exist, such as float64, which has greater precision, and float16, which is a half-precision type that usually only runs on some GPUs.

The other point to note is that JAX tensors have shape. This is usually a tuple, so (3,) means a three-dimensional vector along the first axis. A matrix has two axes, and a tensor has three or more axes.

Now we come to places where JAX differs from NumPy. It is really important to pay attention to "JAX—The Sharp Bits" (*https://oreil.ly/qqcFM*) to understand these differences. JAX's philosophy is about speed and purity. By making functions pure (without side effects) and by making data immutable, JAX is able to make some guarantees to the underlying accelerated linear algebra (XLA) library that it uses to talk to GPUs. JAX guarantees that these functions applied to data can be run in parallel and have deterministic results without side effects, and thus XLA is able to compile these functions and make them run much faster than if they were run just on NumPy.

You can see that modifying one element in x results in an error. JAX would prefer that the array x is replaced rather than modified. One way to modify elements in an array is to do it in NumPy rather than JAX and convert NumPy arrays to JAX—for example, using jnp.array(np_array)—when the subsequent code needs to run fast on immutable data.

Indexing and Slicing

Another important skill to learn is that of indexing and slicing arrays:

```
x = jnp.array([[1, 2, 3], [4, 5, 6], [7, 8, 9]], dtype=jnp.int32)

# Print the whole matrix.
print(x)
[[1 2 3]
 [4 5 6]
 [7 8 9]]

# Print the first row.
print(x[0])
[1 2 3]


# Print the last row.
print(x[-1])
[7 8 9]

# Print the second column.
print(x[:, 1])
[2 5 8]

# Print every other element
print(x[::2, ::2])
[[1 3]
 [7 9]]
```

NumPy introduced indexing and slicing operations that allow us to access different parts of an array. In general, the notation follows a `start:end:stride` convention. The first element indicates where to start, the second indicates where to end (but not inclusive), and the stride indicates the number of elements to skip over. The syntax is similar to that of the Python `range` function.

Slicing allows us to access views of a tensor elegantly. Slicing and indexing are important skills to master, especially when we start to manipulate tensors in batches, which we typically do to make the most use of acceleration hardware.

Broadcasting

Broadcasting is another feature of NumPy and JAX to be aware of. When a binary operation such as addition or multiplication is applied to two tensors of different sizes, the tensor with axes of size 1 is lifted up in rank to match that of the larger-sized tensor. For example, if a tensor of shape (3,3) is multiplied by a tensor of shape (3,1), the rows of the second tensor are duplicated before the operation so that it looks like a tensor of shape (3,3):

```
x = jnp.array([[1, 2, 3], [4, 5, 6], [7, 8, 9]], dtype=jnp.int32)

# Scalar broadcasting.
y = 2 * x
print(y)
[[ 2  4  6]
 [ 8 10 12]
 [14 16 18]]

# Vector broadcasting. Axes with shape 1 are duplicated.
vec = jnp.reshape(jnp.array([0.5, 1.0, 2.0]), [3, 1])
y = vec * x
print(y)
[[ 0.5  1.   1.5]
 [ 4.   5.   6. ]
 [14.  16.  18. ]]

vec = jnp.reshape(vec, [1, 3])
y = vec * x
print(y)
[[ 0.5  2.   6. ]
 [ 2.   5.  12. ]
 [ 3.5  8.  18. ]]
```

The first case is the simplest, that of scalar multiplication. The scalar is multiplied throughout the matrix. In the second case, we have a vector of shape (3,1) multiplying the matrix. The first row is multiplied by 0.5, the second row is multiplied by 1.0, and the third row is multiplied by 2.0. However, if the vector has been reshaped to (1,3), the columns are multiplied by the successive entries of the vector instead.

Random Numbers

Along with JAX's philosophy of pure functions comes its particular way of handling random numbers. Because pure functions do not cause side effects, a random-number generator cannot modify the random number seed, unlike other random-number generators. Instead, JAX deals with random-number keys whose state is updated explicitly:

```
import jax.random as random

key = random.PRNGKey(0)
x = random.uniform(key, shape=[3, 3])
print(x)
[[0.35490513 0.60419905 0.4275843 ]
 [0.23061597 0.6735498  0.43953657]
 [0.25099766 0.27730572 0.7678207 ]]

key, subkey = random.split(key)
x = random.uniform(key, shape=[3, 3])
print(x)
```

```
[[0.0045197  0.5135027  0.8613342 ]
 [0.06939673 0.93825936 0.85599923]
 [0.706004   0.50679076 0.6072922 ]]

y = random.uniform(subkey, shape=[3, 3])
print(y)
[[0.34896135 0.48210478 0.02053976]
 [0.53161216 0.48158717 0.78698325]
 [0.07476437 0.04522789 0.3543167 ]]
```

JAX first requires you to create a random-number key from a seed. This key is then passed into random-number generation functions like uniform to create random numbers in the 0 to 1 range.

To create more random numbers, however, JAX requires that you split the key into two parts: a new key to generate other keys, and a subkey to generate new random numbers. This allows JAX to deterministically and reliably reproduce random numbers even when many parallel operations are calling the random-number generator. We just split a key into as many parallel operations as needed, and the random numbers resulting are now randomly distributed but also reproducible. This is a nice property when you want to reproduce experiments reliably.

Just-in-Time Compilation

JAX starts to diverge from NumPy in terms of execution speed when we start using JIT compilation. JITing code—transforming the code to be compiled just in time— allows the same code to run on CPUs, GPUs, or TPUs:

```
import jax

x = random.uniform(key, shape=[2048, 2048]) - 0.5

def my_function(x):
  x = x @ x
  return jnp.maximum(0.0, x)

%timeit my_function(x).block_until_ready()
302 ms ± 9 ms per loop (mean ± std. dev. of 7 runs, 1 loop each)

my_function_jitted = jax.jit(my_function)

%timeit my_function_jitted(x).block_until_ready()
294 ms ± 5.45 ms per loop (mean ± std. dev. of 7 runs, 1 loop each)
```

The JITed code is not that much faster on a CPU but will be dramatically faster on a GPU or TPU backend. Compilation also carries some overhead when the function is called the first time, which can skew the timing of the first call. Functions that can be JITed have restrictions, such as mostly calling JAX operations inside and having restrictions on loop operations. Variable-length loops trigger frequent recompilations. The "Just-in-Time Compilation with JAX" documentation (*https://oreil.ly/c8ywT*) covers a lot of the nuances of getting functions to JIT compile.

Summary

While we haven't done much math yet, we have gotten to the point where we can begin providing recommendations and implementing deeper logic into these components. We'll start doing things that look like ML soon enough.

So far, we have defined what a recommendation problem is, set up the core architecture of our recommendation system—the collector, the ranker, and the server—and shown a couple of trivial recommenders to illustrate how the pieces come together.

Next we'll explain the core relationship that recommendation systems seek to exploit: the user-item matrix. This matrix lets us build a model of personalization that will lead to ranking.

## CHAPTER 2

User-Item Ratings and Framing the Problem

If you were asked to curate the selection for a cheese plate at a local café, you might start with your favorites. You might also spend a bit of time asking for your friends' favorites. Before you order a large stock in these cheeses for the café, you would probably want to run a small experiment—maybe asking a group of friends to taste your selections and tell you their preferences.

In addition to receiving your friends' feedback, you'd also learn about your friends and the cheeses. You'd learn which kinds of cheeses your friends like and which friends have similar tastes. You can also learn which cheeses are the most popular and which cheeses are liked by the same people.

This data would start to give you hints about your first cheese recommender. In this chapter, we'll talk about how to turn this idea into the right stuff for a recommendation system. By way of this example, we'll discuss one of the underlying notions of a recommender: how to predict a user's affinity for things they've never seen.

The User-Item Matrix

It's extremely common to hear those who work on recommendation systems talk about matrices, and in particular the user-item matrix. While linear algebra is deep, both mathematically and as it applies to RecSys, we will begin with simple relationships.

Before we get to the matrix forms, let's write down some binary relationships between a set of users and a set of items. For the sake of this example, think of a group of five friends (mysteriously named *A, B, C, D, E*) and a blind cheese tasting where of four cheeses (*gouda, chèvre, emmentaler, brie*). The friends are asked to rate the cheeses, 1–4:

1. *A* starts, "OK, I really enjoy *gouda*, so give that a 5; *chèvre* and *emmentaler* are yummy too, 4; and *brie* is awful, 1."

2. *B* replies, "What?! *brie* is my favorite! 4.5! *chèvre* and *emmentaler* are fine, 3; and *gouda* is just OK, 2."

3. *C* gives ratings of 3, 2, 3, and 4, respectively.

4. *D* gives 4, 4, 5, but we run out of *brie* before *D* can try it.

5. *E* starts to not feel well, and tries only *gouda*, giving it a 3.

The first thing you may notice is that such expository writing is a bit tedious to read and parse. Let's summarize these results in a convenient table (Table 2-1):

Table 2-1. Cheeses and ratings

Cheese taster	Gouda	Chèvre	Emmentaler	Brie
A	5	4	4	1
B	2	3	3	4.5
C	3	2	3	4
D	4	4	5	-
E	3	-	-	-

Your first instinct may be to write this in a form more appropriate for computers. You might create a collection of lists:

$A : [5, 4, 4, 1]$
$B : [2, 3, 3, 4.5]$
$C : [3, 2, 3, 4]$
$D : [4, 4, 5, -]$
$E : [3, -, -, -]$

This may work in some scenarios, but you might want to more clearly indicate the positional meaning in each list. You could simply visualize this data with a heatmap (Figure 2-1):

```
import seaborn as sns

_ = np.nan
scores = np.array([[5,4,4,1],
    [2,3,3,4.5],
    [3,2,3,4],
    [4,4,5,_],
    [3,_,_,_]])
sns.heatmap(
    scores,
    annot=True,
    fmt=".1f",
    xticklabels=['Gouda', 'Chevre', 'Emmentaler', 'Brie',],
    yticklabels=['A','B','C','D','E',]
)
```

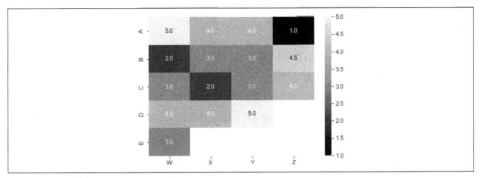

Figure 2-1. Cheese ratings matrix

As we observe datasets with huge numbers of users or items, and with more and more sparsity, we will need to employ a data structure more well suited to representing only the necessary data. A variety of so-called *dense representations* exists, but for now we will use the simplest form: tuples of user_id, item_id, and rating. In practice, the structure is often a dictionary with indices provided by the IDs.

Dense and Sparse Representations

Two types of structures for these kinds of data are dense and sparse representations. Loosely, a *sparse representation* is one such that a datum exists for each nontrivial observation. A *dense representation* always contains a datum for each possibility even when trivial (null or zero).

Let's see what this data looks like as a dictionary:

```
'indices': [
  (0,0),(0,1),(0,2),(0,3),
  (1,0),(1,1),(1,2),(1,3),
  (2,0),(2,1),(2,2),(2,3),
  (3,0),(3,1),(3,2),
  (4,0)
]
'values': [
  5,4,4,1,
  2,3,3,4.5,
  3,2,3,4,
  4,4,5,
  3
]
```

A few natural questions emerge:

1. What's the most popular cheese? From the observations so far, it's looking like *emmentaler* is potentially the favorite, but *E* didn't try *emmentaler*.

2. Would *D* like *brie*? It seems to be a contentious cheese.

3. If you were asked to buy only two cheeses, which should you buy to best satisfy everyone?

This example and associated questions are intentionally simple, but the point is clear that this matrix representation is at least convenient for capturing these ratings.

What may not be obvious is that beyond the convenience of this data visualization is the mathematical utility of this representation. Question 2 suggests an inherent RecSys problem: "predict how much a user will like an item they haven't seen." This question may also be recognizable as a problem from a linear algebra class: "How can we fill in unknown elements of a matrix from the ones we know?" This is called *matrix completion.*

The back-and-forth between creating user experiences that capture their needs and the mathematical formulations to model this data and needs is at the heart of recommendation systems.

User-User Versus Item-Item Collaborative Filtering

Before we dive into the linear algebra, let's consider the purely data science perspective called *collaborative filtering* (*CF*), a term originally used by David Goldberg et al. in their 1992 paper "Using Collaborative Filtering to Weave an Information Tapestry" (*https://oreil.ly/Nd3oe*).

The underlying idea of CF is that those with similar tastes help others to know what they like without having to try it themselves. The *collaboration* terminology was originally intended to mean among similar-taste users, and *filtering* was originally intended to mean filtering out choices people will not like.

You can think of this CF strategy in two ways:

- Two users with similar tastes will continue to have similar tastes.
- Two items with similar user fans will continue to be popular with other users who are similar to those fans.

These may sound identical, but they appear differently in the mathematical interpretations. At a high level, the difference is in deciding which kind of similarity your recommender should prioritize: user similarity or item similarity.

If you prioritize *user similarity*, then to provide a recommendation for a user *A*, you find a similar user *B* and then choose a recommendation from *B*'s list of liked content that *A* hasn't seen yet.

If you prioritize *item similarity*, then to provide a recommendation for a user *A*, you find an item that *A* liked, *chèvre*, and then you find an item similar to *chèvre* that *A* hasn't seen, *emmentaler*, and recommend it for *A*.

Later we will dive deeper into similarity, but let's quickly link these ideas to our preceding discussion. *Similar users* are rows of the user-item matrix that are similar as vectors; *similar items* are columns of the user-item matrix that are similar as vectors.

Vector Similarity

Dot product similarity is more precisely defined in Chapter 10. For now, consider similarity to be computed by normalizing the vectors and then taking their cosine similarity. Given entities of any kind that you've associated to vectors (lists of numbers), *vector similarity* compares which entities are most alike with respect to the characteristics captured by those lists of numbers (called the *latent space*).

The Netflix Challenge

In 2006, Netflix kicked off an online competition called the Netflix Prize. This competition challenged teams to improve on the performance of Netflix CF algorithms on a dataset released as open source by the company. While such a competition is common today via websites like Kaggle or conference, at that time, it was very exciting and novel for those interested in RecSys.

The competition consisted of several intermediate rounds awarding a Progress Prize and the final Netflix Prize awarded in 2009. The data provided was a collection of 2,817,131 triples consisting of (user, movie, date_rated). And half of these additionally included the rating itself. Notice that as in our preceding example, the user-item information is nearly enough to specify the problem. In this particular dataset, the date was provided. Later, we will dig into how time might be a factor, and in particular, for sequential recommendation systems.

The stakes were quite high in this competition. Requirements for beating the internal performance were a 10% increase in root mean square error (RMSE); we will discuss this loss function later. And the spoils added up to over $1.1 million. The final winners were BellKor's Pragmatic Chaos (which incidentally won the two previous Progress Prizes) with a test RMSE of 0.8567. In the end, only a 20-minute earlier submission time kept BellKor ahead of the competitors The Ensemble.

To read in detail about the winning submissions, check out "The BigChaos Solution to the Netflix Grand Prize" (*https://oreil.ly/joaqu*) by Andreas Töscher and Michael Jahrer and "The BigChaos Solution to the Netflix Prize 2008" (*https://oreil.ly/D51iM*) by the same authors. Meanwhile, let's review a few important lessons from this competition:

First, we see that the user-item matrix we've discussed appears in these solutions as the critical mathematical data structure. The model selection and training is important, but parameter tuning provided a huge improvement in several algorithms. We will return to parameter tuning in later chapters. The authors state that several model innovations came from reflecting on the business use case and human behavior and trying to capture those patterns in the model architectures. Next, linear-algebraic approaches resulted in the first reasonably performant solutions, and building on top of them led to the winning model. Finally, eking out the performance that Netflix originally demanded to win the competition took so long that business circumstances changed and the solution was no longer useful (*https://oreil.ly/fz6rz*).

That last point might be the *most* important thing an ML developer needs to learn about recommendation systems; see the following tip.

Start with Simplicity

Build a working usable model quickly and iterate while the model is still relevant to the needs of the business.

Soft Ratings

In our cheese-tasting example, each cheese either received a numerical rating or was not tried by a guest. These are *hard ratings*: regardless of whether the cheese is a brie or a chèvre, the ratings are explicit, and their absence indicates a lack of interaction between the user and item. In some contexts, we'll want to accommodate data indicating a user does interact with an item and yet provides no rating.

A common example is a movies app; a user may have watched a movie with the app but not provided a star rating. This indicates that the item (in this case, a movie) has been observed, but we don't have the rating for our algorithms to learn from. However, we can still use this implicit data to do the following:

- Exclude this item from future recommendations
- Use this data as a separate term in our learner
- Assign a default rating value to indicate "interesting enough to watch, not significant enough to rate"

It turns out that implicit ratings are critical for training effective recommendation systems, not only because users often don't give hard ratings, but also because implicit ratings provide a different level of signal. Later, when we wish to train multilevel models to predict both click likelihood and buy likelihood, these two levels will prove extremely important.

To sum up:

- A hard rating occurs when the user directly responds to a prompt for feedback on an item.
- A soft rating occurs when the user's behavior implicitly communicates feedback on an item without responding to a direct prompt.

Data Collection and User Logging

We've established that we learn from both explicit ratings and implicit ratings, so how and where do we get this data? To dive into this, we'll need to start worrying about application code. In many businesses, the data scientists and ML engineers are separate from the software engineers, but working with recommendation systems requires alignment between the two functions.

What to Log

The simplest and most obvious data collection is user ratings. If users are given the option to provide ratings, or even a thumbs-up or thumbs-down, that component will need to be built and that data will need to be stored. These ratings must be stored not only for the opportunity to build recommendations, but also to prevent the bad user experience of rating something and then shortly thereafter not having the rating appear when revisiting the page.

Similarly, it's useful to understand a few other key interactions that can improve and expand your recommendation system: page loads, page views, clicks, and add-to-bag.

For these types of data, let's use a slightly more complicated example: the ecommerce website Bookshop.org. This one site has multiple applications of recommendation systems, almost all of which we will return to in time. For now, let's focus on some interactions (Figure 2-2).

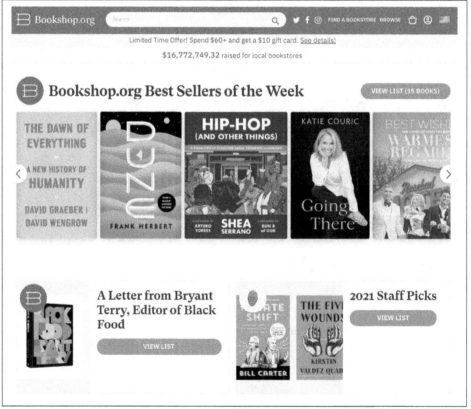

Figure 2-2. Bookshop.org landing page

Page loads

When you first load up Bookshop.org, it starts with items on the page. The Best Sellers of the Week are all clickable images to those book listings. Despite the user having no choice in loading this initial page, it's actually quite important to log the contents of this initial page load.

These options represent the population of books that the user has seen. If a user has seen an option, they have the opportunity to click it, which will ultimately be an important implicit signal.

Propensity Scores

The consideration of the population of all items a user has seen is deeply tied to propensity score matching. In mathematics, *propensity scores* are the probability that an observational unit will be assigned to the treatment group versus the control group.

Compare this setup to the simple 50-50 A/B test: every unit has a 50% chance of being exposed to your treatment. In a feature-stratified A/B test, you purposely change the probability of exposure dependent on a certain feature or collection of features (often called *covariates* in this context). Those probabilities of exposure are the propensity scores.

Why bring up A/B testing here? Later, we'll be interested in mining our soft ratings for signal on user preference, but we must consider the possibility that the lack of a soft rating is not an implicit bad rating. Thinking back to the cheeses: taster *D* never had a chance to rate *brie*, so there's no reason to think *D* has a preference for aversion on *brie*. This is because *D* was not *exposed to brie*.

Now thinking back to Bookshop.org: the landing page does not show *The Hitchhiker's Guide to the Galaxy*, so the user has no way to click it and implicitly communicate interest in that book. The user could use the search option, but that's a different kind of signal—which we'll talk about later and is, in fact, a much stronger signal.

When understanding implicit ratings like "did the user look at something," we need to properly account for the entire population of choices they were exposed to, and use the inverse of that population size to weigh the importance of clicking. For this reason, understanding *all* page loads is important.

Page views and hover

Websites have gotten much more complicated, and now users must contend with a variety of interactions. Figure 2-3 demonstrates what happens if the user clicks the right arrow in the Best Sellers of the Week carousel and then moves their mouse over the Cooking at Home option.

Figure 2-3. Bookshop.org top sellers

The user has unveiled a new option, and by mousing over it, has made it larger and given it a visual effect. These are ways to communicate more information to the user, and remind the user that these options are clickable. To the recommender, these clicks can be used as more implicit feedback.

First, the user clicked the carousel scroll—so some of what they saw in the carousel was interesting enough to dig further. Second, they moused over *Cooking at Home*, which they might click or might just want to see if additional information becomes available when hovering. Many websites use a hover interaction to provide a pop-up detail. While Bookshop.org doesn't implement something like this, internet users have been trained to expect this behavior by all the websites that do, and so the signal is still meaningful. Third, the user has now uncovered a new potential item in their carousel scroll—which we should add to our page loads but with a higher rating because it required interaction to uncover.

All this and more can be encoded into the website's logging. Rich and verbose logging is one of the most important ways to improve a recommendation system. Having more logging data than you need is almost always better than having the opposite.

Clicks

If you thought hovering meant interest, wait until you consider clicking! Not in all cases, but in the large majority, clicking is a strong indicator of product interest. For ecommerce, clicking often is computed as part of the recommendation team's core key performance indicators (KPIs).

This is for two reasons:

- Clicking is almost always required to purchase, so it's an upstream filter for most business transactions.
- Clicking requires explicit user action, so it's a good measure of intent.

Noise will always exist of course, but clicks are the go-to indicator of a client's interest. Many production recommendation systems are trained on click data—not ratings data—because of the much higher data volume and the strong correlation between click behavior and purchase behavior.

Click-Stream Data

Sometimes in recommendation systems you hear people talk about *click-stream* data. This important view into click data also considers the order of a user's clicks in a single *session*. Modern recommendation systems put a lot of effort into utilizing the order of items a user clicks, calling this *sequential recommendations*, and have shown dramatic improvements via this additional dimension. We will discuss sequence-based recommendations in Chapter 7.

Add-to-bag

We've finally arrived; the user has added an item to their bag or cart or queue. This is an extremely strong indicator of interest and is often quite correlated with purchasing. There are even reasons to argue that add-to-bag is a better signal than purchase/order/watch. Add-to-bag is essentially the end of the line for soft ratings, and usually beyond this you'd want to start collecting ratings and reviews.

Impressions

We might also wish to log *impressions* of an item that wasn't clicked. This supplies the recommendation system with negative feedback on items that the user isn't interested in. For example, if the cheeses *gouda*, *chèvre* and *emmentaler* are offered to the user but the user tastes only *chèvre*, perhaps the user doesn't like *gouda*. They might not have gotten around to tasting *emmentaler*, on the other hand, so these impressions may carry only noisy signal.

Collection and Instrumentation

Web applications frequently instrument all the interactions we've discussed via events. If you don't yet know what events are, maybe ask a buddy in your engineering org—but we'll also give you the skinny. Like logging, *events* are specially formatted messages that the application sends out when a certain block of code is executed.

As in the example of a click, the application needs to make a call to get the next content to show the user, it's common to also "fire an event" at this moment, indicating information about the user, what they clicked, the session-ID for later reference, the time, and various other useful details. This event can be handled downstream in any number of ways, but there's an increasingly prevalent pattern of path bifurcation to the following:

- A log database, like a mySQL application database tied to the service
- An event stream for real-time handling

The latter will be interesting: event streams are often connected to listeners via technologies like Apache Kafka. This kind of infrastructure can get complicated fast (consult your local data engineer or MLOps person), but a simple model for what happens is that all of a particular kind of log are sent to several destinations that you think can make use of these events.

In the recommender case, an event stream can be connected up to a sequence of transformations to process the data for downstream learning tasks. This will be enormously useful if you want to build a recommendation system that uses those logs. Other important uses are real-time metrics logging for what is going on at any given time on the website.

Funnels

We've just worked through our first example of a funnel, which no good data scientist can avoid thinking about. Like them or hate them, funnel analyses are crucial for critical evaluation of your website, and by extension your recommendation system.

Click-Streams

A *funnel* is a collection of steps a user must take to get from one state to another; it's called a funnel because at each of the discrete steps, a user may stop proceeding through, or *drop off*, thus reducing the population size at each step.

In our discussion of events and user logging, each step is relevant for a subset of the previous. This means that the process is a funnel, as shown in Figure 2-4. Understanding the drop-off rate at each step reveals important characteristics of your website and your recommendations.

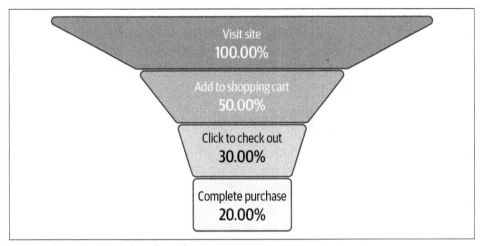

Figure 2-4. An onboarding funnel

Three important funnel analyses can be considered in Figure 2-4:

1. Page view to add-to-bag user flow
2. Page view to add-to-bag per recommendation
3. Add-to-bag to complete purchase

The first funnel is merely identifying, at a high level, the percentage of users who take each step in the flow. This is a high-level measure of your website optimization, the general interestingness of your product offering, and the quality of your user leads.

The second funnel, which is more fine-grained, takes into consideration the recommendations themselves. As mentioned previously in terms of propensity scoring, users can proceed through the funnel for a particular item only if they're shown the item. This concept intersects with the use of funnels because you want to understand at a high level how certain recommendations correlate with funnel drop-off, but also, when using a recommendation system, the confidence in your recommendations should correlate well with the funnel metrics. We will return to this in more detail in Part III, but for now you should remember to think about different categories of recommendation-user pairs and how their funnels may look compared to the average.

Finally, we can consider add-to-bag to completion. This actually isn't part of the RecSys problem but should be on your mind as a data scientist or ML engineer trying to improve the product. *No matter how good your recommendations are, this funnel may destroy any of your hard work.* Before working on a recommender problem, you should almost always investigate the funnel performance in getting a user from add-to-bag to check-out-completed. If there's something cumbersome or difficult about this flow, it will almost certainly provide a bigger bang for your buck to fix this than to improve recommendations. Investigate the drop-offs, do user studies to understand what might be confusing, and work with product and engineering teams to ensure that everyone is aligned on this flow before you start building a recommender for ecommerce.

Business Insight and What People Like

In the previous example from Bookshop.org, Top Sellers of the Week is the primary carousel on the page. Recall our earlier work on `get_most_popular_recs`; what powers the carousel is simply that recommender but applied to a specific collector—one that looks only in the last week.

This carousel is an example of a recommender providing business insight in addition to driving recommendations. A common mission of a growth team is to understand weekly trends and KPIs, often metrics like weekly active users and new sign-ups. For many digital-first companies, growth teams are additionally interested in understanding the primary drivers of engagement.

Let's take an example: as of this writing, the Netflix show *Squid Game* became the company's most popular series of all time, breaking a huge number of records in the process. *Squid Game* reached 111 million viewers in the first month. Most obviously, *Squid Game* needs to be featured in the Top Shows of the Week or Hottest Titles carousels, but where else should a breakout hit like this matter?

The first important insight companies almost always ask for is *attribution*: if the numbers go up in a week, what led to that? Is there something important or special about launches that drove additional growth? How can we learn from those signals to do better in the future? In the case of *Squid Game*—a foreign-language show that saw massive interest from an English-speaking audience—executives might take away the inclination to invest more in shows from South Korea or in subtitled shows with high drama. The flip side of this coin is also important: when growth metrics lag, executives nearly always ask why. Being able to point to what was the most popular, and how it may have deviated from expectation, helps a lot.

The other important insight can feed back into recommendations; during exciting debuts like *Squid Game*, it's easy to get caught up in the excitement as you see all your metrics go up and to the right, but might this negatively affect metrics also? If you have a show debuting the same week or two as *Squid Game*, you'll be less enthusiastic about all this success. Overall, successes like this usually drive *incremental* growth, which is great for business, and in total, metrics will all probably look up. Other items, however, may have less successful launches due to a zero-sum game among the core user base. This can have a negative effect on longer-term metrics and can even make later recommendations less effective.

Later, you will learn about diversity of recommendations; there are many reasons to care about diversifying your recommendations, but here we observe one: diversifying can increase the overall ability to match your users with items. As you keep a broad base of users highly engaged, you increase your future opportunity for growth.

Incremental Gains

Incremental gains is an economics term now used in growth marketing and growth analytics. Incremental gains refer to a margin of increase in addition to the gains expected from an expended effort.

A simple example is a business that usually adds a user for every $100 in marketing spending, gets some positive press, and the next week gets a user for every $80 in marketing spending. By keeping the marketing budget fixed that week at $1,600, the business would get 20 new users instead of 16—an incremental gain of 4 users. This framework is especially common when testing new treatments or programs.

Finally, beyond surfacing the trending hits, another benefit of knowing what's really hot on your platform or service is advertising. When a phenomenon starts, a huge advantage can result from priming the pump—making noise and driving publicity of the success. This sometimes leads to a network effect, and in these days of viral content and easy distribution, this can have multiplicative impacts on your platform's growth.

Summary

This constitutes the most basic aspects of formulating your recommendation problems and preparing yourself to solve them.

The user-item matrix gave us a tool to summarize the relationship between users and items in the simplest case of numerical ratings and will generalize to more complicated models later. We saw our first notion of vector similarity, which will be expanded to a deep geometric notion of relevance. Next, we learned about the kinds of signals that users can provide via explicit and implicit actions. Finally, we learned how to capture these actions for training models.

Now that we've finished our problem framing, we've got a bit of a math review for you. Don't worry, you can keep your ruler and compass packed away, and you won't be required to prove anything or compute any integrals. You will, however, see some important mathematical notions that will help you think clearly about expectations for your recommendation systems and ensure you're asking the right questions.

## CHAPTER 3

Mathematical Considerations

Most of this book is focused on implementation and on practical considerations necessary to get recommendation systems working. In this chapter, you'll find the most abstract and theoretical concepts of the book. The purpose of this chapter is to cover a few of the essential ideas that undergird the field. It's important to understand these ideas as they lead to pathological behavior in recommendation systems and motivate many architectural decisions.

We'll start by discussing the shape of data you often see in recommendation systems, and why that shape can require careful thought. Next we'll talk about the underlying mathematical idea, similarity, that drives most modern recommendation systems. We'll briefly cover a different way of thinking about what a recommender does, for those with a more statistical inclination. Finally, we'll use analogies to NLP to formulate the popular approach.

Zipf's Laws in RecSys and the Matthew Effect

In a great many applications of ML, a caveat is given early: the distribution of observations of unique items from a large corpus is modeled by *Zipf's law*—the frequency of occurrence drops exponentially. In recommendation systems, the *Matthew effect* appears in the popular item's click rates or the popular user's feedback rates. For example, popular items have dramatically larger click counts than average, and more-engaged users give far more ratings than average.

The Matthew Effect

The Matthew effect—or *popularity bias*—states that the most popular items continue to attract the most attention and widen the gap with other items.

Take, for example, the MovieLens dataset (*https://oreil.ly/xiUaq*), an extremely popular dataset for benchmarking recommendation systems. Jenny Sheng (*https://oreil.ly/Uzm2G*) observes the behavior shown in Figure 3-1 for a number of movie ratings:

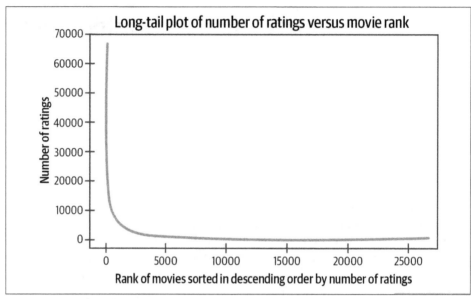

Figure 3-1. Zipfian distribution of movie-rank ratings

At first glance, the rapid decline in ratings is obvious and stark, but is it a problem? Let's assume our recommender will be built as a user-based collaborative filtering (CF) model—as alluded to in Chapter 2. Then how might these distributions affect the recommender?

We will consider the distributional ramifications of this phenomenon. Let the probability mass function be described by the simple Zipf's law:

$$f(k, M) = \frac{1/k}{\sum_{n=1}^{M}(1/n)}$$

For M number of tokens in the corpus (in our example, the number of movies), k is the rank of a token when sorted by number of occurrences.

Let's consider users A and B, with $N_A = |\mathcal{I}_A|$ and $N_B = |\mathcal{I}_B|$ ratings, respectively. Observe that the probability of V_i, the ith most popular video, appearing in $\mathcal{I}_X$ for a user X is given by the following:

$$P(i) = \frac{f(i, M)}{\sum_{j=1}^{M} f(j, M)} = \frac{1/i}{\sum_{j=1}^{M} 1/j}$$

Thus the joint probability of an item appearing in two user's ratings is shown here:

$$P\left(i^2\right) = \left(\frac{1/i}{\Sigma_{j=1}^{M} 1/j}\right)^2$$

In words, the probability of two users sharing an item in their rating sets drops off with the square of its popularity rank.

This becomes important when we also consider that our, yet unstated, definition of user-based CF is based on similarity in users' ratings sets. This similarity is *the number of jointly rated items by two users, divided by the total number of items rated by either.*

Taking this definition, we can, for example, compute the similarity score for one shared item among A and B:

$$\sum_{i=1}^{M} \frac{P\left(i^2\right)}{\| \mathscr{I}_A \cup \mathscr{I}_B \|}$$

The average similarity score of two users is then generalized as follows via repeated application of the preceding equation:

$$\sum_{t=1}^{\min\left(N_A, N_B\right)} \left(\prod_{i_k = i_{k-1}+1}^{t-1} \sum_{i=1}^{M} \left(\frac{P\left(i_k^2\right)}{\frac{\| \mathscr{I}_A \cup \mathscr{I}_B \|}{t}} \right) \right)$$

via repeated application of the preceding observation.

These combinatorial formulas not only indicate the relevance of the Zipfian in our algorithms, but we also see an almost direct effect on the output of scores. Consider the experiment in "Quantitative Analysis of Matthew Effect and Sparsity Problem of Recommender Systems" (*https://oreil.ly/m6iw7*) by Hao Wang et al. on the Last.fm dataset (*https://oreil.ly/NqJOw*). Last.fm is a music-listening tracker enabling users to keep track of all the songs they listen to; for Last.fm users, the authors demonstrate average similarity scores for pairs of users, and they find that this Matthew effect persists into the similarity matrix (Figure 3-2).

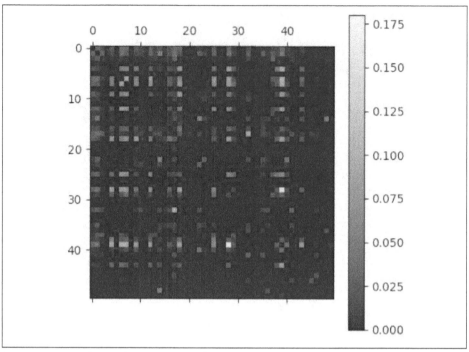

Figure 3-2. Matthew effect as seen on the Last.fm dataset

Observe the radical difference between "hot" cells and all the others. The bright cells are few among the mostly dark, suggesting a difficult combination of some extremely popular items among the far more common frequency close to zero. While these results might seem scary, later we'll consider diversity-aware loss functions that can mitigate the Matthew effect. A simpler way is to use downstream sampling methods, which we will discuss as part of our explore-exploit algorithms. Finally, the Matthew effect is only the first of two major impacts of this Zipfian; let's turn our attention to the second.

Sparsity

We must now reckon with sparsity. As the ratings skew more and more toward the most popular items, the least popular items are starved for data and recommendations, which is called *data sparsity*. This connects to the linear-algebraic definition: mostly zeros or not populated elements in a vector. When you consider again our user-item matrix, less popular items constitute columns with few entries; these are sparse vectors. Similarly, at scale we see that the Matthew effect pushes more and more of the total ratings into certain columns, and the matrix becomes sparse in the traditional mathematical sense. For this reason, sparsity is an extremely well-known challenge for recommendation systems.

As before, let's consider the implication on our CF algorithms from these sparse ratings. Again observe that the probability of V_i, the ith most popular item, appearing in $\mathscr{I}_X$ for a user X is given by the following:

$$P(i) = \frac{f(i, M)}{\sum_{j=1}^{M} f(j, M)} = \frac{1/i}{\sum_{j=1}^{M} 1/j}$$

Then

$$(M-1) * P(i)$$

is the expected number of other users who click the ith most popular item, so summing over all, i yields the total number of other users who will share a rating with X:

$$\sum_{i=1}^{M} (M-1) * P(i)$$

Again, as we pull back to the overall trends, we observe this sparsity sneaking into the actual computations for our CF algorithms, consider the trend of users of different ranks, and see how much their rankings are used to *collaborate* in other users' rankings (Figure 3-3).

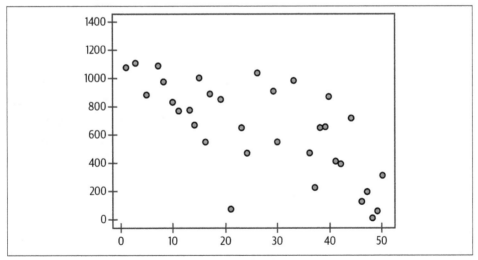

Figure 3-3. User similarity counts for the Last.fm dataset

We see that this is an important result to always be aware of: sparsity pushes emphasis onto the most popular users and has the risk of making your recommender myopic.

Item-Based Collaborative Filtering

While the equations are different, in this section, they apply similarly to item-based CF. Similarity in items exhibits the same inheritance of the Zipfian in their scores, and items consulted in the CF process drop off by rank.

User Similarity for Collaborative Filtering

In mathematics, it's common to hear discussion of *distances*. Even back to the Pythagorean theorem, we are taught to think of relationships between points as distances or dissimilarity. Indeed, this fundamental idea is canonized in mathematics as part of the definition of a metric:

$$d(a, c) \leq d(a, b) + d(b, c)$$

In ML, we often instead concern ourselves with the notion of similarity—an extremely related topic. In many cases, we can compute similarity or dissimilarity, as they are complements of each other; when $d: X \times X \to [0, 1] \subset \mathbb{R}$ is a *dissimilarity function*, then we often define the following:

$$Sim(a, b): = 1 - d(a, b)$$

This may seem like a needlessly precise statement, but in fact you'll see that a variety of options are available for framing similarity (*https://oreil.ly/9xAT6*). Furthermore, sometimes we even formulate similarity measures where the associated distance measure does not establish a metric on the set of objects. These so-called pseudospaces can still be incredibly important, and we'll show where they come up in Chapter 10.

In the literature, you'll find that papers commonly start by introducing a new similarity measure and then training a model you've seen before on that new measure. As you'll see, the way you choose to relate objects (users, items, features, etc.) can have a large effect on what your algorithms learn.

For now, let's laser in on some specific similarity measures. Consider a classic ML problem of clustering: we have a space (usually $\mathbb{R}^n$) in which our data is represented and are asked to partition our data into subcollections of the population and assign these collections names. Frequently, these collections are intended to capture a certain meaning, or at the very least be useful for summarizing the collection elements' features.

When you do that clustering, you frequently are considering points near to one another in that space. Further, if you're given a new observation and asked to assign it to a collection as an inference task, you normally compute the new observation's *nearest neighbors*. This could be the *k*-nearest neighbors or simply the nearest neighbor among cluster centers; either way, your task is to use the notion of similarity to associate—and thus classify. In CF, this same notion is used to relate a user for whom you wish to make recommendations to those you already have data from.

Nearest Neighbors

Nearest neighbors is a catchall term that arises from the simple geometric idea that, given some space (points defined by feature vectors) and a point in that space, you can find the other points closest to it. This has applications in all of ML, including classification, ranking/recommendation, and clustering. "Approximate Nearest Neighbors" on page 87 provides more details.

So how can we define similarity for our users in CF? They're not obviously in the same space, so our usual tools seem to be lacking.

Pearson Correlation

Our original CF formulation indicated that users with similar tastes collaborate to recommend items for one another. Let two users A and B have a set of co-rated items—simply the set of items with ratings from each—written as $\mathscr{R}_{A,B}$, and a rating of item x by user A written as $r_{A,x}$. Then the following is the sum of deviation from A's average rating over all of its co-rated items with B:

$$\sum_{x \in \mathscr{R}_{A,B}} \left(r_{A,x} - \bar{r}_A\right)$$

If we think of these ratings as a random variable and consider the analog for B, the correlation between the jointly distributed variables (the population covariance) is our *Pearson correlation*:

$$\text{USim}_{A,B} = \frac{\sum_{x \in \mathscr{R}_{A,B}} \left(r_{A,x} - \bar{r}_A\right)\left(r_{B,x} - \bar{r}_B\right)}{\sqrt{\sum_{x \in \mathscr{R}_{A,B}} \left(r_{A,x} - \bar{r}_A\right)^2}\sqrt{\sum_{x \in \mathscr{R}_{A,B}} \left(r_{B,x} - \bar{r}_B\right)^2}}$$

Keeping in mind a few details here is extremely important:

- This is the similarity of the jointly distributed variables describing the users' ratings.
- We compute this via all co-rated items, so user similarity is defined via item-ratings.
- This is a pairwise similarity measure taking values in $[-1,1] \in \mathbb{R}$.

Correlation and Similarity

In Part III, you will learn about additional definitions of *correlation* and *similarity* that are more well suited for handling ranking data and that accommodate implicit rankings in particular.

Ratings via Similarity

Now that we've introduced user similarity, let's use it! For a user A and item x, we can estimate the rating via similar users' ratings:

$$Aff_{A,i} = \bar{r}_A + \frac{\sum_{U \in \mathcal{N}(A)} USim_{A,U} * (r_{U,i} - \bar{r}_A)}{\sum_{U \in \mathcal{N}(A)} USim_{A,U}}$$

This is the prediction for user A's rating of item x, which takes A's average adjusted rating of the similarity-weighted average ratings of all of A's neighbors. In other words: A's rating will probably be the average of people who have ratings like A's rating, adjusted to how generous A is with ratings in general. We call this estimate the *user-item affinity score*.

But wait! What's $\mathcal{N}(A)$? It's the neighborhood of A, via our USim definition from the preceding section. The idea here is that we are aggregating ratings over the local region of users identified as similar to our target user by the previous USim metric. How many neighbors? How do you pick those neighbors? These will be the subject of later chapters; for now, assume they're k-nearest neighbors and assume that some hyperparameter tuning is used to determine a good value for k.

Correlation Metric Spaces

You might wonder, "Does this Pearson correlation yield a metric space under a transformation?" The answer is yes, but clearly defining the metric space is a bit more complicated than our simple definition. While the preceding equation can get us a distance, it's not good enough to get us a metric space without a more novel transformation.

In particular, for $P(A, B)$, the previously defined correlation, $1 - P(A, B)$ yields a distance that satisfies all metric properties *except* the triangle inequality. There are several known ways to adjust this, though: $\sqrt{1 - P(A, B)^2}$ is the most common. For a survey, see "Metric Distances Derived from Cosine Similarity and Pearson and Spearman Correlations" (*https://oreil.ly/6bmIp*) by Stijn van Dongen and Anton J. Enright.

Explore-Exploit as a Recommendation System

So far we've presented two ideas, slightly in tension with each other:

- The MPIR, a simple, easy-to-understand recommender
- The Matthew effect in recommendation systems and its runaway behavior in distributions of ratings

By now, you likely realize that the MPIR will amplify the Matthew effect and that the Matthew effect will drive the MPIR to the trivial recommender in the limit. This is the classic difficulty of maximizing a loss function with no randomization: it quickly settles into a modal state.

This problem—and many others like it—encourages some modification to the algorithm to prevent this failure mode and continues to expose the algorithm and users to other options. The basic strategy for *explore-exploit schemes,* or *multiarmed bandits* as they're called, is to take not only the outcome-maximizing recommendation but also a collection of alternative *variants,* and randomly determine which to use as a response.

Taking a step back: given a collection of variant recommendations, or *arms,* A, for which the outcome of each recommendation is y_t, we have a prior reward function $R(y_t)$. The bandit (called an *agent* in this literature) would like to maximize $R(y_t)$ but doesn't know the distribution of the outcomes $Y_{a \in A}$. The agent thus assumes some prior distributions for $Y_{a \in A}$ and then collects data to update those distributions; after sufficient observations, the agent can estimate the expected values of each distribution, $\mu_{a \in A} = \mathbb{E}(\mathscr{R}(Y_a))$.

If the agent was able to confidently estimate these reward values, the recommendation problem would be solved: at inference, the agent would simply estimate the reward values for all variants for the user and select the reward-optimizing *arm.* This is, of course, ridiculous in totality, but the basic idea is useful nonetheless: hold prior assumptions about what will be the greatest expected reward, and explore alternatives with some frequency to continue to update the distributions and refine your estimators.

Even when not explicitly using a multiarmed bandit, this insight is a powerful and useful framework for understanding the goal of a recommendation system. Utilizing the ideas of prior estimates for good recommendations and exploring other options to gain signal is a core idea that's recurring. Let's see one practicality of this approach.

ϵ-greedy

How often should you explore versus use your reward-optimizing arm? The first best algorithm is ϵ-greedy: for $\epsilon \in (0, 1)$, at each request the agent has the probability ϵ of choosing a random arm and the probability $1 - \epsilon$ of selecting the currently highest estimated reward arm.

Let's take the MPIR and slightly modify it to include some exploration:

```python
from jax import random
key = random.PRNGKey(0)


def get_item_popularities() -> Optional[Dict[str, int]]:
    ...
        # Dict of pairs: (item-identifier, count item chosen)
        return item_choice_counts
    return None

def get_most_popular_recs_ep_greedy(
    max_num_recs: int,
    epsilon: float
) -> Optional[List[str]]:
    assert epsilon<1.0
    assert epsilon>0

    items_popularity_dict = get_item_popularities()
    if items_popularity_dict:
        sorted_items = sorted(
            items_popularity_dict.items(),
            key=lambda item: item[1]),
            reverse=True,
        )
        top_items = [i[0] for i in sorted_items]
        recommendations = []
        for i in range(max_num_recs): # we wish to return max_num_recs
            if random.uniform(key)>epsilon: # if greater than epsilon, exploit
                recommendations.append(top_items.pop(0))
            else: # otherwise, explore
                explore_choice = random.randint(1,len(top_items))
                recommendations.append(top_items.pop(explore_choice))
        return recommendations

    return None
```

The only modification to our MPIR is that now we have two cases for each potential recommendation from our max_num_recs. If a random probability is less than our ε, we proceed as before and select the most popular; otherwise, we select a random recommendation.

Maximizing Reward

We're interpreting maximization of reward as selecting the most-popular items. This is an important assumption, and as we move into more complicated recommenders, this will be the crucial assumption that we modify to get different algorithms and schemes.

Now let's summarize our recommender components again:

Collector
The collector here need not change; we still want to get the item popularities first.

Ranker
The ranker also does not change! We begin by ranking the possible recommendations by popularity.

Server
If the collector and ranker remain the same, clearly the server is what must be adapted for this new recommender. This is the case; instead of taking the top items to fill max_num_recs, we now utilize our ε to determine at each step if the next recommendation added to our list should be next in line from the ranker or a random selection. Otherwise, we adhere to the same API schema and return the same shape of data.

What Should ε Be?

In the preceding discussion, ε is a fixed number for the entire call, but what should the value be? This is actually an area of great study, and the general wisdom is to start with large ε (to encourage more exploration) and then reduce over time. Determining the rate at which you decrease it, the starting value, and so on, requires serious thought and research. Additionally, this value can be tied into your prediction loop and be part of the training process. See "The Exploration-Exploitation Trade-Off: Intuitions and Strategies" (*https://oreil.ly/wk-OB*) by Joseph Rocca for a deeper dive.

Other—often better—sampling techniques exist for optimization. *Importance sampling* can utilize the ranking functions we build later to integrate the explore-exploit with what our data has to teach.

The NLP-RecSys Relationship

Let's utilize some intuition from a different area of ML, natural language processing. One of the fundamental models in NLP is *word2vec*: a sequence-based model for language understanding that uses the words that occur in sentences together.

For *skipgram-word2vec*, the model takes sentences and attempts to learn the implicit meaning of their words via their co-occurrence relationships with other words in those sentences. Each pair of co-occurring words constitutes a sample that is one-hot encoded and sent into a vocabulary-sized layer of neurons, with a bottleneck layer and a vocabulary-sized output layer for probabilities that words will occur.

Via this network, we reduce the size of our representation to the bottleneck dimension and thus find a smaller dimensional representation of all our words than the original corpus-sized one-hot embedding. The thinking is that similarity of words can now be computed via vector similarity in this new representation space.

Why is this related to recommendation systems? Well, because if we take the ordered sequence of user-item interactions (e.g., the sequence of movies a user has rated), we can utilize the same idea from word2vec to find item similarity instead of word similarity. In this analogy, the user history is the *sentence*.

Previously, using our CF similarity, we decided that similar users can help inform what a good recommendation for a user should be. In this model, we are finding item-item similarity, so instead we assume that a user will like the items similar to those previously liked.

Items as Words

You may have noticed that natural language models treat words as sequences, and in fact, our user history is a sequence too! For now, hold onto this knowledge. Later, this will guide us to sequence-based methods for RecSys.

Vector Search

We have built a collection of vector representations of our items, and we claim that similarity in this space (often called a *latent space*, *representation space*, or *ambient space*) means similarity in *likability* to users.

To convert this similarity to a recommendation, consider a user A with a collection of previously liked items $\mathscr{R}_A$, and consider $\mathscr{A} = \{v_x | x \in \mathscr{R}_A\}$ the set of vectors associated to those items in this latent space. We are looking for a new item y that we think is good for A.

The Old Curse

These latent spaces tend to be of high dimension, which Euclidean distance famously performs poorly in. As regions become sparse, the distance function performance decreases; local distances are meaningful, but global distances are not to be trusted. Instead, cosine distance shows better performance, but this is a topic of deep exploration. Additionally, instead of minimizing the distance, in practice it's better to maximize the similarity.

One simple way to use similarity to produce a recommendation is to take the closest item to the average of those that A likes:

$$\text{argmax}_y\{\text{USim}(v_y, avg(\mathscr{A})) \mid y \in \text{Items}\}$$

Here, $d(-,-)$ is a distance function in the latent space (usually cosine distance).

The argmax essentially treats all of A's ratings equally and suggests something near those. In practice, this process is often fraught. First, you could weight the terms by rating:

$$\text{argmax}_y\left\{\text{USim}\left(v_y, \frac{\Sigma_{v_x \in \mathscr{A}} r_x}{|\mathscr{R}_\mathscr{A}|}\right) \mid y \in \text{Items}\right\}$$

This can potentially improve the representativeness of the user feedback in the recommendations. Alternatively, you might find that a user rates movies across a variety of genres and themes. Averaging here will definitely lead to worse results, so maybe you want to simply find recommendations similar to one movie the user liked, weighted by that rating:

$$\text{argmax}_y\left\{\frac{\text{USim}(v_y, v_x)}{r_x} \mid y \in \text{Items}, v_x \in \mathscr{A}\right\}$$

Finally, you may even want to do this process several times for different items a user liked to get k recommendations:

$$\text{min} - k\left\{\text{argmax}_y\left\{\frac{\text{USim}(v_y, v_x)}{r_x} \mid y \in \text{Items}\right\} \mid v_x \in \mathscr{A}\right\}$$

Now we have k recommendations; each is similar to something that the user has liked and is weighted by how much they liked it. This approach utilized only an implicit geometry of the items formed by their co-occurrences.

Latent spaces and the geometric power that comes with them for recommendations will be a through line for the rest of the book. We will often formulate our loss functions via these geometries, and we'll exploit the geometric intuition to brainstorm where to expand our technique next.

Nearest-Neighbors Search

A reasonable question to ask is "How do I get these vectors that minimize this distance?" In all the preceding schemes, we are computing many distances and then finding minimums. In general, the problem of nearest neighbors is an extremely important and well-studied question.

While finding the exact nearest neighbors can sometimes be slow, a lot of great progress has been made on approximate nearest neighbors (ANN) searches. These algorithms not only return very close to the actual nearest neighbors, but they also perform orders of complexity faster. In general, when you see us (or other publications) computing an argmin (the argument that minimized the function) over some distances, there's a good chance ANN is what's used in practice.

Summary

Recommendation systems in the preceding chapter discussed data distribution principles such as Zipf's law and the Matthew Effect. These principles lead to challenges, such as skewed user similarity scores and data sparsity. In the world of ML, while the traditional math focuses on distance, the emphasis is on the concept of similarity. Different measures of similarity can drastically alter algorithm learning outcomes, with clustering being a primary application.

In the realm of recommendations, items are often represented in high-dimensional latent spaces. Similarity in these spaces hints at user preferences. Methods include recommending items close to a user's average liked items, and this may be improved by adding a weighting by user-rating. However, individual preferences necessitate diverse recommendations. Latent spaces continue to be influential, driving recommendation techniques.

Locating these vectors effectively requires the nearest-neighbors search. Though exact methods are resource-intensive, approximate nearest-neighbors offer a fast, precise solution, providing the foundation for the recommendation systems discussed in the current chapter.

## CHAPTER 4

System Design for Recommending

Now that you have a foundational understanding of how recommendation systems work, let's take a closer look at the elements needed and at designing a system that is capable of serving recommendations at industrial scale. *Industrial scale* in our context will primarily refer to *reasonable scale* (a term introduced by Ciro Greco, Andrea Polonioli, and Jacopo Tagliabue in "ML and MLOps at a Reasonable Scale" (*https:// oreil.ly/jNIRY*))—production applications for companies with tens to hundreds of engineers working on the product, not thousands.

In theory, a recommendation system is a collection of math formulas that can take historical data about user-item interactions and return probability estimates for a user-item-pair's affinity. In practice, a recommendation system is 5, 10, or maybe 20 software systems, communicating in real time and working with limited information, restricted item availability, and perpetually out-of-sample behavior, all to ensure that the user sees *something*.

This chapter is heavily influenced by "System Design for Recommendations and Search" (*https://oreil.ly/UBMB2*) by Eugene Yan and "Recommender Systems, Not Just Recommender Models" (*https://oreil.ly/G2aiH*) by Even Oldridge and Karl Byleen-Higley.

Online Versus Offline

ML systems consist of the stuff that you do in advance and the stuff that you do on the fly. This division, between online and offline, is a practical consideration about the information necessary to perform tasks of various types. To observe and learn large-scale patterns, a system needs access to lots of data; this is the offline component. Performing inference, however, requires only the trained model and relevant input data. This is why many ML system architectures are structured in this way. You'll frequently encounter the terms *batch* and *real-time* to describe the two sides of the online-offline paradigm (Figure 4-1).

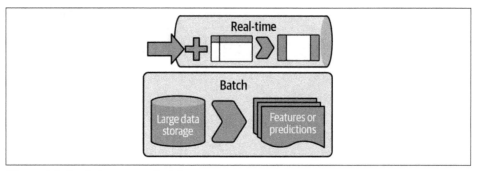

Figure 4-1. Real-time versus batch

A *batch process* does not require user input, often has longer expected time periods for completion, and is able to have all the necessary data available simultaneously. Batch processes often include tasks like training a model on historical data, augmenting one dataset with an additional collection of features, or transforming computationally expensive data. Another characteristic you see more frequently in batch processes is that they work with the full relevant dataset involved, not only an instance of the data sliced by time or otherwise.

A *real-time process* is carried out at the time of the request; said differently, it is evaluated during the inference process. Examples include providing a recommendation upon page load, updating the next episode after the user finishes the last, and re-ranking recommendations after one has been marked *not interesting*. Real-time processes are often resource constrained because of the need for rapidity, but like many things in this domain, as the world's computational resources expand, we change the definition of resource constrained.

Let's return to the components introduced in Chapter 1—the collector, ranker, and server—and consider their roles in offline and online systems.

Collector

The collector's role is to know what is in the collection of items that may be recommended and the necessary features or attributes of those items.

Offline Collector

The *offline collector* has access to and is responsible for the largest datasets. Understanding all user-item interactions, user similarities, item similarities, feature stores for users and items, and indices for nearest-neighbor lookup are all under the purview of the offline collector. The offline collector needs to be able to access the relevant data extremely fast, and sometimes in large batches. For this purpose, offline collectors often implement sublinear search functions or specifically tuned indexing structures. They may also leverage distributed compute for these transformations.

It's important to remember that the offline collector not only needs access and knowledge of these datasets but will also be responsible for writing the necessary downstream datasets to be used in real time.

Online Collector

The *online collector* uses the information indexed and prepared by the offline collector to provide real-time access to the parts of this data necessary for inference. This includes techniques like searching for nearest neighbors, augmenting an observation with features from a feature store, and knowing the full inventory catalog. The online collector will also need to handle recent user behavior; this will become especially important when we see sequential recommenders in Chapter 17.

One additional role the online collector may take on is encoding a request. In the context of a search recommender, we want to take the query and encode it into the *search space* via an embedding model. For contextual recommenders, we need to encode the context into the *latent space* via an embedding model also.

 Embedding Models

One popular subcomponent in the collector's work will involve an embedding step; see *Machine Learning Design Patterns* by Valliappa Lakshmanan et al. (O'Reilly). The embedding step on the offline side involves both training the embedding model and constructing the latent space for later use. On the online side, the embedding transformation will need to embed a query into the right space. In this way, the embedding model serves as a transformation that you include as part of your model architecture.

Ranker

The ranker's role is to take the collection provided by the collector, and order some or all of its elements according to a model for the context and user. The ranker actually gets two components itself, the filtering and the scoring.

Filtering can be thought of as the coarse inclusion and exclusion of items appropriate for recommendation. This process is usually characterized by rapidly cutting away a lot of potential recommendations that we definitely don't wish to show. A trivial example is not recommending items we know the user has already chosen in the past.

Scoring is the more traditional understanding of ranking: creating an ordering of potential recommendations with respect to the chosen objective function.

Offline Ranker

The goal of the *offline ranker* is to facilitate filtering and scoring. What differentiates it from the online ranker is how it runs validation and how the output can be used to build fast data structures that the online ranker can utilize. Additionally, the offline ranker can integrate with a human review process for *human-in-the loop ML*.

An important technology that will be discussed later is the *bloom filter*. A bloom filter allows the offline ranker to do work in batches, so that filtering in real time can happen much faster. An oversimplification of this process would be to use a few features of the request to quickly select subsets of all possible candidates. If this step can be completed quickly—in terms of computational complexity, striving for something less than quadratic in the number of candidates—then downstream complex algorithms can be made much more performant.

Second to the filtering step is the ranking step. In the offline component, ranking is training the model that learns how to rank items. As you will see later, learning to rank items to perform best with respect to the objective function is at the heart of the recommendation models. Training these models, and preparing the aspects of their output, is part of the batch responsibility of the ranker.

Online Ranker

The *online ranker* gets a lot of praise but really utilizes the hard work of other components. The online ranker first does filtering, utilizing the filtering infrastructure built offline—for example, an index lookup or a bloom filter application. After filtering, the number of candidate recommendations has been tamed, and thus we can actually come to the most infamous of the tasks: rank recommendations.

In the online ranking phase, usually a feature store is accessed to take the candidates and embellish them with the necessary details, and then a scoring and ranking model is applied. Scoring or ranking may happen in several independent dimensions and then be collated into one final ranking. In the multiobjective paradigm, you may have several of these ranks associated with the list of candidates returned by a ranker.

Server

The server's role is to take the ordered subset provided by the ranker, ensure that the necessary data schema is satisfied (including essential business logic), and return the requested number of recommendations.

Offline Server

The *offline server* is responsible for high-level alignment of the hard requirements of recommendations returned from the system. In addition to establishing and enforcing schema, these rules can be more nuanced things like "never return this pair of pants when also recommending this top." Often waved off as "business logic," the offline server is responsible for creating efficient ways to impose top-level priorities on the returned recommendations.

An additional responsibility for the offline server is handling tasks like experimentation. At some point, you'll likely want to run online experiments to test out all the amazing recommendation systems you build with this book. The offline server is the place where you'll implement the logic necessary to make experimentation decisions and provide the implications in a way the online server can use them in real time.

Online Server

The *online server* takes the rules, requirements, and configurations established and makes their final application to the ranked recommendations. A simple example is diversification rules; as you will see later, diversification of recommendations can have a significant impact on the quality of a user's experience. The online server can read the diversification requirements from the offline server and apply them to the ranked list to return the expected number of diverse recommendations.

Summary

It's important to remember that the online server is the endpoint from which other systems will be getting a response. While it's usually where the message is coming from, many of the most complicated components in the system are upstream. Be careful to instrument this system in a way that when responses are slow, each system is observable enough that you can identify where those performance degradations are coming from.

Now that we've established the framework and you understand the functions of the core components, we will discuss the aspects of ML systems next and the kinds of technologies associated with them.

In this next chapter, we'll get our hands dirty with the aforementioned components and see how we might implement the key aspects. We'll wrap it up by putting it all together into a production-scale recommender using only the content of each item. Let's go!

## CHAPTER 5

Putting It All Together: Content-Based Recommender

Throughout this part of the book, we've introduced some of the most basic components in a recommendation system. In this chapter, we'll get hands-on. We're going to design and implement a recommendation system for images from Pinterest. This chapter, along with the book's other "Putting It All Together" chapters, will show you how to work with datasets by using open source tools. The material for this kind of chapter refers to code hosted on GitHub that you will need to download and play with in order to properly experience the content.

Since this is the first practical hands-on chapter, here are some extra setup instructions for the development environment. We developed this code on Windows running in a Windows Subsystem for Linux (WSL) Ubuntu virtual machine. The code should run fine on Linux machines, with more technical adaptation for macOS and a lot more for Windows, in which case it would be better to run it on a WSL2 Ubuntu virtual machine. You can look at the setup for WSL in the Microsoft documentation for Windows (*https://oreil.ly/VWPhi*). We picked Ubuntu for the image. You will also need NVIDIA CUDA (*https://oreil.ly/rnCw4*) and cuDNN (*https://oreil.ly/LHa-I*) if you have an NVIDIA GPU and want to use it.

We will be using the Shop the Look (STL) dataset (*https://oreil.ly/PxfJn*) from "Complete the Look: Scene-Based Complementary Product Recommendation" (*https://oreil.ly/2EDnZ*) by Wang-Cheng Kang et al.

In this chapter, we will show you how to build a content-based recommender. Recall that a content-based recommender uses indirect, generalizable representations of the items you wish to represent. Imagine, for instance, that you want to recommend a cake but cannot use the name of a cake. Instead, you might use descriptions of the cake or its ingredients as the content features.

With the STL dataset, we will try to match scenes, which are pictures of a person in a particular setting, with products that might go well with the scene. The training set contains pairs of scenes with single products, and we want to use the content recommender to extend recommendations to the entire catalog of products and sort them in some kind of ranking order. The content recommender, because it uses indirect content features to make recommendations, can be used to recommend new products that haven't been in the recommendation system or to warm-start a recommendation system with manually curated data before users start using it and a feedback loop is established. In the case of the STL dataset, we'll focus on the visual appearance of the scene and the products.

We will generate content embeddings via a convolutional neural network (CNN) architecture, and then train the embedding via a triplet loss and show how to create a content recommendation system.

This chapter covers the following topics:

- Revision control software
- Python build systems
- Random-item recommender
- Obtaining the STL dataset images
- Definition of CNN
- Model training in JAX, Flax, and Optax
- Input pipeline

Revision Control Software

Revision control software is a software system that keeps track of code changes. Think of it as a database that tracks versions of code you have written, while providing added functionality like showing the differences between each version of code and allowing you to revert to a previous version.

There are many kinds of revision control systems. We host the code for this book on GitHub (*https://oreil.ly/DsolH*).

The revision control software we use is called Git (*https://git-scm.com*). Code changes are done in batches called a *patch*, and each patch is uploaded to a source control repository like GitHub so that it can be cloned and worked on by many people at the same time.

You can use this command to clone the book code sample repository:

```
git clone git@github.com:BBischof/ESRecsys.git
```

For this chapter, look in the directory *ESRecsys/pinterest* for instructions on how to run the code in detail. This chapter will mostly focus on descriptions and pointers to the repository so that you'll able to get a feel for these systems in practice.

Python Build Systems

Python *packages* are libraries that provide functionality beyond the standard Python libraries. These include ML packages such as TensorFlow and JAX but also more utilitarian packages like the absl flags library or machine learning operations (MLOps) libraries like Weights & Biases (*https://wandb.ai*).

These packages are usually hosted on the Python Package Index (*https://pypi.org*).

Take a look at the file *requirements.txt*:

```
absl-py==1.1.0
tensorflow==2.9.1
typed-ast==1.5.4
typing_extensions==4.2.0
jax==0.3.25
flax==0.5.2
optax==0.1.2
wandb==0.13.4
```

You can see that we have picked a small set of Python packages to install for our dependencies. The format is package name, two equal signs, and then the version of the package.

Other build systems that work with Python include the following:

- pip (*https://oreil.ly/QNevQ*)
- Bazel (*https://oreil.ly/3BdIC*)
- Anaconda (*https://oreil.ly/4z182*)

For this chapter, we will use pip.

Before installing the packages, however, you might want to read up on Python virtual environments (*https://oreil.ly/fnQKD*). Python virtual environments are a way to keep track of Python package dependencies per project so that if different projects use different versions of the same package, they won't interfere with one another because each project has its own Python virtual environment to run in.

You can create and activate a Python virtual environment by typing the following into a Unix shell:

```
python -m venv pinterest_venv
source pinterest_venv/bin/activate
```

The first command creates a Python virtual environment, and the second one activates it. You will have to activate a virtual environment every time you open a new shell so that Python knows what environment to work in.

After the virtual environment is created, you can then use pip to install packages into the virtual environment, and those newly installed packages will not affect the system-level packages.

You can do this by running this command in the *ESRecsys/pinterest* directory:

```
pip install -r requirements.txt
```

This will install the specified packages and any subpackages that they might depend on into the virtual environment.

Random-Item Recommender

The first program we will look at is a random-item recommender (Example 5-1).

Example 5-1. Setting up flags

```
FLAGS = flags.FLAGS
_INPUT_FILE = flags.DEFINE_string(
  "input_file", None, "Input cat json file.")
_OUTPUT_HTML = flags.DEFINE_string(
  "output_html", None, "The output html file.")
_NUM_ITEMS = flags.DEFINE_integer(
  "num_items", 10, "Number of items to recommend.")

# Required flag.
flags.mark_flag_as_required("input_file")
flags.mark_flag_as_required("output_html")

def read_catalog(catalog: str) -> Dict[str, str]:
    """
    Reads in the product to category catalog.
    """
    with open(catalog, "r") as f:
        data = f.read()
    result = json.loads(data)
    return result

def dump_html(subset, output_html:str) -> None:
    """
    Dumps a subset of items.
```

```
    """
    with open(output_html, "w") as f:
        f.write("<HTML>\n")
        f.write("""
        <TABLE><tr>
        <th>Key</th>
        <th>Category</th>
        <th>Image</th>
        </tr>""")
        for item in subset:
            key, category = item
            url = pin_util.key_to_url(key)
            img_url = "<img src=\"%s\">" % url
            out = "<tr><td>%s</td><td>%s</td><td>%s</td></tr>\n" %
            (key, category, img_url)
            f.write(out)
        f.write("</TABLE></HTML>")

def main(argv):
    """
    Main function.
    """
    del argv  # Unused.

    catalog = read_catalog(_INPUT_FILE.value)
    catalog = list(catalog.items())
    random.shuffle(catalog)
    dump_html(catalog[:_NUM_ITEMS.value], _OUTPUT_HTML.value)
```

Here we use the absl flags library to pass in arguments to the program such as the path to the JSON catalog file that contains the STL scene, and product pairs.

Flags can have different types like string and integer, and you can mark them as required. If a required flag is not passed to the program, it will complain and stop running. Flags can be accessed via their value method.

We load and parse the STL dataset by using the JSON Python library, and then we randomly shuffle the catalog and dump the top few results in HTML.

You can run the random-item recommender via the following command:

```
python3 random_item_recommender.py
--input_file=STL-Dataset/fashion-cat.json --output_html=output.html
```

After completion, you can open the *output.html* file with your web browser and see some random items from the catalog. Figure 5-1 shows a sample.

Figure 5-1. Random-item recommender

The *fashion-catalog.json* file contains descriptions of products and their Pinterest ID, while *fashion.json* contains pairings of a scene with a recommended product.

Next, we'll look at how to recommend multiple new items for a single scene by training an ML model on scene-product pairings.

It is generally a good idea to create a random-item recommender the first time you encounter a corpus just so you have an idea of the kind of items in the corpus and you have a baseline to compare to.

Obtaining the STL Dataset Images

The first step in the process of creating a content-based recommender is fetching the content. In this case, the STL dataset's content is mostly images, with some metadata about the image (like the type of product). We will be using just the image content for this chapter.

You can look at the code in *fetch_images.py* to see how this is done, by using the Python standard library urllib to fetch the images. Be aware that doing too much fetching on someone else's website might trigger their bot defenses and cause them to blacklist your IP address, so it might be a wise idea to rate-limit fetches or find some other way to get the data.

We have downloaded thousands of image files and put them together into an archive as a Weights & Biases artifact. Since the archive is already in this artifact, you don't need to scrape the images yourself, but the code we've supplied will allow you to do so.

You can read up on artifacts in the Weights & Biases documentation (*https://oreil.ly/ NXTYP*). Artifacts are an MLOps concept that version and package together archives of data and track producers and consumers of the data.

You can download the image artifact by running the following:

```
wandb artifact get building-recsys/recsys-pinterest/shop_the_look:latest
```

The images will then be in the local directory *artifacts/shop_the_look:v1*.

Convolutional Neural Network Definition

Now that we have the images, the next step is figuring out how to represent the data. Images come in different sizes and are a complex type of content to analyze. We can use the raw pixels as the representation of our content, but the drawback is that tiny changes in pixel values can cause large differences in the distance between images. We do not want that. Rather, we want to somehow learn what is important in the images and ignore parts of the image, such as the background color, that might not be as important.

For this task, we will use a convolutional neural network (CNN) (*https://oreil.ly/r6KpS*) to compute an embedding vector for the image. An *embedding vector* is a kind of feature vector for the image that is learned from data and is of fixed size. We use embedding vectors for our representation because we want our database to be small and compact, easy to score over large numbers of images in the corpus, and relevant to the task at hand, which is to match products to a given scene image.

The neural network architecture we use is a variant of residual networks, or Resnet. Refer to "Deep Residual Learning for Image Recognition" (*https://oreil.ly/XQYUh*) by Kaiming He et al. for details about the architecture and for references on CNNs. Briefly, a convolution layer repeatedly applies a small filter of typically 3 × 3 size over an image. This results in a feature map of the same resolution as the input if the stride is (1, 1) (which means apply the filter with a 1-pixel step in the x direction and a 1-pixel step in the y direction), or quarter size if the stride is (2, 2). The residual skip connection is just a shortcut from the previous input layer to the next, so in effect, the nonlinear part of the networks learns the residual from the linear skip part, hence the name residual network.

Additionally, we use the BatchNorm layer, details of which can be found at "Batch Normalization: Accelerating Deep Network Training by Reducing Internal Covariate Shift" (*https://oreil.ly/qM-yg*) by Sergey Ioffe and Christian Szegedy, and the "Searching for Activation Functions" (*https://oreil.ly/9Zlqb*) by Prajit Ramachandran, Barret Zoph, and Quoc V. Le.

Once we specify the model, we also need to optimize it for the task.

Model Training in JAX, Flax, and Optax

Optimizing our model should be pretty straightforward in any ML framework. Here we show how to do it easily with JAX (*https://oreil.ly/pcmCU*), Flax (*https://oreil.ly/RtzDn*), and Optax (*https://oreil.ly/vOCvF*). JAX is a lower-level NumPy-like ML library, and *Flax* is a higher-level neural network library that provides functionality such as neural network modules and embedding layers. *Optax* is a library that does optimization that we will use to minimize our loss function.

If you are familiar with NumPy, JAX is quite easy to pick up. JAX shares the same API as NumPy but has the capability of running the resulting code on vector processors such as GPUs or TPUs by doing JIT compilation. JAX device arrays and NumPy arrays can be easily converted back and forth, which makes it easy to develop for the GPU and yet easy to debug on the CPU.

In addition to learning how to represent the images, we also need to specify how they are related to one another.

Since the embedding vectors are of fixed dimensions, the easiest similarity score is simply the dot product of the two vectors. See "Similarity from Co-occurrence" on page 163 for other kinds of similarity measures. So, given an image for a scene, we compute the scene embedding and do the same for the product to obtain a product embedding, and take the dot product of the two to obtain a score for the closeness of fit of a scene $\vec{s}$ to a product $\vec{p}$:

$$score\left(\vec{s}, \vec{p}\right) = \vec{s} * \vec{p}$$

We use CNNs to obtain the embedding of an image.

We use separate CNNs for the scene and product, however, because they come from different kinds of images. Scenes tend to show the context we're matching products to and contain people and the setting, whereas products tend to be catalog images of shoes and bags with a blank background, so we need different neural networks to determine what is important in the image.

Once we have the score, that alone is not sufficient, though. We need to make sure that a good match of a scene and product, which we call the *positive product*, is higher scoring than a negative product. The positive product is a good match for the scene, and the negative product is a not-so-good match for the scene. The positive product comes from the training data, and the negative product comes from randomly sampling the catalog. A loss that can capture the relationship between a positive scene-product pair (A, B) and negative scene-product pair (A, C) is called *triplet loss*. Let's go into some detail for defining the triplet loss (*https://oreil.ly/alBxu*).

Suppose we want the score for the positive scene-product pair to be one more than a negative scene-product pair. We then have the following inequality:

$$score(scene, pos_{product}) > score(scene, neg_{product}) + 1$$

The 1 is just an arbitrary constant we use, called a *margin*, to make sure that the positive scene-product score is larger than the negative scene-product score.

Since the process of gradient descent minimizes a function, we then convert the preceding inequality into a loss function by moving all terms to one side:

$$0 > 1 + score(scene, neg_{product}) - score(scene, pos_{product})$$

As long as the quantity on the right side is larger than 0, we want to minimize it; but if it is already less than 0, we do not. Therefore, we encode the quantity in a rectified linear unit, which is represented by the function `max(0, x)`. We can thus write out our loss function as follows:

$$loss(scene, pos_{product}, neg_{product}) =$$
$$max(0, 1 + score(scene, neg_{product}) - score(scene, pos_{product}))$$

Since we usually minimize loss functions, this ensures that as long as the `score(scene, neg_product)` is 1 more than `score(scene, pos_product)`, the optimization procedure will try to minimize the score of the negative pair while increasing the score of the positive pair.

The next example covers the following modules in order so that they make sense as they follow the flow of data from reading to training to making recommendations:

input__pipeline.py
How the data is read

models.py
How the neural networks are specified

train_shop_the_look.py
How the neural network is fit using Optax

make_embeddings.py
How to make a compact database of scene and products

make_recommendations.py
    How to use the compact database of embeddings to create a list of product
    recommendations per scene

Input Pipeline

Example 5-2 shows the code for *input_pipeline.py*. We use the ML library TensorFlow
(*https://oreil.ly/hsqPr*) for its data pipeline.

Example 5-2. TensorFlow data pipeline

```
import tensorflow as tf

def normalize_image(img):
  img = tf.cast(img, dtype=tf.float32)
  img = (img / 255.0) - 0.5
  return img

def process_image(x):
  x = tf.io.read_file(x)
  x = tf.io.decode_jpeg(x, channels=3)
  x = tf.image.resize_with_crop_or_pad(x, 512, 512)
  x = normalize_image(x)
  return x

def process_image_with_id(id):
  image = process_image(id)
  return id, image

def process_triplet(x):
  x = (process_image(x[0]), process_image(x[1]), process_image(x[2]))
  return x

def create_dataset(
    triplet: Sequence[Tuple[str, str, str]]):
    """Creates a triplet dataset.
    Args:
      triplet: filenames of scene, positive product, negative product.
    """
    ds = tf.data.Dataset.from_tensor_slices(triplet)
    ds = ds.map(process_triplet)
    return ds
```

You can see that `create_dataset` takes in three filenames: that of a scene, then a
positive match and a negative match. For this example, the negative match is simply
selected at random from the catalog. We cover more sophisticated ways of picking
the negative in Chapter 12. The image filenames are processed by reading the file,
decoding the image, cropping it to a fixed size, and then rescaling the data so that it

---

becomes a floating-point image centered around 0 and with small values between −1 and 1. We do this because most neural networks are initialized with the assumption that the data they get is roughly normally distributed, and so if you pass in too large a value, it would be far out of the norm of the expected input range.

Example 5-3 shows how to specify our CNN and STL model with Flax.

Example 5-3. Defining the CNN model

```
from flax import linen as nn
import jax.numpy as jnp

class CNN(nn.Module):
    """Simple CNN."""
    filters : Sequence[int]
    output_size : int

    @nn.compact
    def __call__(self, x, train: bool = True):
        for filter in self.filters:
            # Stride 2 downsamples 2x.
            residual = nn.Conv(filter, (3, 3), (2, 2))(x)
            x = nn.Conv(filter, (3, 3), (2, 2))(x)
            x = nn.BatchNorm(
              use_running_average=not train, use_bias=False)(x)
            x = nn.swish(x)
            x = nn.Conv(filter, (1, 1), (1, 1))(x)
            x = nn.BatchNorm(
              use_running_average=not train, use_bias=False)(x)
            x = nn.swish(x)
            x = nn.Conv(filter, (1, 1), (1, 1))(x)
            x = nn.BatchNorm(
              use_running_average=not train, use_bias=False)(x)
            x = x + residual
            # Average pool downsamples 2x.
            x = nn.avg_pool(x, (3, 3), strides=(2, 2), padding="SAME")
        x = jnp.mean(x, axis=(1, 2))
        x = nn.Dense(self.output_size, dtype=jnp.float32)(x)
        return x

class STLModel(nn.Module):
    """Shop the look model that takes in a scene
       and item and computes a score for them.
    """
    output_size : int

    def setup(self):
        default_filter = [16, 32, 64, 128]
        self.scene_cnn = CNN(
          filters=default_filter, output_size=self.output_size)
        self.product_cnn = CNN(
```

```
        filters=default_filter, output_size=self.output_size)

    def get_scene_embed(self, scene):
        return self.scene_cnn(scene, False)

    def get_product_embed(self, product):
        return self.product_cnn(product, False)

    def __call__(self, scene, pos_product, neg_product,
                 train: bool = True):
        scene_embed = self.scene_cnn(scene, train)

        pos_product_embed = self.product_cnn(pos_product, train)
        pos_score = scene_embed * pos_product_embed
        pos_score = jnp.sum(pos_score, axis=-1)

        neg_product_embed = self.product_cnn(neg_product, train)
        neg_score = scene_embed * neg_product_embed
        neg_score = jnp.sum(neg_score, axis=-1)

        return pos_score, neg_score, scene_embed,
            pos_product_embed, neg_product_embed
```

Here we use Flax's neural network class Module. The annotation nn.compact is there so we do not have to specify a setup function for simple neural network architectures like this one and can simply specify the layers in the call function. The call function accepts two parameters, an image *x* and a Boolean train that tells the module whether we are calling it in training mode. The reason we need the Boolean training is that the BatchNorm layers are updated only during training and are not updated when the network is fully learned.

If you look at the CNN specification code, you can see how we set up the residual network. We can freely mix neural network functions like swish with JAX functions like mean. The swish function is a nonlinear activation for the neural network that transforms the input in such a way as to weight some values of activation more than others.

The STL model, on the other hand, has a more complicated setup, so we have to specify the setup code to create two CNN towers: one for the scene and another for the product. A *CNN tower* is just a copy of the same architecture but has different weights for different image types. As mentioned earlier, we have a different tower for each type of image because each represents different things; one tower is for the scene (which provides the context to which we are matching products), and a separate tower is for the products. As a result, we add in two different methods for converting scene and product images into scene and product embeddings.

The call is also different. It doesn't have the annotation compact because we have a more complicated setup. In the call function for the STL model, we first compute the scene embedding, then the positive product embedding, and then the positive score. After that, we do the same for the negative score. We then return the positive score, negative score, and all three embedding vectors. We return the embedding vectors as well as the scores because we want to ensure that the model generalizes to new, unseen data as in a held-out validation set, so we want to make sure the embedding vectors are not too large. The concept of capping their size is called *regularization*.

Now let's take a look at *train_shop_the_look.py* (Example 5-4). We'll break it into separate function calls and discuss them one by one.

Example 5-4. Generating triplets for training

```
def generate_triplets(
    scene_product: Sequence[Tuple[str, str]],
    num_neg: int) -> Sequence[Tuple[str, str, str]]:
    """Generate positive and negative triplets."""
    count = len(scene_product)
    train = []
    test = []
    key = jax.random.PRNGKey(0)
    for i in range(count):
        scene, pos = scene_product[i]
        is_test = i % 10 == 0
        key, subkey = jax.random.split(key)
        neg_indices = jax.random.randint(subkey, [num_neg], 0, count - 1)
        for neg_idx in neg_indices:
            _, neg = scene_product[neg_idx]
            if is_test:
                test.append((scene, pos, neg))
            else:
                train.append((scene, pos, neg))
    return train, test

def shuffle_array(key, x):
    """Deterministic string shuffle."""
    num = len(x)
    to_swap = jax.random.randint(key, [num], 0, num - 1)
    return [x[t] for t in to_swap]
```

The code fragment reads in the scene-product JSON database and generates triplets of scene, positive product, and negative products for the input pipeline. The interesting part to note here is how JAX handles random numbers. JAX's philosophy is functional in nature, meaning that functions are pure and have no side effects. Random-number generators carry state, so in order to make JAX random-number generators function, you have to pass in the state to the random-number generator. The mechanism for this is to have a pseudo random number generator key,

PNRGKey, as the object-carrying state. We initialize one arbitrarily from the number 0. Whenever we wish to use the key, though, we have to split it into two by using `jax.random.split`, then use one to generate the next random number and a subkey to perform the random action. In this case, we use the subkey to select a random negative from the entire corpus of products for our negative. We cover more complex ways to sample the negative in Chapter 12, but randomly selecting a negative is the simplest way to construct the triplet for triplet loss.

Similar to the way the negatives are selected, we again use JAX's random functionality to generate a list of indices to swap, in order to shuffle the array for the training step. Random shuffling is important in stochastic gradient descent to break up any kind of structure in the training data to ensure that the gradients are stochastic. We use JAX's random shuffling mechanism for better reproducibility so that experiments are more likely to be the same, given the same initial data and settings.

The next pair of functions we will look at are listed in Example 5-5 and show how the train and eval steps are written. The train step takes the state of the model, which contains the model parameters as well as the gradient information, which varies depending on the optimizer being used. This step also takes in batches of scenes, positive products, and negative products in order to construct the triplet loss. In addition to optimizing for the triplet loss, we want to minimize the size of the embeddings whenever they go outside the unit sphere. The process of minimizing the size of the embeddings is called *regularization*, so we add it to the triplet loss to obtain the final loss.

Example 5-5. Training and evaluation steps

```
def train_step(state, scene, pos_product,
               neg_product, regularization, batch_size):
    def loss_fn(params):
        result, new_model_state = state.apply_fn(
            params,
            scene, pos_product, neg_product, True,
            mutable=['batch_stats'])
        triplet_loss = jnp.sum(nn.relu(1.0 + result[1] - result[0]))
        def reg_fn(embed):
            return nn.relu(
                jnp.sqrt(jnp.sum(jnp.square(embed), axis=-1)) - 1.0)
        reg_loss = reg_fn(result[2]) +
                   reg_fn(result[3]) + reg_fn(result[4])
        reg_loss = jnp.sum(reg_loss)
        return (triplet_loss + regularization * reg_loss) / batch_size

    grad_fn = jax.value_and_grad(loss_fn)
    loss, grads = grad_fn(state.params)
    new_state = state.apply_gradients(grads=grads)
    return new_state, loss
```

```
def eval_step(state, scene, pos_product, neg_product):
    def loss_fn(params):
        result, new_model_state = state.apply_fn(
            state.params,
            scene, pos_product, neg_product, True,
            mutable=['batch_stats'])
        # Use a fixed margin for the eval.
        triplet_loss = jnp.sum(nn.relu(1.0 + result[1] - result[0]))
        return triplet_loss
```

Flax, being written on top of JAX, is also functional in philosophy, so the existing state is used to compute the gradient of the loss function, which when applied returns a new state variable. This ensures that the functions remain pure and the state variables are mutable.

This functional philosophy is what allows JAX to JIT compile or use JIT functions so they run fast on CPU, GPU, or TPU.

The eval step, in comparison, is rather simple. It just computes the triplet loss without the regularization loss as our evaluation metric. Again, we cover more sophisticated evaluation metrics in Chapter 11.

Finally, let's take a look at the body of the training program, shown in Example 5-6. We store our hyperparameters such as learning rate, regularization, and output size in a config dictionary. We do this so we can pass the config dictionary on to the Weights & Biases MLOps service for safekeeping and also so we can do hyperparameter sweeps.

Example 5-6. Main body of code for training the model

```
def main(argv):
    """Main function."""
    del argv  # Unused.
    config = {
        "learning_rate" : _LEARNING_RATE.value,
        "regularization" : _REGULARIZATION.value,
        "output_size" : _OUTPUT_SIZE.value
    }

    run = wandb.init(
        config=config,
        project="recsys-pinterest"
    )

    tf.config.set_visible_devices([], 'GPU')
    tf.compat.v1.enable_eager_execution()
    logging.info("Image dir %s, input file %s",
        _IMAGE_DIRECTORY.value, _INPUT_FILE.value)
    scene_product = pin_util.get_valid_scene_product(
```

```
    _IMAGE_DIRECTORY.value, _INPUT_FILE.value)
logging.info("Found %d valid scene product pairs." % len(scene_product))

train, test = generate_triplets(scene_product, _NUM_NEG.value)
num_train = len(train)
num_test = len(test)
logging.info("Train triplets %d", num_train)
logging.info("Test triplets %d", num_test)

 # Random shuffle the train.
key = jax.random.PRNGKey(0)
train = shuffle_array(key, train)
test = shuffle_array(key, test)
train = np.array(train)
test = np.array(test)

train_ds = input_pipeline.create_dataset(train).repeat()
train_ds = train_ds.batch(_BATCH_SIZE.value).prefetch(
  tf.data.AUTOTUNE)

test_ds = input_pipeline.create_dataset(test).repeat()
test_ds = test_ds.batch(_BATCH_SIZE.value)

stl = models.STLModel(output_size=wandb.config.output_size)
train_it = train_ds.as_numpy_iterator()
test_it = test_ds.as_numpy_iterator()
x = next(train_it)
key, subkey = jax.random.split(key)
params = stl.init(subkey, x[0], x[1], x[2])
tx = optax.adam(learning_rate=wandb.config.learning_rate)
state = train_state.TrainState.create(
    apply_fn=stl.apply, params=params, tx=tx)
if _RESTORE_CHECKPOINT.value:
    state = checkpoints.restore_checkpoint(_WORKDIR.value, state)

train_step_fn = jax.jit(train_step)
eval_step_fn = jax.jit(eval_step)

losses = []
init_step = state.step
logging.info("Starting at step %d", init_step)
regularization = wandb.config.regularization
batch_size = _BATCH_SIZE.value
eval_steps = int(num_test / batch_size)
for i in range(init_step, _MAX_STEPS.value + 1):
    batch = next(train_it)
    scene = batch[0]
    pos_product = batch[1]
    neg_product = batch[2]

    state, loss = train_step_fn(
        state, scene, pos_product, neg_product,
```

```
            regularization, batch_size)
        losses.append(loss)
        if i % _CHECKPOINT_EVERY_STEPS.value == 0 and i > 0:
            logging.info("Saving checkpoint")
            checkpoints.save_checkpoint(
              _WORKDIR.value, state, state.step, keep=3)
        metrics = {
            "step" : state.step
        }
        if i % _EVAL_EVERY_STEPS.value == 0 and i > 0:
            eval_loss = []
            for j in range(eval_steps):
                ebatch = next(test_it)
                escene = ebatch[0]
                epos_product = ebatch[1]
                eneg_product = ebatch[2]
                loss = eval_step_fn(
                  state, escene, epos_product, eneg_product)
                eval_loss.append(loss)
            eval_loss = jnp.mean(jnp.array(eval_loss)) / batch_size
            metrics.update({"eval_loss" : eval_loss})
        if i % _LOG_EVERY_STEPS.value == 0 and i > 0:
            mean_loss = jnp.mean(jnp.array(losses))
            losses = []
            metrics.update({"train_loss" : mean_loss})
            wandb.log(metrics)
            logging.info(metrics)

    logging.info("Saving as %s", _MODEL_NAME.value)
    data = flax.serialization.to_bytes(state)
    metadata = { "output_size" : wandb.config.output_size }
    artifact = wandb.Artifact(
        name=_MODEL_NAME.value,
        metadata=metadata,
        type="model")
    with artifact.new_file("pinterest_stl.model", "wb") as f:
        f.write(data)
    run.log_artifact(artifact)


if __name__ == "__main__":
    app.run(main)
```

A *hyperparameter sweep* is a tuning service that helps you find optimal values for hyperparameters such as learning rate by running many trials of different values and searches for the best one. Having the configuration as a dictionary allows us to reproduce the best parameters by running a hyperparameter sweep and then saving the best one for the final model.

In Figure 5-2, you can see what a Weights & Biases hyperparameter sweep looks like. On the left, we have all the runs in the sweep; each run is trying a different set of values that we have specified in the config dictionary. In the middle, we see how the final evaluation loss changes over time with the number of trials on the sweep. On the right, we have a plot indicating the importance of the hyperparameter in affecting the evaluation loss. Here we can see that the learning rate has the most effect on the eval loss, followed by the regularization amount.

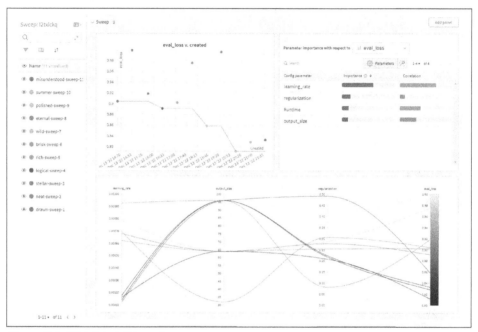

Figure 5-2. Weights & Biases hyperparameter sweep

On the bottom right of the figure, a parallel coordinates plot shows how each parameter affects the evaluation loss. To read the plot, follow each line and see where it ends up on the final evaluation loss. The optimal hyperparameters can be found by tracing the line from the bottom-right target value of evaluation loss back to the left, through the values chosen for the hyperparameters. In this case, the optimal value selected is a learning_rate of 0.0001618, a regularization of 0.2076, and an output_size of 64.

The rest of the code is mostly setting up the model and hooking up the input pipeline to the model. Deciding when to log metrics and model serialization is mostly self-explanatory. The details can be read in the Flax documentation.

In saving the model, notice that two methods are used. One is a checkpoint, and the other is Flax serialization. We have both because the checkpoint is used when training jobs are canceled and we need to recover the step at which the job was canceled so we can resume training. The final serialization is used when the training is done.

We also save a copy of the model as a Weights & Biases artifact (*https://oreil.ly/ gmGGt*). This way, the Weights & Biases platform can keep track of the hyperparameters that created the model, the exact code and the exact Git hash that generated the model, and the lineage of the model. This lineage consists of upstream artifacts used to generate the model (such as the training data), the state of the job used to create the model, and an added back link to all future jobs that might use the artifact. This makes it easier to reproduce models at a point in time or trace back which model was used and at what time in production. This comes in super handy when you have a larger organization and folks are hunting around for information on how a model was created. By using artifacts, they can simply look in one place for the code and training data artifacts to reproduce a model.

Now that we have trained the models, we want to generate embeddings for the scene and the product database. The nice thing about using the dot product as a scoring function as opposed to using a model is that you can generate scene and product embeddings independently and then scale out these computations at inference time. This kind of scaling will be introduced in Chapter 8, but for now the relevant part of *make_embeddings.py* is shown in Example 5-7.

Example 5-7. Finding the top-k recommendations

```
model = models.STLModel(output_size=_OUTPUT_SIZE.value)
state = None
logging.info("Attempting to read model %s", _MODEL_NAME.value)
with open(_MODEL_NAME.value, "rb") as f:
    data = f.read()
    state = flax.serialization.from_bytes(model, data)
assert(state != None)

@jax.jit
def get_scene_embed(x):
  return model.apply(state["params"], x, method=models.STLModel.get_scene_embed)
@jax.jit
def get_product_embed(x):
  return model.apply(
  state["params"],
  x,
  method=models.STLModel.get_product_embed
  )

ds = tf.data.Dataset
  .from_tensor_slices(unique_scenes)
  .map(input_pipeline.process_image_with_id)
ds = ds.batch(_BATCH_SIZE.value, drop_remainder=True)
it = ds.as_numpy_iterator()
scene_dict = {}
count = 0
for id, image in it:
```

```
    count = count + 1
    if count % 100 == 0:
      logging.info("Created %d scene embeddings", count * _BATCH_SIZE.value)
    result = get_scene_embed(image)
    for i in range(_BATCH_SIZE.value):
      current_id = id[i].decode("utf-8")
      tmp = np.array(result[i])
      current_result = [float(tmp[j]) for j in range(tmp.shape[0])]
      scene_dict.update({current_id : current_result})
  scene_filename = os.path.join(_OUTDIR.value, "scene_embed.json")
  with open(scene_filename, "w") as scene_file:
    json.dump(scene_dict, scene_file)
```

As you can see, we simply use the same Flax serialization library to load the model, and then call the appropriate method of the model by using the apply function. We then save the vectors in a JSON file, since we have already been using JSON for the scene and product databases.

Finally, we'll use the scoring code in *make_recommendations.py* to generate product recommendations for sample scenes (Example 5-8).

Example 5-8. Core retrieval definition

```
def find_top_k(
  scene_embedding,
  product_embeddings,
  k):
  """
  Finds the top K nearest product embeddings to the scene embedding.
  Args:
    scene_embedding: embedding vector for the scene
    product_embedding: embedding vectors for the products.
    k: number of top results to return.
  """

  scores = scene_embedding * product_embeddings
  scores = jnp.sum(scores, axis=-1)
  scores_and_indices = jax.lax.top_k(scores, k)
  return scores_and_indices

top_k_finder = jax.jit(find_top_k, static_argnames=["k"])
```

The most relevant code fragment is the scoring code, where we have a scene embedding and want to use JAX to score all the product embeddings instead of a single scene embedding. Here we use Lax, a sublibrary of JAX that supplies direct API calls to XLA, the underlying ML compiler for JAX, in order to access accelerated functions like top_k. In addition, we compile the function find_top_k by using JAX's JIT. You can pass pure Python functions that contain JAX commands to jax.jit in order to compile them to a specific target architecture such as a GPU using XLA. Notice we have a special argument called `static_argnames`; this allows us to inform JAX that k is fixed and doesn't change much so that JAX is able to compile a purpose-built `top_k_finder` for a fixed value of k.

Figure 5-3 shows sample product recommendations for a scene in which a woman is wearing a red shirt. The products recommended include red velvet and dark pants.

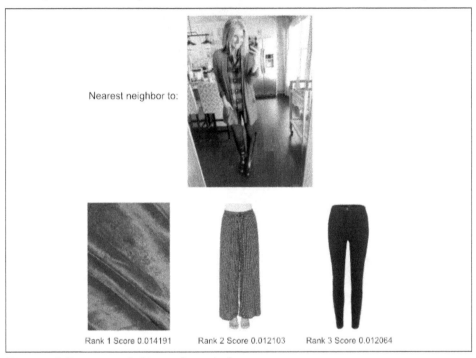

Nearest neighbor to:

Rank 1 Score 0.014191   Rank 2 Score 0.012103   Rank 3 Score 0.012064

Figure 5-3. Recommended items for an indoor scene

Figure 5-4 shows another scene: a woman is wearing a red coat outdoors, and the matching accessories are a yellow handbag and yellow pants.

We have pregenerated some results that are stored as an artifact that you can view by typing in the following command:

```
wandb artifact get building-recsys/recsys-pinterest/scene_product_results:v0
```

One thing you may notice is that the yellow bag and pants get recommended a lot. It may be possible that the embedding vector for the yellow bag is large, so it gets matched to a lot of scenes. This is called the *popular item problem* and is a common issue with recommendation systems. We cover some business logic to handle diversity and popularity in later chapters, but this is a problem that can happen with recommendation systems that you might want to keep an eye out for.

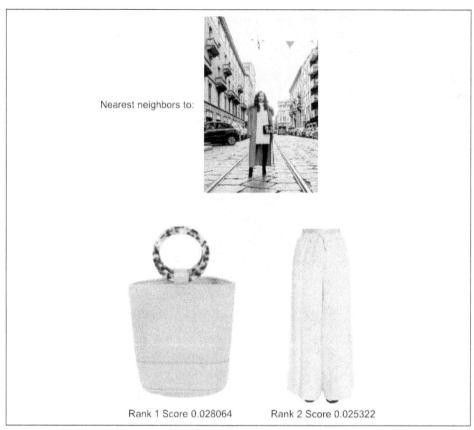

Nearest neighbors to:

Rank 1 Score 0.028064   Rank 2 Score 0.025322

Figure 5-4. Recommended items for an outdoor scene

Summary

And with that, we conclude the first "Putting It All Together" chapter. We covered how to use JAX and Flax to read real-world data, train a model, and find the top recommended items for a look. If you haven't played with the code yet, hop on over to the GitHub repo to give it a whirl! We hope that providing a real-world working example of an end-to-end content-based recommender will give you a better feel for how the theory translates into practice. Enjoy playing with the code!

## PART II

Retrieval

How do we get all the data in the right place to train a recommendation system? How do we build and deploy systems for real-time inference?

Reading **research papers** about recommendation systems will often give the impression that they're built via a bunch of math equations, and all the really hard work of using recommendation systems is in connecting these equations to the features of your problem. More realistically, the first several steps of building a production recommendation system fall under systems engineering. Understanding how your data will make it into your system, be manipulated into the correct structure, and then be available in each of the relevant steps of the training flow often constitutes the bulk of the initial recommendation system's work. But even beyond this initial phase, ensuring that all the necessary components are fast enough and robust enough for production environments requires yet another significant investment in platform infrastructure.

Often you'll build a component responsible for processing the various types of data and storing them in a convenient format. Next, you'll construct a model that takes that data and encodes it in a latent space or other representation model. Finally, you'll need to transform an input request into the representation as a query in this space. These steps usually take the form of jobs in a workflow management platform or services deployed as endpoints. The next few chapters will walk you through the relevant technologies and concepts necessary to build and deploy these systems—and the awareness of important aspects of reliability, scalability, and efficiency.

You might be thinking, "I'm a data scientist! I don't need to know all this!" But you should know that RecSys has an inconvenient duality: model architecture changes often affect the systems architecture. Interested in trying out those fancy transformers? Your deployment strategy is going to need a new design. Maybe your clever feature embeddings can solve the cold-start problem! Those feature embeddings will need to serve your encoding layers and integrate with your new NoSQL feature store. Don't panic! This part of the book is a walk through the Big Data Zoo.

## CHAPTER 6

Data Processing

In the trivial recommender that we defined in Chapter 1, we used the method `get_availability`; and in the MPIR, we used the method `get_item_popularities`. We hoped the choice of naming would provide sufficient context about their function, but we did not focus on the implementation details. Now we will start unpacking the details of some of this complexity and present the toolsets for online and offline collectors.

Hydrating Your System

Getting data into the pipeline is punnily referred to as *hydration*. The ML and data fields have a lot of water-themed naming conventions; "(Data ∩ Water) Terms" (*https://oreil.ly/XVlzd*) by Pardis Noorzad covers this topic.

PySpark

Spark is an extremely general computing library, with APIs for Java, Python, SQL, and Scala. PySpark's role in many ML pipelines is for data processing and transforming the large-scale datasets.

Let's return to the data structure we introduced for our recommendation problem; recall that the user-item matrix is the linear-algebraic representation of all the triples of users, items, and the user's rating of the item. These triples are not naturally occurring in the wild. Most commonly, you begin with log files from your system; for example, Bookshop.org may have something that looks like this:

```
'page_view_id': 'd15220a8e9a8e488162af3120b4396a9ca1',
'anonymous_id': 'e455d516-3c08-4b6f-ab12-77f930e2661f',
'view_tstamp': 2020-10-29 17:44:41+00:00,
'page_url': 'https://bookshop.org/lists/best-sellers-of-the-week',
'page_url_host': 'bookshop.org',
```

```
'page_url_path': '/lists/bookshop-org-best-sellers-of-the-week',
'page_title': 'Best Sellers of the Week',
'page_url_query': None,
'authenticated_user_id': 15822493.0,
'url_report_id': 511629659.0,
'is_profile_page': False,
'product_viewed': 'list',
```

This is a made-up log file that may look similar to the backend data for Book-shop.org's best sellers of the week. These are the kinds of events that you consume from engineering and are likely stored in your columnar database. For data like this, utilizing SQL syntax will be our entry point.

PySpark provides a convenient SQL API. Based on your infrastructure, this API will allow you to write what looks like SQL queries against a potentially massive dataset.

Example Schemas

These example database schemas are only guesses at what Book-shop.org may use, but they are modeled on the authors' experience of looking at hundreds of database schemas at multiple companies over many years. Additionally, we attempt to distill these schemas to the components relevant to our topic. In real systems, you'd expect much more complexity but the same essential parts. Each data warehouse and event stream will have its own quirks. Please consult a data engineer near you.

Let's use Spark to query the preceding logs:

```
user_item_view_counts_qry = """
SELECT
  page_views.authenticated_user_id
  , page_views.page_url_path
  , COUNT(DISTINCT page_views.page_view_id) AS count_views

FROM prod.page_views
JOIN prod.dim_users
        ON page_views.authenticated_user_id = dim_users.authenticated_user_id

WHERE DATE page_views.view_tstamp >= '2017-01-01'
        AND dim_users.country_code = 'US'

GROUP BY
  page_views.authenticated_user_id
  , page_views.page_url_path

ORDER BY 3, page_views.authenticated_user_id
"""

user_item_view_counts_sdf = spark.sql(user_item_view_counts_qry)
```

This is a simple SQL query, assuming the preceding log schema, that would allow us to see, for each user-item pair, how many times that user has viewed that pair. The convenience of writing pure SQL here means that we can use our experience in columnar databases to quickly ramp up on Spark.

The major advantage of Spark, however, is not yet on display. When executing the preceding code in a Spark session, this query will not be immediately run. It will be staged for execution, but Spark waits until you use this data downstream in a way that *requires immediate execution* before it begins doing so. This is called *lazy evaluation*, and it allows you to work on your data object without every change and interaction immediately being applied. For more details, it's worth consulting a more in-depth guide like *Learning Spark* by Jules Damji et al. (O'Reilly), but there's one more important characteristic of the Spark paradigm that is essential to discuss.

Spark is natively a distributed computing language. In particular, this means that the preceding query—even after we force it to execute—will store its data on multiple computers. Spark works via a *driver program* in your program or notebook, which drives a *cluster manager*, which in turn coordinates *executors* on *worker nodes*. When we query data with Spark, instead of all that data being returned into a DataFrame in memory on the computer we're using, parts of that data are sent to memory on the executors. And when we do a transformation on the DataFrame, it is applied appropriately on the pieces of the DataFrame that are stored on each of the executors.

If this sounds a bit like magic, that's because it's obscuring a lot of technical details behind several convenience layers. Spark is a layer of technology that allows the ML engineer to program as if they're working on one machine, and have those changes take effect on an entire cluster of machines. It's not important to understand the network structure when querying, but it is important to be aware of some of these details in case things go wrong; the ability to understand what the error output is referring to is crucial in troubleshooting. This is all summarized in Figure 6-1, which is a diagram from the Spark documentation (*https://oreil.ly/89kAm*).

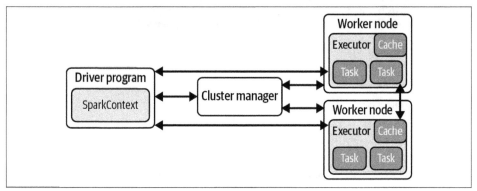

Figure 6-1. Component architecture of Spark 3.0

It's important to note that all this does not come for free; both lazy evaluation and distributed DataFrames come at the cost of needing additional thought when writing programs. Even though Spark makes a lot of this work far easier, understanding how to write efficient code in this paradigm that works with the architecture but still achieves complicated goals can require a year's worth of experience.

Returning to recommendation systems—and in particular, the offline collector—we want to use PySpark to build the types of datasets needed to train our models. One simple thing to do with PySpark is to transform our logs data into the appropriate form for training a model. In our simple query, we applied a few filters to our data and grouped by user and item to get the number of views. A variety of other tasks may fit naturally into this paradigm—perhaps adding user or item features stored in other databases, or high-level aggregations.

In our MPIR, we asked for `get_item_popularities`; and we sort of assumed a few things:

- This would return the number of times each item was chosen.
- This method would be fast.

The second point is important if the endpoint is going to be called in real time. So how might Spark come into play?

First, let's assume we have a lot of data, enough that we can't get it all to fit into our little MacBook Pro's memory. Additionally, let's continue to use the preceding schema. We can write an even simpler query:

```
item_popularity_qry = """
SELECT
  page_views.page_url_path
  , COUNT(DISTINCT page_views.authenticated_user_id) AS count_viewers

FROM prod.page_views
JOIN prod.dim_users
        ON page_views.authenticated_user_id = dim_users.authenticated_user_id

WHERE DATE page_views.view_tstamp >= '2017-01-01'
        AND dim_users.country_code = 'US'

GROUP BY
  page_views.page_url_path

ORDER BY 2
"""

item_view_counts_sdf = spark.sql(item_popularity_qry)
```

We can now write this aggregated list of (`item`, `count`) pairs to an app database to serve `get_item_popularities` (something that doesn't require us to do any parsing when this is called), or potentially we can take a subset of the top-N of this list and store it in memory to get the best items with respect to a particular ranking. Either way, we've separated concerns of parsing all our log data, and doing aggregation, from the `get_item_popularities` function call in real time.

This example used an overly simple data aggregation, one just as easy to do in something like PostgreSQL, so why bother? The first reason is scalability. Spark is really built to scale horizontally, which means that as the data we need to access grows, we merely add more worker nodes.

The second reason is that PySpark is more than just SparkSQL; anyone who's done complicated SQL queries can probably agree that the power and flexibility of SQL is enormous, but frequently certain tasks that you want to achieve require a lot of creativity to carry out in the fully SQL environment. PySpark gives you all the expressiveness of pandas DataFrames, Python functions and classes, and a simple interface to apply Python code to the PySpark data structure's user-defined functions (UDFs). UDFs are similar to lambda functions that you'd use in pandas, but they're built and optimized for PySpark DataFrames. As you've probably experienced when writing ML programs in smaller data regimes, at some point you switch away from using only SQL to using pandas API functions to perform data transformations—so too will you appreciate this power at the Spark data scale.

PySpark allows you to write what looks very much like Python and pandas code and have that code executed in a distributed fashion! You don't need to write code to specify which worker nodes operations should happen; that's handled for you by PySpark. This framework isn't perfect; some things you expect to work may require a bit of care, and optimization of your code can require an additional level of abstraction, but generally, PySpark gives you a rapid way to move your code from one node to a cluster and utilize that power.

To illustrate something a bit more useful in PySpark, let's return to collaborative filtering (CF) and compute some features more relevant for ranking.

Example: User Similarity in PySpark

A user similarity table allows you to map a user to other users who are relevant to the recommender. This recalls the assumption that two similar users like similar things, and thus you can recommend to both users the items that one hasn't seen. Constructing this user similarity table is an example of a PySpark job that you might see as part of the offline collector's responsibility. Even though in many cases ratings would continue to stream in all the time, for the purposes of large offline jobs, we often think of a daily batch to update the essential tables for our model. In practice, in many cases this daily batch job suffices to provide features that are good enough for most of the ML work downstream. Other important paradigms exist, but those frequently *marry* the more frequent updates with these daily batch jobs, instead of totally eliminating them.

This architecture of daily batch jobs with smaller, more frequent batch jobs is called the *lambda architecture*, and we'll get more into the details of how and why later. In brief, the two layers—batch and speed—which are distinguished (inversely) by the frequency of processing and the volume per run of data they process. Note that the speed layer may have varying frequencies associated with it, and it's possible to have different speed layers for hourly, and another speed layer for minute-frequency jobs that do different things. Figure 6-2 provides an overview of the architecture.

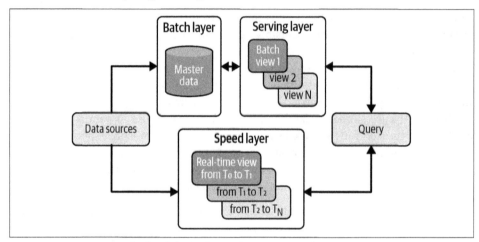

Figure 6-2. Overview of a lambda architecture

In the case of user similarity, let's work on a batch job implementation of computing a daily table. First we'll need to get ratings from our schema before today. We'll also include a few other filters that simulate how this query might look in real life:

```
user_item_ratings_qry = """
SELECT
  book_ratings.book_id
  book_ratings.user_id
  , book_ratings.rating_value
  , book_ratings.rating_tstamp

FROM prod.book_ratings
JOIN prod.dim_users
        ON book_ratings.user_id = dim_users.user_id
JOIN prod.dim_books
        ON book_ratings.book_id = dim_books.dim_books

WHERE
        DATE book_ratings.rating_tstamp
```

```
                    BETWEEN (DATE '2017-01-01')
                      AND (CAST(current_timestamp() as DATE)
        AND book_ratings.rating_value IS NOT NULL
              AND dim_users.country_code = 'US'
        AND dim_books.book_active
    """

    user_item_ratings_sdf = spark.sql(user_item_ratings_qry)
```

As before, utilizing the SQL syntax to get the dataset into a Spark DataFrame is the first step, but now we have additional work on the PySpark side. A common pattern is to get the dataset you want to work with via simple SQL syntax and logic, and then use the PySpark API to do more detailed data processing.

Let's first observe that we have no assumptions about uniqueness of a user-item rating. For the sake of this table, let's decide that we'll use the most recent rating for a pair:

```
from pyspark.sql.window import Window

windows = Window().partitionBy(
        ['book_id', 'user_id']
).orderBy(
        col("rating_tstamp").desc()
)

user_item_ratings_sdf.withColumn(
        "current_rating",
        first(
                user_item_ratings_sdf("rating_tstamp")
        ).over(windows).as("max_rating_tstamp")
).filter("rating_tstamp = max_rating_tstamp")
```

We'll now use `current_rating` as our ratings column for the purpose of downstream calculation. Recall from before our ratings-based definition of user similarity:

$$\text{USim}_{A,B} = \frac{\Sigma_{x \in \mathscr{R}_{A,B}}\left(r_{A,x} - \bar{r}_A\right)\left(r_{B,x} - \bar{r}_B\right)}{\sqrt{\Sigma_{x \in \mathscr{R}_{A,B}}\left(r_{A,x} - \bar{r}_A\right)^2}\sqrt{\Sigma_{x \in \mathscr{R}_{A,B}}\left(r_{B,x} - \bar{r}_B\right)^2}}$$

The important values we'll need are as follows:

$r_{(-,-)}$
    The rating corresponding to a user-item pair

$\bar{r}_{(-)}$
    The average rating across all items for a user

The rows are already the $r_{(-, -)}$ values, so let's compute user average ratings, $\bar{r}_{(-)}$, and the rating deviations:

```
from pyspark.sql.window import Window
from pyspark.sql import functions as F

user_partition = Window.partitionBy('user_id')

user_item_ratings_sdf = user_item_ratings_sdf.withColumn(
        "user_average_rating",
        F.avg("current_rating").over(user_partition)
)

user_item_ratings_sdf = user_item_ratings_sdf.withColumn(
        "rating_deviation_from_user_mean",
        F.col("current_rating") - F.col("user_average_rating")
)
```

Now our schema should look like this (we've formatted it slightly nicer than the default Spark output):

```
+-------+-------+------------+------------+
|book_id|user_id|rating_value|rating_tstamp|
+-------+-------+------------+------------+

+--------------+-------------------+--------------------------------+
current_rating|user_average_rating|rating_deviation_from_user_mean|
+--------------+-------------------+--------------------------------+
```

Let's finish creating a dataset that contains our User Similarity calculations:

```
user_pair_item_rating_deviations = user_item_ratings_sdf.alias("left_ratings")
.join(user_item_ratings_sdf.alias("right_ratings"),
   (
F.col("left_ratings.book_id") == F.col("right_ratings.book_id") &\
F.col("left_ratings.user_id") != F.col("right_ratings.user_id")
        ),
        "inner"
).select(
        F.col("left_ratings.book_id"),
        F.col("left_ratings.user_id").alias("user_id_1"),
        F.col("right_ratings.user_id").alias("user_id_2"),
   F.col("left_ratings.rating_deviation_from_user_mean").alias("dev_1"),
   F.col("right_ratings.rating_deviation_from_user_mean").alias("dev_2")
).withColumn(
        'dev_product',
        F.col("dev_1")*F.col("dev_2")
)

user_similarities_sdf = user_pair_item_rating_deviations.groupBy(
        "user_id_1", "user_id_2"
).agg(
        sum('dev_product').alias("dev_product_sum"),
        sum(F.pow(F.col("dev_1"),2)).alias("sum_of_sqrd_devs_1"),
```

```
        sum(F.pow(F.col("dev_2"),2)).alias("sum_of_sqrd_devs_2")
).withColumn(
        "user_similarity",
        (
                F.col("dev_product_sum") / (
                        F.sqrt(F.col("sum_of_sqrd_devs_2")) *
                        F.sqrt(F.col("sum_of_sqrd_devs_2"))
                )
        )
)
```

In constructing this dataset, we begin by taking a self-join, which avoids matching the same users with themselves but rather joins on books that match. As we do this join, we take the rating deviation from the user's mean ratings that we computed previously. We also use this opportunity to multiply them together for the numerator in our user similarity function. In the last step, we'll groupBy again so that we can sum over all matching book IDs (by groupBy on user_id_1 and user_id_2); we sum the product and the powers of each set of deviations so that we can finally divide and generate a new column for our user similarity.

While this computation isn't particularly complex, let's take note of a few things that we might appreciate. First, we built our user similarity matrix in full from our records. This matrix may now be stored in a faster-access format so that if we wish to do operations in real time, it's ready to go. Second, we did all these data transformations in Spark, so we can run these operations on massive datasets and let Spark handle the parallelization onto the cluster. We even were able to do this while writing code that looks a lot like pandas and SQL. Finally, all our operations were columnar and required no iteration-based calculation. This means this code will scale much better than some approaches. This also ensures that Spark can parallelize our code well, and we can expect good performance.

We've seen how PySpark can be used to prepare our user similarity matrix. We have this definition of affinity estimating the appropriateness of an item for a user; we can collect each of those scores into a tabular form—user rows and item columns—to yield a matrix. As an exercise, can you take this matrix and generate the affinity matrix?

$$\text{Aff}_{A, i} = \bar{r}_A + \frac{\Sigma_{U \in \mathcal{N}(A)} \text{USim}_{A, U} * (r_{U, i} - \bar{r}_A)}{\Sigma_{U \in \mathcal{N}(A)} \text{USim}_{A, U}}$$

Feel free to assume that $\mathcal{N}(A)$ is just the five nearest neighbors to A with respect to user similarity.

DataLoaders

DataLoaders is a programming paradigm originating from PyTorch, but it has been embraced in other gradient-optimized ML workflows. As we begin to integrate gradient-based learning into our recommendation system architectures, we will face challenges in our MLOps tooling. The first is related to training data size and available memory. DataLoaders are a way to prescribe how data is batched and sent to the training loop efficiently; as datasets get large, careful scheduling of these training sets can have major effects on learning. But why must we think about *batches* of data? That's because we'll use a variant of gradient descent appropriate for large amounts of data.

First, let's review the basics of *mini-batched gradient descent*. During training via gradient descent, we make a forward pass of our training sample through our model to yield a prediction, and we then compute the error and the appropriate gradient backward through our model to update parameters. Batched gradient descent takes all our data in a single pass to compute the gradient for the training set and push it back through; this implies you have the entire training dataset in memory. As the dataset scales, this ranges from expensive to impossible; to avoid this, we can instead compute gradients of the loss function for only a subset of the dataset at a time. The simplest paradigm for this, called *stochastic gradient descent* (SGD), computes these gradients and parameter updates one sample at a time. The mini-batched version performs our batched gradient descent, but over a series of subsets to form a partition of our dataset. In mathematical notation, we write the update rule in terms of Jacobians on the smaller batches:

$$\theta = \theta - \eta * \nabla_\theta J\left(\theta; x^{(i:i+n)}; y^{(i:i+n)}\right)$$

This optimization serves a few purposes. First, it requires only potentially small subsets of our data held in memory during the steps. Second, it requires far fewer passes than the purely iterative version in SGD. Third, the gradient operating on these mini-batches can be organized as a Jacobian, and thus we have linear-algebraic operations that may be highly optimized.

Jacobians

The mathematical notion of a Jacobian in the simplest sense is an organizational tool for a set of vector derivatives with relevant indexes. You may recall that for functions of several variables, you can take the derivative *with respect to* each of those variables. For a single multivariable scalar function, the Jacobian is simply the row vector of first derivatives of the function—which happens to be the transpose of the gradient.

This is the simplest case; the gradient of a multivariable scalar function may be written as a Jacobian. However, once we have a vector of (vector) derivatives, we can write that as a matrix; the utility here is really only in the notation, though. When you collect a series of multivariable scalar functions into a vector of functions, the associated vector of gradients is a vector of vectors of derivatives. This is called a *Jacobian matrix*, and it generalizes the gradient to vector-valued functions. As you've likely realized, layers of neural networks are a great source of vector-valued functions for which you'd like to derivate.

If you're convinced mini-batches are useful, it's time to discuss *DataLoaders*—a simple PyTorch API for facilitating mini-batch access from a large dataset. The key parameters for a DataLoader are `batch_size`, `shuffle`, and `num_workers`. The batch size is easy to understand: it's the number of samples included in each batch (often an integer factor of the total size of the dataset). Often a shuffle operation is applied in serving up these batches; the shuffle allows batches in each epoch to be shown to the network in a randomized order; this is intended to improve robustness. Finally, `num_workers` is a parallelization parameter for the CPU's batch generation.

The utility of a DataLoader is really best understood via demonstration:

```
params = {
        'batch_size': _,
        'shuffle': _,
        'num_workers': _
}

training_generator = torch.utils.data.DataLoader(training_set, params)

validation_generator = torch.utils.data.DataLoader(validation_set, params)

// Loop over epochs
for epoch in range(max_epochs):
    // Training
    for local_batch, local_labels in training_generator:

        // Model computations
        [...]
```

```
// Validation
with torch.set_grad_enabled(False):
    for local_batch, local_labels in validation_generator:

        // Model computations
        [...]
```

The first important detail in this code is that any of its generators will be reading in mini-batches from your total dataset and can be instructed to load those batches in parallel. Note also that any differential steps in the model computations will now be operating on these mini-batches.

It's easy to think of DataLoaders as merely a tool for code cleanliness (which, admittedly, it does improve), but it's important to not underestimate how the control of batch order, parallelization, and shape are significant features for training your model. Lastly, the structure of your code now looks like batch gradient descent, but it is taking advantage of mini-batching, further exposing what your code actually does instead of the steps necessary to do it.

Database Snapshots

Let's round out this section by stepping back from these fancy technologies to discuss something important and classic: snapshotting a production database.

An extremely likely scenario is that the engineers (potentially also you) who have built the recommendations server are writing their logs and other application data to an SQL database. More likely than not, this database architecture and deployment are optimized for fast querying by the application across its most common use cases. As we've discussed, those logs may be in an event-style schema, and there are other tables that may require aggregation and roll-up to make any sense. For example, a *current inventory* table may require knowledge of start-of-day inventory and then aggregate a list of purchase events.

All told, the production SQL database is usually a crucial component in the stack that's geared to specific use. As the downstream consumer of this data, you may find yourself wanting different schemas, wanting lots of access to this database, and performing serious operations on this data. The most common paradigm is *database snapshotting*. Snapshotting is a functionality provided by various flavors of SQL to performantly make a clone of a database. While this snapshotting may take form in a variety of ways, let's focus on a few that serve to simplify our systems and ensure they have the necessary data on hand:

- A daily table snapshot may be tied to an as_of field, or *the state of this table on this day*.

- A daily table snapshot may be limited by time to see *what records have been added today*.

- An event table snapshot may be used to feed a set of events into an event stream processor like Segment (note that you may also set up live event streams like Kafka).

- An hourly aggregated table can be used for status logging or monitoring.

In general, the paradigm is usually to operate on snapshots for downstream data processing. Many of the kinds of data processing we mentioned earlier—like computing user similarity—are operations that may require significant data reads. *It's important to not build ML applications that require extensive querying on the production database*, because doing so would likely decrease performance of the app and result in a slower user experience. This decrease will undermine the improvement made possible by your recommendations.

Once you've snapshotted the tables you're interested in, you can often find a collection of data pipelines useful to transform that data into even more specific tables in your *data warehouse* (where you should be doing most of your work anyway). Tools like Dagster, dbt, Apache Airflow, Argo, and Luigi are popular data-pipeline and workflow orchestration tools for extract, transform, load (ETL) operations.

Data Structures for Learning and Inference

This section introduces three important data structures that will enable our recommendation system to perform complex operations quickly. The goal of each structure is to sacrifice precision as little as possible, while speeding up access to the data in real time. As you'll see, these data structures form the backbone of the real-time inference pipeline and approximate what takes place in the batch pipeline as accurately as possible.

The three data structures are as follows:

- Vector search/ANN index
- Bloom filters for candidate filtering
- Feature stores

So far, we've discussed the necessary components for getting data flowing in your system. These help organize data to make it more accessible during the learning and inference processes. Also, we'll find some shortcuts to speed up inference during retrieval. Vector search will allow us to identify similar items at scale. Bloom filters will allow us to rapidly evaluate many criteria for excluding results. Feature stores will provide us with necessary data about users for recommendation inference.

Vector Search

We have discussed user similarity and item similarity in terms of understanding the relationships between those entities, but we haven't talked about any *acceleration structures* for these processes.

First let's discuss a bit of terminology;. If we think of a collection of vectors that represent entities with a similarity metric provided by a distance function, we refer to this as a *latent space*. The simple goal is to utilize our latent space and its associated similarity metric (or complementary distance metric) to be able to retrieve *similar* items quickly. In our previous examples with similarity, we talked about neighborhoods of users and how they can be utilized to build an affinity score between users and unseen items. But how do you find the neighborhood?

To understand this, recall that we defined neighborhoods of an element x, written $\mathcal{N}(x)$, as the set of k elements in the latent space with the maximum similarity; or said differently, the set of jth order statistics for $j \leq k$ from the sample of item similarities to x. These *k-nearest neighbors*, as they're often called, will be used as the set of elements considered similar to x.

These vectors from CF yield a few other useful side effects:

- A simple recommender that randomly samples unseen items from a user neighborhood's liked items
- Predictions about features of a user, from known features of users in the neighborhood
- User segmentation via taste similarity

So how can we speed up these processes? One of the first significant improvements in this area came from inverted indices. Utilizing inverted indices is at its core carefully constructing a large hash between tokens of the query (for text-based search) and the candidates.

This approach is great for tokenizable entities like sentences or small-lexicon collections. Given the ability to look up items that share one or many tokens with the query, you can even use a general latent embedding to rank the candidate responses by similarity. This approach deserves extra consideration as you scale: it incurs a speed cost because it entails two steps, and because the similarity distribution may not be well correlated with the token similarity required to return many more candidates than we need.

Classic approaches to building a search system are based on large lookup tables and feel deterministic. As we move toward ANN lookup, we want to relax some of that strong deterministic behavior and introduce data structures that make assumptions to *prune* these large indices. Instead of building indices for only tokenizable components of your elements, you could precompute the k-d tree and use the indices as the index. The k-d tree would precompute the nearest neighbors in a batch process (which may be slow), to populate a top-k response for fast lookup. k-d trees are an efficient data structure for encoding the preceding neighborhoods but are notoriously slow to read from in higher dimensions. Using them instead to build inverted indices, though, can be a great improvement.

More recently, explicitly using vector databases with vector search is becoming much more possible and feasible. Elasticsearch has added this capability; Faiss (*https://oreil.ly/AZ-Ai*) is a Python library that helps you implement this functionality in your systems; Pinecone (*https://oreil.ly/LSaos*) is a vector-database system explicitly targeting this goal; and Weaviate (*https://oreil.ly/Z6la_*) is a native vector-database architecture that allows you to layer the previous token-based inverted indices and vector similarity search.

Approximate Nearest Neighbors

What are this element's k-nearest neighbors? Incredibly, approximate nearest neighbors (ANN) can get very high accuracy compared to the actual nearest neighbors, and you get there faster with head-spinning speedups. You often are satisfied with approximate solutions to these problems.

One open source library that specializes in these approximations is PyNNDescent (*https://oreil.ly/i5LyM*), which uses clever speedups via both optimized implementation and careful mathematical tricks. With ANN, you are opened up to two strategies as discussed:

- The pre-index can be dramatically improved.
- On queries without a pre-indexing option, you can still expect good performance.

In practice, these similarity lookups are incredibly important for making your applications actually work. While we've mostly talked about recommendations for full known catalogs of items, we cannot assume this in other recommendation contexts. These include the following:

- Query-based recommendations (like search)
- Contextual recommendations
- Cold-starting new items

As we go, you will see more and more references to similarity in spaces and nearest neighbors; at each of those moments, think: "I know how to make this fast!"

Bloom Filters

Bloom filters are probabilistic data structures that allow us to test for set inclusion very efficiently but with a downside: set exclusion is deterministic, but set inclusion is probabilistic. *In practice, this means that asking the question "Is x in this set" never results in a false negative but may result in a false positive!* Note that this type-I error increases as the size of the bloom increases.

Via vector search, we have identified a large pool of potential recommendations for the user. From this pool, we need to do some immediate elimination. The most obvious type of high-level filtering that's essential is to remove those items that the *user has previously not shown interest in or has already purchased.* You've probably had the experience of being recommended the same item, over and over, and thinking, "I don't want this; stop showing me this." From the simple CF models we've introduced, you may now see why this could happen.

The system has identified a set of items via CF that you're more likely to pick. Without any outside influence, those computations will continue to return the same results, and you'll never escape those recommendations. As the system designer, you may start with a heuristic:

> If the user has seen this item recommended three times and never clicked, let's not show it to them anymore.

This is a totally reasonable strategy to improve *freshness* (the idea of ensuring users see new item recommendations) in your recommendation system. While this is a simple strategy to improve your recommendations, how might you implement this at scale?

A bloom filter may be used by defining the sets in question with the following: "Has this user seen this item recommended three times and never clicked?" Bloom filters have a caveat that they're additive only: once something is in the bloom, you can't remove it. This is not a problem when observing a binary state like this heuristic.

Let's construct a user-item ID to use as our hash in the bloom. Remember that the key feature of the bloom filter is to quickly determine whether the hashed item is in the bloom. When we observe a user-item pair that satisfies the preceding criteria, take that pair as an ID and hash it. Now, because that hashed pair can be easily reconstructed from a list of items for a user, we have a very fast way to filter.

Let's discuss a few technical details on this topic. First, you might want to do a variety of kinds of filtering—maybe freshness is one, and another may be items the user has already bought, and a third could exclude items that have sold out.

Here it would be good to implement each of these filters independently; the first two can follow our user-item ID hashing as before, and the third one can be a hash only on item IDs.

Another consideration is populating the bloom filters. It's best practice to build these blooms from a database during the offline batch jobs. On whatever schedule your batch training is run, rebuild your blooms from the records storage to ensure you're keeping your blooms accurate. Remember that blooms don't allow deletion, so in the previous example, if an item goes from sold out to restocked, your batch refresh of your blooms can pick up the availability again. In between batch retraining, adding to a bloom is also very performant, so you can continue to add to the bloom as you observe more data that needs to be considered for the filtering in real time. Be sure these transactions are logged to a table, though! That logging will be important when you want to refresh.

Fun Aside: Bloom Filters as the Recommendation System

Bloom filters not only provide an effective way to eliminate some recommendations based on conditions for inclusion, but can also be used to do the recommending itself! In particular, "An Item/User Representation for Recommender Systems Based on Bloom Filters" (*https://oreil.ly/VsvN2*) by Manuel Pozo et al. shows that for high-dimensional feature sets with a lot of sparsity (as we discussed in Chapter 3), the type of hashing bloom filters do can help overcome some of the key challenges in defining good similarity functions!

Let's observe that we can do two natural operations on sets via the bloom filter data structures. First, consider two sets A and B, and associate to them bloom filters $\mathcal{BF}_A$ and $\mathcal{BF}_B$. Then what's the definition of $A \cap B$? Can we come up with a bloom filter for this intersection? Yep! Recall that our bloom filters are guaranteed to tell us when an element is not contained in the set, but if an element is in the set, the bloom filter can respond with only a certain probability. In this case, we'd simply look for elements that are *in* according to $\mathcal{BF}_A$ AND *in* according to $\mathcal{BF}_B$. Of course, the set of items returned as *in* each set is larger than the actual set (i.e., $A \subset \mathcal{BF}_A$), so the intersection will also be larger:

$$A \cap B \subset \mathcal{BF}_A \cap \mathcal{BF}_B$$

Note that you can compute the exact difference in cardinality via information about your choice of hashing functions. Also note that the equation is an abuse of notation by calling $\mathcal{BF}_A$ the set of things returned by the bloom filter corresponding to A.

Second, we also need to construct the union. This is similarly easy by considering elements that are *in* according to $\mathcal{BF}_A$ OR *in* according to $\mathcal{BF}_B$. And so, similarly:

$$A \cup B \subset \mathcal{BF}_A \cup \mathcal{BF}_B$$

Now, if we consider items X and Y as concatenated vectors of potentially many features, and hash those concatenated features, we are representing each of them as the bitwise vectors of our bloom. From before, we saw that the intersection of two blooms makes sense, and in fact is equivalent to the bitwise *AND* of their bloom representations. This means two items' feature similarities can be expressed by the bitwise *and* similarity of their bloom hashes:

$$\text{sim}(X, Y) = |\mathcal{BF}(X) \cap \mathcal{BF}(Y)| = \mathcal{BF}(X) *_{\text{bitwise}} \mathcal{BF}(X)$$

For static datasets, this method has real advantages, including speed, scalability, and performance. Limitations are based on a variety of features and on the ability to change the set of possible items. Later we will discuss *locally sensitive hashing*, which further iterates on lookup speed with lower risks of collision in high-dimensional spaces, and some similar ideas will reemerge.

Feature Stores

So far, we have focused on recommendation systems that we might call *pure collaborative filtering*. We've made use of the user- or item-similarity data only when attempting to make good recommendations. If you've been wondering, "Hey, what about information about the actual users and items?" your curiosity will now be sated.

There are a huge variety of reasons you could be interested in features in addition to your previous CF methods. Let's list a few high-level concerns:

- You may wish to show new users a specific set of items first.
- You may wish to consider geographic boundaries in your recommendations.
- Distinguishing between children and adults may be important for the types of recommendations they're given.
- Item features may be used to ensure high-level diversity in the recommendations (more to come in Chapter 15).
- User features can enable various kinds of experimental testing.
- Item features could be used to group items into sets for contextual recommendations (more to come in Chapter 15).

In addition to these issues, another kind of feature is often essential: real-time features. While the point of feature stores is to provide real-time access to all the necessary features, it's worthwhile to distinguish stable features that change infrequently from real-time features that we anticipate will change often.

Some important examples of a real-time feature store are dynamic prices, current item availability, *trending* status, wish-list status, and so on. These features may change throughout the day, and we want their values in the feature store to be mutable in real-time via other services and systems. Therefore, the real-time feature store will need to provide API access for feature mutation. This is something you may not want to provide for *stable* features.

When we design our feature store, we're likely to want the stable features to be built from data warehouse tables via ETLs and transformations, and we likely want the real-time features to be built this way as well, but on a faster schedule or allowing API access for mutation. In either case, the key quality of a feature store is *very fast read access*. It's often a good idea to separately build feature stores for offline training of models that can be built in test to ensure support for new models.

So how might the architecture and implementation look? See Figure 6-3.

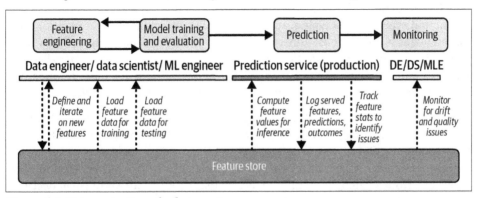

Figure 6-3. Demonstration of a feature store

Designing a feature store involves designing pipelines that define and *transform the features into that store* (coordinated via things like Airflow, Luigi, Argo, etc.) and often look similar to the type of data pipelines used in building our collector. One additional complication that the feature store needs to concern itself with is a speed layer. During our discussion of the lambda architecture earlier in this chapter, we mentioned that we can think of batch data processing for the collector and a more rapid speed layer for intermediary updates, but this is even more important for the feature store. The feature store may also need a *streaming layer*. This layer operates on continuous streams of data and can perform data transformations on those; it then writes the appropriate output to the online feature store in real time. This adds complexity because data transformations on streaming data present a very different set of challenges and often require different algorithmic strategies. Some technologies that help here are Spark Streaming and Kinesis. You'll also need to configure the system to properly handle the data stream, the most common of which is Kafka. Data streaming layers involve many components and architectural considerations that fall outside our scope; if you're considering getting started with Kafka, check out *Kafka: The Definitive Guide* by Gwen Shapira et al. (O'Reilly).

A feature store also needs a *storage layer*; many approaches exist here, but using a NoSQL database is common, especially in the online feature store. The reason is faster retrieval and the nature of the data storage. Feature stores for recommendation systems tend to be very key based (i.e., *get the features for this user*, or *get the features for this item*), which lend themselves well to key-value stores. Some example technologies here are DynamoDB, Redis, and Cassandra. The storage layer for an offline feature store may simply be an SQL-style database to reduce complexity, but instead you'll pay a tax of a delta between offline and online. This delta and others like it are called *training-serving skew* (*https://oreil.ly/IcE1R*).

A unique but essential aspect of feature stores is the *registry*. A registry is incredibly useful for a feature store because it coordinates existing features and information on how they're defined. A more sophisticated instance of a registry also includes input and output schemas with typing, and distributional expectations. These are contracts that the data pipelines must adhere to and satisfy to avoid populating your feature store with garbage data. Additionally, the registry's definitions allow parallel data scientists and ML engineers to develop new features, use one another's features, and generally understand the assumptions of features their models may utilize.

One important advantage of these registries is that they incentivize alignment between teams and developers. In particular, if you decide you care about *country* for your user, and you see a feature *country* in the registry, you're more likely to use that (or ask the developer who's assigned to this feature in the registry) than to make a new one from scratch. Practically, data scientists make hundreds of small decisions and assumptions when defining their models, and this removes some of that load that's relying on the existing resources.

Model Registries

A closely related concept to feature registries is model registries. The concepts have a lot in common, but we caution you to think of them differently. A great model registry can have type contracts for the input and output of your models, and can serve many of the same benefits around alignment and clarity. A feature registry should really be focused on definitions of the business logic and features. Because feature engineering can also be model driven, speaking clearly about the differences between these two things can be challenging, so to sum it up, we'll focus on what they serve: a model registry concerns itself with ML models and the relevant metadata, whereas a feature registry concerns itself with features that models will use.

Finally, we need to talk about *serving* these features. Backed by the appropriately performant storage layer, we need to serve via API request the necessary feature vectors. Those feature vectors are details about the user that the model will need when serving recommendations—for example, the user's location or content age restrictions. The API can serve back the entire set of features for the key or allow for more specification. Often the responses are JSON serialized for fast data transfer. It's important that the features being served are the *most up-to-date set of features*, and latency here is expected to be < 100 ms for more serious industrial applications.

One important caveat here is that for offline training, these feature stores need to accommodate *time travel*. Because our goal during training is to give the model the appropriate data to learn in the *most generalizable way*, when training our model, it's crucial to not give it access to features out of time. This is called *data leakage* and can cause massive divergence in performance between training and production. The feature store for offline training thus must have knowledge of the features through time, so that during training, a time index may be provided to get the features as they were then. These `as_of` keys can be tied to the historical training data as we *replay* the history of what the user-item interactions looked like.

With these pieces in place—and the important monitoring this system needs—you'll be able to serve offline and online features to your models. In Part III, you will see model architectures that make use of them.

Data Leakage

You're likely familiar with the concept of leakage based on what you know about ML: corrupted performance metrics result because the training of the model had access to data that was supposed to be reserved for model performance evaluation.

Data leakage in ML is divided into *feature leakage* and *training example leakage*. For recommendation systems, data leakage has the additional challenge of temporal leakage, or nonstationarity leakage. The real danger is that in recommendation systems, we see the same observational unit, a user, over and over, and observe a datum each time we see them. When we see them, other aspects of the system may have changed, and in reality we want to use features in our model that are the most up to date as of that observation. Both in features and training examples, to avoid leakage we need to always be thinking of our system's timeline. This is why data preparation for recommendation systems is inherently time dependent. You will see in Chapter 11 that our accuracy metrics will need to explicitly consider train-test splitting with respect to this time axis, and then be further grouped by the user. This also means that training recommendation systems often requires more resources than many other task types.

Summary

We've discussed not only the crucial components necessary to hydrate your system and serve recommendations, but also some of the engineering building blocks needed to make those components a reality. Equipped with data loaders, embeddings, feature stores, and retrieval mechanisms, we are ready to start constructing our pipeline and system topology.

In the next chapter, we'll focus our sights on MLOps and the rest of the engineering work required to build and iterate on these systems. It's going to be important for us to think carefully about deployment and monitoring so our recommendation systems are constrained to life in IPython Notebooks.

Continue onward to see the architectural considerations to move to production.

## CHAPTER 7

Serving Models and Architectures

As we think about how recommendation systems utilize the available data to learn and eventually serve recommendations, it's crucial to describe how the pieces fit together. The combination of the data flow and the jointly available data for learning is called the *architecture*. More formally, the architecture is the connections and interactions of the system or network of services; for data applications, the architecture also includes the available features and objective functions for each subsystem. Defining the architecture typically involves identifying components or individual services, defining the relationships and dependencies among those components, and specifying the protocols or interfaces through which they will communicate.

In this chapter, we'll spell out some of the most popular and important architectures for recommendation systems.

Architectures by Recommendation Structure

We have returned several times to the concept of collector, ranker, and server, and we've seen that they may be regarded via two paradigms: the online and the offline modes. Further, we've seen how many of the components in Chapter 6 satisfy some of the core requirements of these functions.

Designing large systems like these requires several architectural considerations. In this section, we will demonstrate how these concepts are adapted based on the type of recommendation system you are building. We'll compare a mostly standard item-to-user recommendation system, a query-based recommendation system, context-based recommendations, and sequence-based recommendations.

Item-to-User Recommendations

We'll start by describing the architecture of the system we've been building in the book thus far. As proposed in Chapter 4, we built the collector offline to ingest and process our recommendations. We utilize representations to encode relationships between items, users, or user-item pairs.

The online collector takes the request, usually in the form of a user ID, and finds a neighborhood of items in this representation space to pass along to the ranker. Those items are filtered when appropriate and sent for scoring.

The offline ranker learns the relevant features for scoring and ranking, training on the historical data. It then uses this model and, in some cases, item features as well for inference.

In the case of recommendation systems, this inference computes the scores associated to each item in the set of potential recommendations. We usually sort by this score, which you'll learn more about in Part III. Finally, we integrate a final round of ordering based on some business logic (described in Chapter 14). This last step is part of the serving, where we impose requirements like test criteria or recommendation diversity requirements.

Figure 7-1 is an excellent overview of the retrieval, ranking, and serving structure, although it depicts four stages and uses slightly different terminology. In this book, we combine the filtering stage shown here into retrieval.

Query-Based Recommendations

To start off our process, we want to make a query. The most obvious example of a query is a text query as in text-based search engines; however, queries may be more general! For example, you may wish to allow search-by-image or search-by-tag options. Note that an important type of query-based recommender uses an *implicit* query: the user is providing a search query via UI choices or by behaviors. While these systems are quite similar in overall structure to the item-to-user systems, let's discover how to modify them to fit our use case.

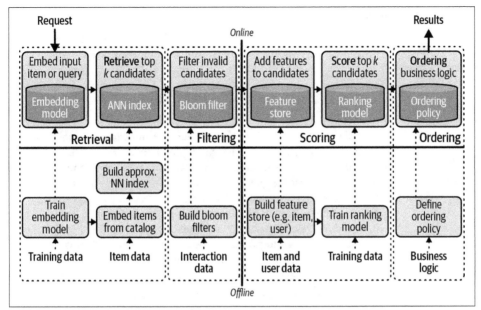

Figure 7-1. A four-stage recommendation system (adapted from an image by Karl Higley and Even Oldridge)

We want to integrate more context about the query into the first step of the request. Note that we don't want to throw out the user-item matching components of this system. Even though the user is performing a search, personalizing the recommendations based on their taste is useful. Instead, we need to utilize the query as well; later we will discuss various technical strategies, but a simple summary for now is to also generate an embedding for the query. Note that the query is like an item or a user but is sufficiently different.

Some strategies might include similarity between the query and items, or co-occurrence of the query and items. Either way, we now have a query representation and user representation, and we want to utilize both for our recommendation. One simple approach is to use the query representation for retrieval, but during the scoring, score via both query-item and user-item, combining them via a multiobjective loss. Another approach is to use the user for retrieval and then the query for filtering.

Different Embeddings

Unfortunately, while we'd love the same embedding space (for nearest-neighbors lookup) to work well for our queries and our documents (items, etc.), this is often not the case. The simplest example is something like asking questions and hoping to find relevant Wikipedia articles. This problem is often referred to as the queries being "out of distribution" from the documents.

Wikipedia articles are written in a declarative informative article style, whereas questions are often brief and casual. If you were to use an embedding model focused on capturing semantic meaning, you'd naively expect the queries to be located in significantly different subspaces than the articles. This means that your distance computations will be affected. This is often *not* a huge problem because you retrieve via relative distances, and you can hope that the shared subspaces are enough to provide a good retrieval. However, it can be hard to predict when these perform poorly.

The best practice is to carefully examine the embeddings on common queries and on target results. These problems can be *especially* bad on implicit queries like a series of actions taken at a particular time of day to look up food recommendations. In this case, we expect the queries to be wildly different from the documents.

Context-Based Recommendations

A context is quite similar to a query but tends to be more obviously feature based and frequently less similar to the items/users distributions. *Context* is usually the term used to represent exogenous features to the system that may have an effect on the system—i.e., auxiliary information such as time, weather, or location. Context-based recommendation is similar to query based in that context is an additional signal that the system needs to consider during recommendation, but more often than not, the query should dominate the signal for recommendation, whereas the context should not.

Let's take a simple example of ordering food. A query for a food-delivery recommendation system would look like *Mexican food*; this is an extremely important signal from the user looking for burritos or quesadillas of how the recommendations should look. A context for a food-delivery recommendation system would look like *it's almost lunchtime*. This signal is useful but may not outweigh user personalization. Putting hard-and-fast rules on this weighting can be difficult, so usually we don't, and instead we learn parameters via experimentation.

Context features fit into the architecture similar to the way queries do, via learned weightings as part of the objective function. Your model will learn a representation between context features and items, and then add that affinity into the rest of the pipeline. Again, you can make use of this early in the retrieval, later in the ranking, or even during the serving step.

Sequence-Based Recommendations

Sequence-based recommendations build on context-based recommendations but with a specific type of context. Sequential recommendations are based on the idea that the recent items the user has been exposed to should have a significant influence on the recommendations. A common example here is a music-streaming service, as the last few songs that have been played can significantly inform what the user might want to hear next. To ensure that this *autoregressive*, or sequentially predictive, set of features has an influence on recommendations, we can treat each item in the sequence as a weighted context for the recommendation.

Usually, the item-item representation similarities are weighted to provide a collection of recommendations, and various strategies are used for combining these. In this case, we normally expect the user to be of high importance in the recommendations, but the sequence is also of high importance. One simple model is to think of the sequence of items as a sequence of tokens, and form a single embedding for that sequence—as in NLP applications. This embedding can be used as the context in a context-based recommendation architecture.

Naive Sequence Embeddings

The combinatorics of one-embedding-per-sequence explode in cardinality; the number of potential items in each sequential slot is very large, and each item in the sequence multiplies those possibilities together. Imagine, for example, five-word sequences, where the number of possibilities for each item is close to the size of the English lexicon, and thus it would be that size to the fifth power. We provide simple strategies for dealing with this in Chapter 17.

Why Bother with Extra Features?

Sometimes it is useful to step back and ask if a new technology is actually worth caring about. So far in this section, we've introduced four new paradigms for thinking about a recommender problem. That level of detail may seem surprising and potentially even unnecessary.

One of the core reasons that things like context- and query-based recommendations become relevant is to deal with some of the issues mentioned before around sparsity and cold starting. Sparsity makes things that aren't cold seem cold via the learner's underexposure to them, but true cold starting also exists because of new items being added to catalogs with high frequency in most applications. We will address cold starting in detail, but for now, suffice it to say that one strategy for warm starting is to use other features that *are* available even in this regime.

In applications of ML that are explicitly feature based, we rarely battle the cold-start problem to such a degree, because at inference time we're confident that the model parameters useful for prediction are well aligned with those features that are available. In this way, feature-included recommendation systems are bootstrapping from a potentially weaker learner that has more guaranteed performance via always-available features.

The second analogy that the previous architectures are reflecting is that of boosting. Boosted models operate via the observation that ensembles of weaker learners can reach better performance. Here we are asking for some additional features to help these networks ensemble with weak learners, to boost their performance.

Encoder Architectures and Cold Starting

The previous problem framings of various types of recommendation problems point out four model architectures, each fitting into our general framework of collector, ranker, and server. With this understanding, let's discuss in a bit more detail how model architecture can become intertwined with serving architecture. In particular, we also need to discuss feature encoders.

The key opportunity from encoder-augmented systems is that for users, items, or contexts without much data, we can still form embeddings on the fly. Recall from before that our embeddings make the rest of our system possible, but cold-starting recommendations is a huge challenge.

The *two-towers architecture*—or dual-encoder networks—introduced in "Sampling-Bias-Corrected Neural Modeling for Large Corpus Item Recommendations" (*https://oreil.ly/gQHfo*) by Xinyang Yi et al. is shown in Figure 7-2 explicit model architecture is aimed at prioritizing features of both the user and items when building a scoring model for a recommendation system. We'll see a lot more discussion of matrix factorization (MF), which is a kind of latent collaborative filtering (CF) derived from the user-item matrix and some linear algebraic algorithms. In the preceding section, we explained why additional features matter. Adding these *side-car* features into an MF paradigm is possible and has shown to be successful—for example, applications CF for implicit feedback (*https://oreil.ly/cbePb*), factorization machines (*http://libfm.org/*), and SVDFeature (*https://oreil.ly/cN7fP*). However, in this model we will take a more direct approach.

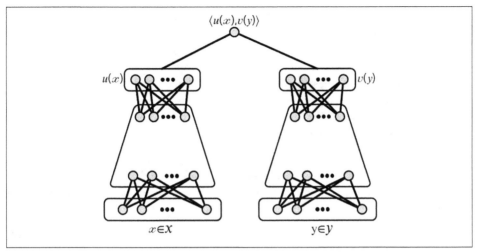

Figure 7-2. The two towers responsible for the two embeddings

In this architecture, we take the left tower to be responsible for items and the right tower to be responsible for the user and, when appropriate, context. These two tower architectures are inspired by the NLP literature and, in particular, "Learning Text Similarity with Siamese Recurrent Networks" (*https://oreil.ly/m7IrK*) by Paul Neculoiu et al.

Let's detail how this model architecture is applied to recommending videos on YouTube. For a full overview of where this architecture was first introduced, see "Deep Neural Networks for YouTube Recommendations" (*https://oreil.ly/aXekc*) by Paul Covington et al. Training labels will be given by clicks, but with an additional regression feature $r_i \in \{0, 1\}$, where the minimum value corresponds to a click but trivial watch time, and the maximum of the range corresponds to a full watch.

As we've mentioned, this model architecture will explicitly include features from both user and items. The video features will consist of categorical and continuous features, like VideoId, ChannelId, VideoTopic, and so on. An embedding layer is used for many of the categorical features to move to dense representations. The user features include watch histories via bag of words and standard user features.

This model structure combines many of the ideas you've seen before but has relevant takeaways for our system architecture. First is the idea of sequential training. Each *temporal batch* of samples should be trained in sequence to ensure that model drift is shown to the model; we will discuss prequential datasets in "Prequential validation" on page 197. Next, we present an important idea for the productionizing of these kinds of models: encoders.

In these models, we have feature encoders as the early layers in both towers, and when we move to inference, we will still need these encoders. When performing the online recommendations, we will be given UserId and VideoId and will first need to collect their features. As discussed in "Feature Stores" on page 90, the feature store will be useful in getting these raw features, but we need to also encode the features into the dense representations necessary for inference. This is something that can be stored in the feature store for known entities, but for unknown entities we will need to do the feature embedding at inference time.

Encoding layers serve as a simple model for mapping a collection of features to a dense representation. When fitting encoding layers as the first step in a neural network, the common strategy is to take the first k layers and reuse them as an encoder model. More specifically, if $\mathscr{L}^i, 0 \leq i \leq k$ are the layers responsible for feature encoding, call $Emb(\widehat{V}) = \mathscr{L}^k(\mathscr{L}^{k-1}(...\mathscr{L}^0(\widehat{V})))$ the function that maps a feature vector $\widehat{V}$ to its dense representation.

In our previous system architecture, we would include this encoder as part of the fast layer, after receiving features from the feature store. It's also important to note that we would still want to utilize vector search; these feature embedding layers are used upstream of the vector search and nearest neighbor searches.

Encoder as a Service

Encoders and retrieval are a key part of the multistage recommendation pipeline. We've spoken briefly about the latent spaces in question (for more details, see "Latent Spaces" on page 167), and we've alluded to an *encoder*. Briefly, an encoder is the model that converts users, items, queries, etc., into the latent space in which you'll perform nearest-neighbors search. These models can be trained via a variety of processes, many of which will be discussed later, but it's important to discuss where they live once trained.

Encoders are often simple API endpoints that take the content to be embedded and return a vector (a list of floats). Encoders often work at the batch layer to encode all the documents/items that will be retrieved, but they must *also* be connected to the real-time layer to encode the queries as they come in. A common pattern is to set up a batch endpoint and a single query endpoint to facilitate optimization for both modalities. These endpoints should be fast and highly available.

If you're working with text data, a good starting place is to use BERT or GPT-based embeddings. The easiest at this time are provided as a hosted service from OpenAI.

Deployment

Like many ML applications, the final output of a recommendation system is itself a small program that runs continuously and exposes an API to interact with it; batch recommendations are often a powerful place to start, performing all the necessary recommendations ahead of time. Throughout this chapter, we've seen the pieces embedded in our backend system, but now we will discuss the components closer to the user.

In our relatively general architecture, the server is responsible for handing over the recommendations, after all the work that comes before, and should adhere to a preset schema. But what does this deployment look like?

Models as APIs

Let's discuss two systems architectures that might be appropriate for serving your models in production: microservice and monolith.

In web applications, this dichotomy is well covered from many perspectives and special use cases. As ML engineers, data scientists, and potentially data platform engineers, it's not necessary to dig deep into this area, but it's essential to know the basics:

Microservice architectures
> Each component of the pipeline should be its own small program with a clear API and output schema. Composing these API calls allows for flexible and predictable pipelines.

Monolithic architectures
> One application should contain all the necessary logic and components for model predictions. Keeping the application self-contained means fewer interfaces that need to be kept aligned and fewer rabbit holes to hunt around in when a location in your pipeline is being starved.

Whatever you choose as your strategy, you'll need to make a few decisions:

How large is the necessary application?
> If your application will need fast access to large datasets at inference time, you'll need to think carefully about memory requirements.

What access does your application need?
> We've previously discussed using technologies like bloom filters and feature stores. These resources may be tightly coupled to your application (by building them in memory in the application) or may be an API call away. Make sure your deployment accounts for these relationships.

Should your model be deployed to a single node or a cluster?
>
> For some model types, even at the inference step we wish to utilize distributed computing. This will require additional configuration to allow for fast parallelization.

How much replication do you need?
>
> Horizontal scaling allows you to have multiple copies of the same service running simultaneously to reduce the demand on any particular instance. This is important for ensuring availability and performance. As we horizontally scale, each service can operate independently, and various strategies exist for coordinating these services and an API request. Each replica is usually its own containerized application, and these APIs like CoreOS and Kubernetes are used to manage these. The requests themselves must also be balanced to the different replicas via something like nginx.

What are the relevant APIs that are exposed?
>
> Each application in the stack should have a clear set of exposed schemas and an explicit communication about the types of other applications that may call to the APIs.

Spinning Up a Model Service

So what can you use to get your model into an application? A variety of frameworks for application development are useful; some of the most popular in Python are Flask, FastAPI, and Django. Each has different advantages, but we'll discuss FastAPI here.

FastAPI is a targeted framework for API applications, making it especially well fit for serving ML models. It calls itself an asynchronous server gateway interface (ASGI) framework, and its specificity grants a ton of simplicity.

Let's take a simple example of turning a fit torch model into a service with the FastAPI framework. First, let's utilize an artifact store to pull down our fit model. Here we are using the Weights & Biases artifact store:

```
import wandb, torch
run = wandb.init(project=Prod_model, job_type="inference")

model_dir = run.use_artifact(
                'bryan-wandb/recsys-torch/model:latest',
                type='model'
).download()

model = torch.load(model_dir)
model.eval(user_id)
```

This looks just like your notebook workflow, so let's see how easy it is to integrate this with FastAPI:

```
from fastapi import FastAPI # FastAPI code

import wandb, torch

app = FastAPI() # FastAPI code

run = wandb.init(project=Prod_model, job_type="inference")

model_dir = run.use_artifact(
        'bryan-wandb/recsys-torch/model:latest',
        type='model'
).download()

model = torch.load(model_dir)

@app.get("/recommendations/{user_id}") # FastAPI code
def make_recs_for_user(user_id: int): # FastAPI code
                endpoint_name = 'make_recs_for_user_v0'
                logger.info(
                        "{'type': 'recommendation_request',"
                        f"'arguments': {'user_id': {user_id}},"
                        f"'response': {None}},",
                        f"'endpoint_name': {endpoint_name}"
                )
                recommendation = model.eval(user_id)
                logger.log(
                        "{'type': 'model_inference',"
                        f"'arguments': {'user_id': {user_id}},"
                        f"'response': {recommendation}},"
                        f"'endpoint_name': {endpoint_name}"
                )
        return { # FastAPI code
                        "user_id": user_id,
                        "endpoint_name": endpoint_name,
                        "recommendation": recommendation
                }
```

I hope you share my enthusiasm that we now have a model as a service in five additional lines of code. While this scenario includes simple examples of logging, we'll discuss logging in greater detail later in this chapter to help you improve observability in your applications.

Workflow Orchestration

The other component necessary for your deployed system is workflow orchestration. The model service is responsible for receiving requests and serving results, but many system components need to be in place for this service to do anything of use. These workflows have several components, so we will discuss them in sequence: containerization, scheduling, and CI/CD.

Containerization

We've discussed how to put together a simple service that can return the results, and we suggested using FastAPI; however, the question of environments is now relevant. When executing Python code, it is important to keep the environment consistent if not identical. FastAPI is a library for designing the interfaces; Docker is the software that manages the environment that code runs in. It's common to hear Docker described as a container or containerization tool: this is because you load a bunch of apps—or executable components of code—into one shared environment.

We have a few subtle things to note at this point. The meaning of *environment* encapsulates both the Python environment of package dependencies and the larger environment, including the operating system or GPU drivers. The environment is usually initialized from a predetermined *image* that installs the most basic aspects of what you'll need access to and in many cases is less variable across services to promote consistency and standardization. Finally, the container is usually equipped with a list of infrastructure code necessary to work wherever it is to be deployed.

In practice, you specify details of the Python environment via your *requirements* file, which consists of a list of Python packages. Note that some library dependencies are outside Python and will require additional configuration mechanisms. The operating system and drivers are usually built as part of a base image; you can find these on DockerHub or similar. Finally, *infrastructure as code* is a paradigm wherein you write code to orchestrate the necessary steps in getting your container configured to run in the infrastructure it will be deployed into. Dockerfile and Docker Compose are specific to the Docker container interfacing with infrastructure, but you can further generalize these concepts to include other details of the infrastructure. This infrastructure as code begins to encapsulate provisioning of resources in your cloud, setting up open ports for network communication, access control via security roles, and more. A common way to write this code is in Terraform. This book doesn't dive into infrastructure specification, but infrastructure as code is becoming a more important tool to the ML practitioner. Many companies are beginning to attempt to simplify these aspects of training and deploying systems including Weights & Biases or Modal.

Scheduling

Two paradigms exist for scheduling jobs: cron and triggers. Later we'll talk more about the continuous training loop and active learning processes, but upstream of those is your ML workflow. ML workflows are a set of ordered steps necessary to prepare your model for inference. We've introduced our notion of collector, ranker, and server, which are organized into a sequence of stages for recommendation systems—but these are the three coarsest elements of the system topology.

In ML systems, we frequently assume that there's an upstream stage of the workflow that corresponds to data transformations, as discussed in Chapter 6. Wherever that stage takes place, the output of those transformations results in our vector store—and potentially the additional feature stores. The handoff between those steps and the next steps in your workflow are the result of a job scheduler. As mentioned previously, tools like Dagster and Airflow can run sequences of jobs with dependent assets. These kinds of tools are needed to orchestrate the transitions and to ensure that they're timely.

Cron refers to a time schedule where a workflow should begin—for example, hourly at the top of the hour or four times a day. *Triggers* refers to the instigation of a job run when another event has taken place—for example, if an endpoint receives a request, or a set of data gets a new version, or a limit of responses is exceeded. These are meant to capture more ad hoc relationships between the next job stage and the trigger. Both paradigms are very important.

CI/CD

Your workflow execution system is the backbone of your ML systems, often the bridge between the data collection process, the training process, and the deployment process. Modern workflow execution systems also include automatic validation and tracking so that you can audit the steps on the way to production.

Continuous integration (CI) is a term taken from software engineering to enforce a set of checks on new code in order to accelerate the development process. In traditional software engineering, this comprises automating unit and integration testing, usually run after checking the code into version control. For ML systems, CI may mean running test scripts against the model, checking the typed output of data transformations, or running validation sets through the model and benchmarking the performance against previous models.

Continuous deployment (CD) is also a term popularized in software engineering to refer to automating the process of pushing new packaged code into an existing system. In software engineering, deploying code when it has passed the relevant checks speeds development and reduces the risk of stale systems. In ML, CD can involve strategies like automatically deploying your new model behind a service endpoint in shadow (which we'll discuss in "Shadowing" on page 115) to test that it works as expected under live traffic. It could also mean deploying a model behind a very small allocation of an A/B test or multiarm bandit treatment to begin to measure effects on target outcomes. CD usually requires effective triggering by the requirements it has to satisfy before being pushed. It's common to hear CD utilizing a model registry, where you house and index variations on your model.

Alerting and Monitoring

Alerting and monitoring take a lot of their inspiration from the DevOps world for software engineering. Here are some high-level principles that will guide our thinking:

- Clearly defined schemas and priors
- Observability

Schemas and Priors

When designing software systems, you almost always have expectations about how the components fit together. Just as you anticipate the input and output to functions when writing code, in software systems you anticipate these at each interface. This is relevant not only for microservice architectures; even in a monolith architecture, components of the system need to work together and often have boundaries between their defining responsibilities.

Let's make this more concrete via an example. You've built a user-item latent space, a feature store for user features, a bloom filter for client avoids (things the client specifically tells you they don't want), and an experiment index that defines which of two models should be used for scoring. First let's examine the latent space; when provided a user_id, we need to look up its representation, and we already have some assumptions:

- The user_id provided will be of the correct type.
- The user_id will have a representation in our space.
- The representation returned will be of the correct type and shape.
- The component values of the representation vector will be in the appropriate domain. (*The support of representations in your latent space may vary day to day.*)

From here, we need look up the k ANN, which incurs more assumptions:

- There are $\geq k$ vectors in our latent space.
- Those vectors adhere to the expected distributional behavior of the latent space.

While these seem like relatively straightforward applications of unit tests, canonizing these assumptions is important. Take the last assumption in both of the two services: how can you know the appropriate domain for the representation vectors? As part of your training procedure, you'll need to calculate this and then store it for access during the inference pipeline.

In the second case, when finding nearest neighbors in high-dimensional spaces, well-discussed difficulties arise in distributional uniformity, but this can mean particularly poor performance for recommendations. In practice, we have observed a spiky nature to the behavior of k-nearest neighbors in latent spaces, leading to difficult challenges downstream in ensuring diversity of recommendations. These distributions can be estimated as priors, and simple checks like KL divergence can be used online; we can estimate the average behavior of the embeddings and the difference between local geometries.

In both cases, collecting and logging the output of this information can provide a rich history of what is going on with your system. This can shorten debugging loops later if model performance is low in production.

Returning to the possibility of `user_id` lacking a representation in our space: this is precisely the cold-start problem! In that case, we need to transition over to a different prediction pipeline: perhaps user-feature-based, explore-exploit, or even hardcoded recommendations. In this setting, we need to understand next steps when a schema condition is not met and then gracefully move forward.

Integration Tests

Let's consider one higher-level challenge that might emerge in a system like this at the level of integration. Some refer to these issues as *entanglement*.

You've learned through experimentation that you should find $k = 20$ ANNs in the item space for a user to get good recommendations. You make a call to your representation space, get your 20 items, and pass them onto the filtering step. However, this user is quite picky; they have previously made many restrictions on their account about the kind of recommendations they allow: no shoes, no dresses, no jeans, no hats, no handbags—what's a struggling recommendation system to do?

Naively, if you take the 20 neighbors and pass them into the bloom, you're likely to be left with nothing! You can approach this challenge in two ways:

- Allow for a callback from the filter step to the retrieval (see "Predicate Push-down" on page 278)
- Build a user distribution and store that for access during retrieval

In the first approach, you give access to your filter step to call the retrieval step with a larger k until the requirements are satisfied after the bloom. Of course, this incurs significant slowdown as it requires multiple passes and ever-growing queries with redundancy! While this approach is simple, it requires building defensively and knowing ahead of time what may go wrong.

In the second approach, during training, you can sample from the user space to build estimates of the appropriate k for varying numbers of avoids by user. Then, giving access to a lookup of total avoids by user to the collector can help defend against this behavior.

Over-Retrieval

Sometimes people in information retrieval perform *over-retrieval* to mitigate issues of conflicting requirements from the search request, which can arise if the user makes a search and applies many filters simultaneously. This is applicable in recommendation systems as well.

If you retrieve only exactly the number of potential recommendations you need to serve to the user, downstream rules or poor personalization scores can sometimes cause a serious issue for serving up recommendations. This is why it is common to retrieve more items than you anticipate showing to the user.

Observability

Many tools in software engineering can assist with observability—understanding the *whys* of what's going on in the software stack. Because the systems we are building become quite distributed, the interfaces become critical monitoring points, but the paths also become complex.

Spans and traces

Common terms in this area are *spans* and *traces,* which refer to two dimensions of a call stack, illustrated in Figure 7-3. Given a collection of connected services, as in our preceding examples, an individual inference request will pass through some or all of those services in a sequence. The sequence of service requests is the *trace.* The potentially parallel time delays of each of these services is the *span.*

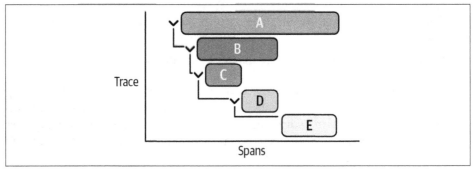

Figure 7-3. The spans of a trace

The graphical representation of spans usually demonstrates how the time for one service to respond comprises several other delays from other calls.

Observability enables you to see traces, spans, and logs in conjunction to appropriately diagnose the behavior of your system. In our example of utilizing a callback from the filter step to get more neighbors from the collector, we might see a slow response and wonder, "What has happened?" By viewing the spans and traces, we'd be able to see that the first call to the collector was as expected, then the filter step made a call to the collector, then another call to the collector, and so on, which built up a huge span for the filter step. Combining that view with logging would help us rapidly diagnose what might be happening.

Timeouts

In the preceding example, we had a long process that could lead to a very bad user experience. In most cases, we impose hard restrictions on how bad we let things get; these are called *timeouts*.

Usually, we have an upper bound on how long we're willing to wait for our inference response, so implementing timeouts aligns our system with these restrictions. It's important in these cases to have a *fallback*. In the setting of recommendation systems, a fallback usually comprises things like the MPIR prepared such that it incurs minimal additional delay.

Evaluation in Production

If the previous section was about understanding what's coming into your model in production, this one might be summarized as what's coming out of your model in production. At a high level, evaluation in production can be thought of as extending all your model-validation techniques to the inference time. In particular, you are looking at *what the model actually is doing*!

On one hand, we already have tools to do this evaluation. You can use the same methods to evaluate performance as you do for training, but now on real observations streaming in. However, this process is not as obvious as we might first guess. Let's discuss some of the challenges.

Slow Feedback

Recommendation systems fundamentally are trying to lead to item selection, and in many cases, purchases. But if we step back and think more holistically about the purpose of integrating recommendation systems into businesses, it's to drive revenue. If you're an ecommerce shop, item selection and revenue may seem easily associated: a purchase leads to revenue, so good item recommendation leads to revenue. However, what about returns? Or even a harder question: is this revenue incremental? One challenge with recommendation systems is that it can be difficult to draw a causal arrow between any metric used to measure the performance of your models to the business-oriented KPIs.

We call this *slow feedback* because sometimes the loop from a recommendation to a meaningful metric and back to the recommender can take weeks or even longer. This is especially challenging when you want to run experiments to understand whether a new model should be rolled out. The length of the test may need to stretch quite a bit more to get meaningful results.

Usually, the team aligns on a proxy metric that the data scientists believe is a good estimator for the KPI, and that proxy metric is measured live. This approach has a huge variety of challenges, but it often suffices and provides motivation for more testing. Well-correlated proxies are often a great start to get directional information indicating where to take further iterations.

Model Metrics

So, what are the key metrics to track for your model in production? Given that we're looking at recommendation systems at inference time, we should seek to understand the following:

- Distribution of recommendation across categorical features
- Distribution of affinity scores
- Number of candidates
- Distribution of other ranking scores

As we discussed before, during the training process, we should be calculating broadly the ranges of our similarity scores in our latent space. Whether we are looking at high-level estimations or finer ones, we can use these distributions to get warning signals that something might be strange. Simply comparing the output of our model during inference, or over a set of inference requests, to these precompute distributions can be extremely helpful.

Comparing distributions can be a long topic, but one standard approach is computing *KL-divergence* between the observed distribution and the expected distribution from training. By computing KL divergence between these, we can understand how *surprising* the model's predictions are on a given day.

What we'd really like is to understand the receiver operating characteristic curve (ROC) of our model predictions with respect to one of our conversion types. However, this involves yet another integration to tie back to logging. Since our model API produces only the recommendation, we'll still need to tie into logging from the web application to understand outcomes! To tie back in outcomes, we must join the model predictions with the logging output to get the evaluation labels, which can be done via log-parsing technologies (like Grafana, ELK, or Prometheus). We'll see more of this in Chapter 8.

Receiver Operating Characteristic Curve

If we assume that the relevance scores are estimating whether the item will be relevant to the user, this forms a binary classification problem. Utilizing these (normalized) scores, we can build an ROC to estimate over the distributions of queries when the relevance score begins to accurately predict a relevant item via retrieval history. This curve can thus be used to estimate parameters like necessary retrieval depth or even problematic queries.

Continuous Training and Deployment

It may feel like we're done with this story since we have models tracked and production monitoring in place, but rarely are we satisfied with set-it-and-forget-it model development. One important characteristic of ML products is that models frequently need to be updated to even be useful. Previously, we discussed model metrics and that sometimes performance in production might look different from our expectations based on the trained models' performance. This can be further exacerbated by model drift.

Model Drift

Model drift is the notion that the same model may exhibit different prediction behavior over time, merely due to changes in the data-generating process. A simple example is a time-series forecasting model. When you build a time-series forecasting model, the especially unique property that is essential for good performance is *autoregression*: the value of the function covaries with previous values of the function. We won't go into detail on time-series forecasting, but suffice it to say: your best hope of making a good forecast is to use up-to-date data! If you want to forecast stock prices, you should always use the most recent prices as part of your predictions.

This simple example demonstrates how models may drift, and forecasting models are not so different from recommendation models—especially when considering the seasonal realities of many recommendation problems. A model that did well two weeks ago needs to be retrained with recent data to be expected to continue to perform well.

One criticism of a model that drifts is "that's the smoking gun of an overfit model," but in reality these models require a certain amount of over-parameterization to be useful. In the context of recommendation systems, we've already seen that quirks like the Matthew effect have disastrous effects on the expected performance of a recommender model. If we don't consider things like new items in our recommender, we are doomed to fail. Models can drift for a variety of reasons, often coming down to exogenous factors in the generating process that may not be captured by the model.

One approach to dealing with and predicting stale models is to simulate these scenarios during training. If you suspect that the model goes stale mostly because of the distribution changing over time, you can employ sequential cross-validation—training on a contiguous period and testing on a subsequent period—but with a specified block of time delay. For example, if you think your model performance is going to decrease after two weeks because it's being trained on out-of-date observations, then during training you can purposely build your evaluation to incorporate a two-week delay before measuring performance. This is called *two-phase prediction comparison*, and by comparing the performances, you can estimate drift magnitudes to keep an eye out in production.

A wealth of statistical approaches can be used to rein in these differences. In lieu of a deep dive into variational modeling for variability and reliability for your predictions, we'll discuss continuous training and deployment and open this peanut with a sledge hammer.

Deployment Topologies

Let's consider a few structures for deploying models that will not only keep your models well in tune but also accommodate iteration, experimentation, and optimization.

Ensembles

Ensembles are a type of model structure in which multiple models are built, and the predictions from those models are pooled together in one of a variety of ways. While this notion of an ensemble is usually packaged into the model called for inference, you can generalize the idea to your deployment topology.

Let's take an example that builds on our previous discussion of prediction priors. If we have a collection of models with comparable performance on a task, we can deploy them in an ensemble, weighted by their deviation from the prior distributions of prediction that we've set before. This way, instead of having a simple yes/no filter on the output of your model's range, you can more smoothly transition potentially problematic predictions into more expected ones.

Another benefit of treating the ensemble as a deployment topology instead of only a model architecture is that you can *hot-swap* components of an ensemble as you make improvements in specific subdomains of your observation feature space. Take, for example, a life-time-value (LTV) model comprising three components: one that predicts well for new clients, another for activated clients, and a third for super-users. You may find that pooling via a voting mechanism performs the best on average, so you decide to implement a bagging approach. This works well, but later you find a better model for the new clients. By using the deployment topology for your ensemble, you can swap in the new model for the new clients and start comparing performance in your ensemble in production. This brings us to the next strategy, model comparison.

Ensemble Modeling

Ensemble modeling is popular in all kinds of ML, built upon the simple notion that the mixture of expert opinions is strictly more effective than a single estimator. In fact, assume for a moment that you have M classifiers with error rate ϵ; then for an N class classification problem, your error would be $P(y \geq k) = \Sigma_k^n * \binom{n}{k} \epsilon^k * (1 - \epsilon)^{n - k}$, and the exciting part is that this is smaller than ϵ for all values less than 0.5!

Shadowing

Deploying two models, even for the same task, can be enormously informative. We call this *shadowing* when one model is "live" and the other is secretly also receiving all the requests and doing inference, and logging the results, of course. By shadowing traffic to the other model, you get the best expectations possible about how the model behaves before making your model live. This is especially useful when wanting to ensure that the prediction ranges align with expectation.

In software engineering and DevOps, there's a notion of *staging* for software. It's a hotly contested question of "how much of the real infrastructure should staging see," but shadowing is the staging of ML models. You can basically build a parallel pipeline for your entire infrastructure to connect for shadow models, or you can just put them both in the line of fire and have the request sent to both but use only one response. Shadowing is also crucial for implementing experimentation.

Experimentation

As good data scientists, we know that without a proper experimental framework, it's risky to advertise much about the performance of a feature or, in this case, model. Experimentation can be handled with shadowing by having a controller layer that is taking the incoming requests and orchestrating which of the deployed models to curry the response along. A simple A/B experimentation framework might ask for a randomization at every request, whereas something like a multiarmed bandit will require the controller layer to have notions of the reward function.

Experimentation is a deep topic that we don't have the knowledge or space to do adequate justice, but it's useful to know that this is where experimentation can fit into the larger deployment pipeline.

Model Cascades

A really nice extension of the concepts of ensembling and shadowing is model cascading (*https://oreil.ly/Ao4t_*), illustrated in Figure 7-4. The simplified idea of a model cascade is that we use model confidence to create a conditional ensemble. In particular, given an inference request, the model provides a prediction with a confidence estimate; when the model confidence is high, that prediction is returned, but if the confidence is below a certain threshold, a downstream model is called and the ensemble is started. There's no reason to stop at two models; this method can be used to iteratively expand the number of ensemble layers for any number of models that in training show improved performance in an ensemble.

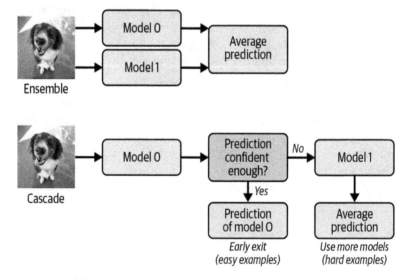

Figure 7-4. Ensembles versus cascades

Here are a few advantages of this approach:

- Better expected performance overall, as ensembles usually increase performance
- Ensemble performance with lower average computation time
- Especially better performance in out-of-sample scenarios

This method scales to larger pools of models and, while it may incur significant training efforts, finding the right ordering of the models can have significant effects on model accuracy and latency.

The Evaluation Flywheel

By now, it's likely obvious that a production ML model is far from a static object. Production ML systems of any kind are subject to as many deployment concerns as a traditional software stack, in addition to the added challenge of dataset shift and new users/items. In this section, we'll look closely at the feedback loops introduced and understand how the components fit together to continuously improve our system— even with little input from a data scientist or ML engineer.

Daily Warm Starts

As we've now discussed several times, we need a connection between the continuous output of our model and retraining. The first simplest example of this is daily warm starts, which essentially ask us to utilize the new data seen each day in our system.

As might already be obvious, some of the recommendation models that show great success are quite large. Retraining some of them can be a massive undertaking, and simply *rerunning everything* each day is often infeasible. So, what can be done?

Let's ground this conversation in the user-user CF example that we've been sketching out; the first step was to build an embedding via our similarity definition. Let's recall:

$$
\text{USim}_{A,B} = \frac{\sum_{x \in \mathcal{R}_{A,B}} \left(r_{A,x} - \bar{r}_A \right)\left(r_{B,x} - \bar{r}_B \right)}{\sqrt{\sum_{x \in \mathcal{R}_{A,B}} \left(r_{A,x} - \bar{r}_A \right)^2} \sqrt{\sum_{x \in \mathcal{R}_{A,B}} \left(r_{B,x} - \bar{r}_B \right)^2}}
$$

Here we remember that the similarity between two users is dependent on the shared ratings and on each user's average rating.

On a given day, let's say $\widetilde{X} = \{\tilde{x} \mid x$ was rated since yesterday by a user $\}$. Then we'd need to update our user similarities, but ideally we'd leave everything else the same. To update the user's data, we see that all $\tilde{x}$ rated by two users, A and $B\bar{r}_A$ and $\bar{r}_B$, would need to change, but we could probably skip these updates in many cases where the number of ratings by those users was large. All in all, this means for each $\tilde{x}$, we should look up which users previously rated x and update the user similarity between them and the new rater.

This is a bit ad hoc, but for many methods you can utilize these tricks to reduce a full retraining. This would avoid a full batch retraining, via a fast layer. Other approaches exist, like building a separate model that can approximate recommendations for low-signal items. This can be done via feature models and can significantly reduce the complexity of these quick retrainings.

Lambda Architecture and Orchestration

On the more extreme end of the spectrum of these strategies is the lambda architecture; as discussed in Chapter 6, the lambda architecture seeks to have a much more frequent pipeline for adding new data into the system. The *speed* layer is responsible for working on small batches to perform the data transformations, and on model fitting to combine with the core model. As a reminder, many other aspects of the pipeline should also be updated during these fast layers, like the nearest neighbors graph, the feature store, and the filters.

Different components of the pipeline can require different investments to keep updated, so their schedules are an important consideration. You might be starting to notice that keeping all of these aspects in sync can be a bit challenging. If you have model training, model updating, feature store updates, redeployment, and new items/users all coming in on potentially different schedules, a *lot* of coordination may be necessary. This is where an *orchestration tool* can become relevant. A variety of approaches exist, but a few useful technologies here are GoCD, MetaFlow, and KubeFlow; the latter is more oriented at Kubernetes infrastructures. Another pipeline orchestration tool that can handle both batch and streaming pipelines is Apache Beam.

Generally, for ML deployment pipelines, we need to have a reliable core pipeline and the ability to keep the systems up to date as more data pours in. Orchestration systems usually define the topology of the systems, the relevant infrastructure configurations, and the mapping of the code artifacts needing to be run—not to mention the CRON schedules of when all these jobs need to run. Code as infrastructure is a popular paradigm that captures these goals as a mantra, so that even all this configuration itself is reproducible and automatable.

In all these orchestration considerations, there's a heavy overlap with containerization and *how* these steps may be deployed. Unfortunately, most of this discussion is beyond the scope of this book, but a simple overview is that containerized deployment with something like Docker is extremely helpful for ML services, and managing those deployments with various container management systems, like Kubernetes, is also popular.

Logging

Logging has come up several times already. Previously in this chapter, you saw that logging was important for ensuring that our system was behaving as expected. Let's discuss some best practices for logging and how they fit into our plans.

When we discussed traces and spans earlier, we were able to get a snapshot of the entire call stack of the services involved in responding to a request. Linking the services together to see the larger picture is incredibly useful, and when it comes to logging, gives us a hint as to how we should be orienting our thinking. Returning to our favorite RecSys architecture, we have the following:

- Collector receiving the request and looking up the embedding relevant to the user
- Computing ANN on items for that vector
- Applying filters via blooms to eliminate potential bad recommendations
- Augmenting features of the candidate items and user via the feature stores
- Scoring of candidates via the ranking model and estimating potential confidence
- Ordering and application of business logic or experimentation

Each of these elements has potential applications of logging, but let's now think about how to link them together. The relevant concept from microservices is correlation IDs; a *correlation ID* is simply an identifier that's passed along the call stack to ensure the ability to link everything later. As is likely obvious at this point, each of these services will be responsible for its own logging, but the services are almost always more useful in aggregate.

These days, Kafka is often used as the log-stream processor to listen for logs from all the services in your pipeline and to manage their processing and storing. Kafka relies on a message-based architecture; each service is a producer, and Kafka helps manage those messages to consumer channels. In terms of log management, the Kafka cluster receives all the logs in the relevant formats, hopefully augmented with correlation IDs, and sends them off to an ELK stack. The *ELK stack*—Elasticsearch, Logstash, Kibana—consists of a Logstash component to handle incoming log streams and apply structured processing, Elasticsearch to build search indices to the log store, and Kibana to add a UI and high-level dashboarding to the logging.

This stack of technologies is focused on ensuring that you have access and observability from your logs. Other technologies focus on other aspects, but what should you be logging?

Collector logs

Again, we wish to log during the following:

- Collector receiving the request and looking up the embedding relevant to the user
- Computing ANN on items for that vector

The collector receives a request, consisting in our simplest example of user_id, requesting_timestamp, and any augmenting keyword elements (kwargs) that might be required. A correlation_id should be passed along from the requester or generated at this step. A log with these basic keys should be fired, along with the timestamp of request received. A call is made to the embedding store, and the collector should log this request. Then the embedding store should log this request when received, along with the embedding store's response. Finally, the collector should log the response as it returns. This may feel like a lot of redundant information, but the explicit parameters included in the API calls become extremely useful when troubleshooting.

The collector now has the vector it will need to perform a vector search, so it will make a call to the ANN service. Logging this call, and any relevant logic in choosing the k for number of neighbors will be important, along with the ANN's received API request, the relevant state for computing ANN, and ANN's response. Back in the collector, logging that response and any potential data augmentation for downstream service requirements are the next steps.

At this point, at least six logs have been emitted—only reinforcing the need for a way to link these all together. In practice, you often have other relevant steps in your service that should be logged (e.g., checking that the distribution of distances in returned neighbors is appropriate for downstream ranking).

Note that if the embedding lookup was a miss, logging that miss is obviously important, as well as logging the subsequent request to the cold-start recommendation pipeline. The cold-start pipeline will incur additional logs.

Filtering and scoring

Now we need to monitor the following steps:

1. Applying filters via blooms to eliminate potential bad recommendations
2. Augmenting features to the candidate items and user via the feature stores
3. Scoring candidates via the ranking model, and potential confidence estimation

We should log the incoming request to the filtering service as well as the collection of filters we wish to apply. Additionally, as we search the blooms for each item and rule them in or out of the bloom, we should build up some structured logging of which items are caught in which filters and then log all this as a blob for later inspection. Responses and requests should be logged as part of feature augmentation—where we should log requests and responses to the feature store.

Also log the augmented features that end up attached to the item entities. This may seem redundant with the feature store itself, but understanding which features were added during a recommendation pipeline is *crucial* when looking back later to figure out why the pipeline might have behaved differently than anticipated.

At the time of scoring, the entire set of candidates should be logged with the features necessary for scoring and the output scores. It's extremely powerful to log this entire dataset, because training later can use these to get a better sense for real ranking sets. Finally, the response is passed to the next step with the ranked candidates and all their features.

Ordering

We have one more step to go, but it's an essential one: *ordering and application of business logic or experimentation*. This step is probably the most important logging step, because of how complicated and ad hoc the logic in this step can get.

If you have multiple intersecting business requirements implemented via filters at this step, while also integrating with experimentation, you can find yourself seriously struggling to unpack how reasonable expectations coming out of the ranker have turned into a mess by response time. Techniques like logging the incoming candidates, keyed to why they're eliminated, and the order of business rules applied will make reconstructing the behavior much more tractable.

Additionally, experimentation routing will likely be handled by another service, but the experiment ID seen in this step and the way that experiment assignment was utilized are the responsibility of the server. As we ship off the final recommendations, or decide to go another round, one last log of the state of the recommendation will ensure that app logs can be validated with responses.

Notes on Formatting

Structured logs are your friend. Implementing a data structure to hold the relevant data for your logs and then utilizing a log-formatter object (*https://oreil.ly/5Nu5N*) will significantly reduce the difficulty in parsing and writing these logs. One often underappreciated feature of building message objects in code, and utilizing them as a running data structure throughout your call stack, is tight coupling between logs and app logic.

Tight coupling is often bemoaned in service-architecture discussions, but when that coupling is between your logs and your actual objects of execution, this saves you a lot of headaches. When changing the objects used for your service, instead of having an additional step to ensure the logs reflect that, you can propagate those changes through automatically by using the same objects in tandem with a log formatter.

These processes can also make good use of testing, to ensure that the objects your code cares about are visible in the logs, and these log-formatter objects can have enforced matching via unit tests. Finally, because we want to connect to downstream log parsing and log searching, it will be invaluable to have a clear relationship between the log stack and the application stack via object parameters and keys in the log data structure.

Active Learning

So far, we have discussed using updating data to train on a much more frequent schedule, and we've discussed how to provide good recommendations, even when the model hasn't seen enough data for those entities. An additional opportunity for the feedback loop of recommendation and rating is active learning.

We won't be able to go deep into the topic, which is a large and active field of research, but we will discuss the core ideas in relation to recommendation systems. *Active learning* changes the learning paradigm a bit by suggesting that the learner should not only be passively collecting labeled (maybe implicit) observations but also attempting to mine relations and preferences from them. Active learning determines which data and observations would be most useful in improving model performance and then seeks out those labels. In the context of RecSys, we know that the Matthew effect is one of our biggest challenges, in that many potentially good matches for a user may be lacking enough or appropriate ratings to bubble to the top during the recommendations.

What if we employed a simple policy: every new item to the store gets recommended as a second option to the first 100 customers. Two outcomes would result:

- We would quickly establish data for our new item to help cold-start it.
- We would likely decrease the performance of our recommender.

In many cases, the second outcome is worth enduring to achieve the first, but when? And is this the right way to approach this problem? Active learning provides a methodical approach to these problems.

Another more specific advantage of active learning schemes is that you can broaden the distribution of observed data. In addition, to just cold-start items, we can use active learning to target broadening users' interests. This is usually framed as an uncertainty-reduction technique, as it can be used to improve the confidence in recommendations in a broader range of item categories. Here's a simple example: a user shops for only sci-fi books, so one day you show them a few extremely well-liked Westerns to see whether that user might be open to occasionally getting recommendations for Westerns. See "Propensity Weighting for Recommendation System Evaluation" on page 208 for more details.

An active learning system is instrumented as a loss function inherited from the model it's trying to enhance—usually tied to uncertainty in some capacity—and it's attempting to minimize that loss. Given a model $\mathcal{M}$ trained on a set of observations and labels $\{x_i, y_i\}$, with loss $\mathcal{L}$, an active learner seeks to find a new observation, $\bar{x}$, such that if a label was obtained, $\bar{y}$, the loss would decrease via the model's training including this new pair. In particular, the goal is to approximate the marginal reduction in loss due to each possible new observation and find the observation that maximizes that reduction in the loss function:

$$\text{Argmax}_{\bar{x}}\left(\mathcal{L}\left(\mathcal{M}_{\{x_i, y_i\}}\right) - \mathcal{L}\left(\mathcal{M}_{\{x_i, y_i\} \cup \{\bar{x}\}}\right)\right)$$

The structure of an active learning system roughly follows these steps:

1. Estimate marginal decrease in loss due to obtaining one of a set of observations.
2. Select the observation with the largest effect.
3. *Query* the user; i.e., provide the recommendation to obtain a label.
4. Update the model.

It's probably clear that this paradigm requires a much faster training loop than our previous fast retraining schemes. Active learning can be instrumented in the same infrastructure as our other setups, or it can have its own mechanisms for integration into the pipeline.

Types of optimization

The optimization procedure carried out by an active learner in a recommendation system has two approaches: personalized and nonpersonalized. Because RecSys is all about personalization, it's no surprise that we would, in time, want to push the utility of our active learning further by integrating the great details we already know about users.

We can think of these two approaches as global loss minimization and local loss minimization. Active learning that isn't personalized tends to be about minimizing the loss over the entire system, not for only one user. (This split doesn't perfectly capture the ontology, but it's a useful mnemonic). In practice, optimization methods are nuanced and sometimes utilize complicated algorithms and training procedures.

Let's talk through some factors to optimize for nonpersonalized active learning:

User rating variance
> Consider which items have the largest variance in user ratings to try to get more data on those we find the most complicated in our observations.

Entropy
> Consider the dispersion of ratings of a particular item across an ordinal feature. This is useful for understanding whether our set of ratings for an item is distributed uniformly at random.

Greedy extend
> Measure which items seem to yield the worst performance in our current model; this attempts to improve our performance overall by collecting more data on the hardest items to recommend well.

Representatives or exemplars
> Pick out items that are extremely representative of large groups of items; we can think of this as "If we have good labels for this, we have good labels for everything like this."

Popularity
> Select items that the user is most likely to have experience with to maximize the likelihood that they'll give an opinion or rating.

Co-coverage
> Attempt to amplify the ratings for frequently occurring pairs in the dataset; this strikes directly at the CF structure to maximize the utility of observations.

On the personalized side:

Binary prediction
> To maximize the chances that the user can provide the requested rating, choose the items that the user is more likely to have experienced. This can be achieved via an MF on the binary ratings matrix.

Influence based
> Estimate the influence of item ratings on the rating prediction of other items, and select the items with the largest influence. This attempts to directly measure the impact of a new item rating on the system.

Rating optimized
> Obviously, there's an opportunity to simply use the best rating or best rating within a class to perform active learning queries, but this is precisely the standard strategy in recommendation systems to serve good recommendations.

User segmented
>When available, use user segmentation and feature clusters within users to anticipate when users have opinions and preferences on an item by virtue of the user-similarity structure.

In general, a soft trade-off exists between active learning that's useful for maximally improving your model globally and active learning that's useful for maximizing the likelihood that a user can and will rate a particular item. Let's look at one particular example that uses both.

Application: User sign-up

One common hurdle to overcome in building recommendation systems is onboarding new users. By definition, new users will be cold-starting with no ratings of any kind and will likely not expect great recommendations from the start.

We may begin with the MPIR for all new users—simply show them *something* to get them started and then learn as you go. But is there something better?

One approach you've probably experienced is the user onboarding flow: a simple set of questions employed by many websites to quickly ascertain basic information about the user, to help guide early recommendation. If discussing our book recommender, this might be asking what genres the user likes, or in the case of a coffee recommender, how the user brews coffee in the morning. It's probably clear that these questions are building up knowledge-based recommender systems and don't directly feed into our previous pipelines but can still provide some help in early recommendations.

If instead we looked at all our previous data and asked, "Which books in particular are most useful for determining a user's taste?," this would be an active learning approach. We could even have a decision tree of possibilities as the user answered each question, wherein the answer determines which next question is most useful to ask.

Summary

Now we have the confidence that we can serve up our recommendations, and even better, we have instrumented our system to gather feedback. We've shown how you can gain confidence before you deploy and how you can experiment with new models or solutions. Ensembles and cascades allow you to combine testing with iteration, and the data flywheel provides a powerful mechanism for improving your product.

You may be wondering how to put all this new knowledge into practice, to which the next chapter will speak. Let's understand how data processing and simple counting can lead to an effective—and useful!—recommendation system.

## CHAPTER 8

Putting It All Together: Data Processing and Counting Recommender

Now that we have discussed the broad outline of recommender systems, this chapter will put it into a concrete implementation so that we can talk about the choices of technologies and specifics of how the implementation works in real life.

This chapter covers the following topics:

- Data representation with protocol buffers
- Data processing frameworks
- A PySpark sample program
- GloVE embedding model
- Additional foundational techniques in JAX, Flax, and Optax

We will show step-by-step how to go from a downloaded Wikipedia dataset to a recommender system that can recommend words from Wikipedia based on the co-occurrence with words in a Wikipedia article. We use a natural language example because words are easily understood, and their relationships are readily grasped because we can see that related words occur near one another in a sentence. Fur-thermore, the Wikipedia corpus is easily downloadable and browsable by anyone with an internet connection. This idea of co-occurrence can be generalized to any co-occurring collection of items, such as watching a video in the same session or purchasing cheeses in the same shopping bag.

This chapter will demonstrate concrete implementations of an item-item and a feature-item recommender. Items in this case are the words in an article, and the features are word-count similarity—a MinHash or a kind of locality sensitive hash for words. Chapter 16 covers locality sensitive hash in more detail, but for now, we'll consider these simple hashing functions to be encoding functions over content, such that content with similar properties maps to similar co-domains. This general idea can be used as a warm-start mechanism on a new corpus in the absence of logging data, and if we have user-item features such as likes, these can be used as features for a feature-item recommender. The principles of co-occurrence are the same, but by using Wikipedia as an example, you can download the data and play with it by using the tools provided.

Warm and Cold Starts

A *cold start* occurs when we do not have any information about a corpus or people's preferences and resort to a best-guess approach such as recommending popular items. On the other hand, if items naturally occur in typical groupings, like the selection and arrangement in the cheese aisle of a grocery store, then we call this a warm start: using information like co-occurrence of cheeses with each other or with other items like salami as a means of starting out the recommender engine more intelligently.

In the Wikipedia example, even before we have users click articles, we'll be able to warm-start the word-to-word recommender simply based on how close words are to each other in a sentence. Similarly, if you had a bunch of items that naturally fall into some kind of hierarchical taxonomy, you might be able to warm-start your recommender by having items that are in the same branch of the taxonomy count as co-occurring with one another.

Tech Stack

A set of technologies used together is commonly called a *technology stack*, or *tech stack*. Each component of a tech stack can usually be replaced by other similar technologies. We will list a few alternatives for each component but not go into detail about their pros and cons, as there can be many, and the situation of the deployment will affect the choice of components. For example, your company might already use a particular component, so for familiarity and support, you might wish to use that one.

This chapter covers some of the technology choices for processing the data that goes into building a concrete implementation of a collector.

The sample code is available on GitHub (*https://github.com/BBischof/ESRecsys*). You might want to clone the code into a local directory.

Data Representation

The first choice of technology we need to make will determine how we represent the data. Some of the choices are as follows:

- Protocol buffers (*https://oreil.ly/Oc0cE*)
- Apache Thrift (*https://oreil.ly/BUHkW*)
- JSON (*https://oreil.ly/_QwWR*)
- XML (*https://oreil.ly/JigfM*)
- CSV (*https://oreil.ly/it5TA*)

In this implementation, we're mostly using protocol buffers because of the ease of specifying a schema and then subsequently serializing and deserializing it.

Protocol Buffers

Before protocol buffers were invented, people used to store their binary data in all sorts of custom formats that involved various syntax and specifications (like starting a file with a magic number, followed by rules on how to parse and store various data types like integers, strings, bytes, and floating-point numbers). Protocol buffers unified the storage of custom binary data by allowing users to specify a *schema*, or a named representation of each field and the type of each field (like `first_name` being a string and `age` being an integer). This enables us to easily read and write structured data in a binary format, and the parsing of the data is handled automatically by the protocol buffer library.

For the file format, we're using serialized protocol buffers that are uuencoded and written as a single line per record and then bzipped up for compression. This is just for convenience so that we can parse the files easily without having dependencies on too many libraries. Your company might instead store data in a data warehouse that is accessible by SQL, for example.

Protocol buffers are generally easier to parse and handle than raw data. In our implementation, we will parse the Wikipedia XML into protocol buffers for easier handling using *xml2proto.py*. You can see from the code that XML parsing is a complicated affair, whereas protocol buffer parsing is as simple as calling the `ParseFromString` method, and all the data is then subsequently available as a convenient Python object.

As of June 2022, the Wikipedia dump is about 20 GB in size, and converting to protocol buffer format takes about 10 minutes. Please follow the steps described in the README in the GitHub repo for the most up-to-date steps to run the programs.

In the *proto* directory, take a look at some of the protocol messages defined. This, for example, is how we might store the text from a Wikipedia page:

```
// Generic text document.
message TextDocument {
  // Primary entity, in wikipedia it is the title.
  string primary = 1;
  // Secondary entity, in wikipedia it is other titles.
  repeated string secondary = 2;
  // Raw body tokens.
  repeated string tokens = 3;
  // URL. Only visible documents have urls, some e.g. redirect shouldn't.
  string url = 4;
}
```

The types supported and the schema definitions can be found on the protocol buffer documentation page. This schema is converted into code by using the protocol buffer compiler. This compiler's job is to convert the schema into code that you can call in different languages, which in our case is Python. The installation of the protocol buffer compiler depends on the platform, and installation instructions can be found in the protocol buffer documentation (*https://oreil.ly/k2QEv*).

Each time you change the schema, you will have to use the protocol buffer compiler to get a new version of the protocol buffer code. This step can easily be automated by using a build system like Bazel, but this is out of scope for this book. For the purposes of this book, we will simply generate the protocol buffer code once and check it into the repository for simplicity.

Following the directions on the GitHub README, download a copy of the Wikipedia dataset and then run *xml2proto.py* to convert the data to a protocol buffer format. Optionally, use *codex.py* to see what the protocol buffer format looks like. These steps took 10 minutes on a Windows workstation using Windows Subsystem for Linux. The XML parser used doesn't parallelize very well, so this step is fundamentally serial. We'll next discuss how we would distribute the work in parallel either among multiple cores locally or on a cluster.

Big Data Frameworks

The next technology we choose will process data at scale on multiple machines. Some options are listed here:

- Apache Spark (*https://spark.apache.org*)
- Apache Beam (*https://beam.apache.org*)
- Apache Flink (*https://flink.apache.org*)

In this implementation, we're using Apache Spark in Python, or PySpark. The README in the repository shows how to install a copy of PySpark locally using `pip install`.

The first step implemented in PySpark is tokenization and URL normalization. The code is in *tokenize_wiki_pyspark.py* (*https://oreil.ly/TF_vU*), but we won't go over it here because a lot of the processing is simply distributed natural language parsing and writing out the data into protocol buffer format. We will instead talk in detail about the second step, which is to make a dictionary of tokens (the *words* in the article) and some statistics about the word counts. However, we will run the code just to see what the Spark usage experience looks like. Spark programs are run using the program `spark-submit` as follows:

```
bin/spark-submit
--master=local[4]
--conf="spark.files.ignoreCorruptFiles=true"
tokenize_wiki_pyspark.py
--input_file=data/enwiki-latest-parsed --output_file=data/enwiki-latest-tokenized
```

Running the Spark submit script allows you to execute the controller program, in this case, *tokenize_wiki_pyspark.py* (*https://oreil.ly/pQp7r*), on a local machine as we have in the command line—note that the line `local[4]` means use up to four cores. The same command can be used to submit the job to a YARN cluster for running on hundreds of machines, but for the purposes of trying out PySpark, a decent enough workstation should be able to process all the data in minutes.

This tokenization program converts from a source-specific format (in this case, a Wikipedia protocol buffer) into a more generic text document used for NLP. In general, it's a good idea to use a generic format that all your sources of data can be converted into because that simplifies the data processing downstream. The data conversion can be done from each corpus into a standard format that is handled uniformly by all the later programs in the pipeline.

After submitting the job, you can navigate to the Spark UI (shown in Figure 8-1) on your local machine at *localhost:4040/stages/*. You should see the job executing in parallel, using up all the cores in your machine. You might want to play with the `local[4]` parameter; using `local[*]` will use up all the free cores on your machine. If you have access to a cluster, you can also point to the appropriate cluster URL.

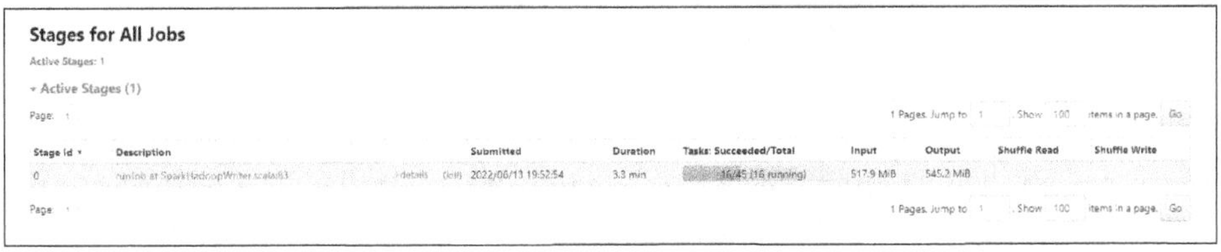

Figure 8-1. Spark UI

Cluster Frameworks

The nice thing about writing a Spark program is that it can scale from a single machine with multiple cores to a cluster of many machines with thousands of cores. The full list of cluster types can be found in the Spark "Submitting Applications" documentation (*https://oreil.ly/0apFm*).

Spark can run on the following cluster types:

- Spark Standalone cluster (*https://oreil.ly/NIiwB*)
- Mesos cluster (*https://oreil.ly/lHzRG*)
- YARN cluster (*https://oreil.ly/nuEQh*)
- Kubernetes cluster (*https://oreil.ly/sXIfK*)

Depending on the kind of cluster your company or institution has set up, most of the time submitting the job is just a matter of pointing to the correct URL. Many companies such as Databricks and Google also have fully managed Spark solutions that allow you to set up a Spark cluster with little effort.

PySpark Example

Counting words turns out to be a powerful tool in information retrieval, as we can use handy tricks like term frequency, inverse document frequency (TF-IDF), which is simply the count of words in the documents divided by the number of documents the word has occurred in. This is represented as follows:

$$tfidf_{\text{word}}(i) = \frac{\log_{10} (\text{number of times } word_i \text{ has occurred in corpus})}{\text{number of documents in corpus containing } word_i}$$

For example, because the word *the* appears frequently, we might think it is an important word. But by dividing by the document frequency, *the* becomes less special and drops in importance. This trick is quite handy in simple NLP to get a better-than-random weighting of word importance.

Therefore, our next step is to run *make_dictionary.py* (*https://oreil.ly/lESlx*). As the name indicates, this program simply counts the words and documents and makes a dictionary with the number of times a word has occurred.

We have some concepts to cover in order for you to properly grok how Spark helps process data in a distributed manner. The entry point of most Spark programs is SparkContext. This Python object is created on the controller. The *controller* is the central program that launches workers that actually process the data. The workers can be run locally on a single machine as a process or on many machines on the cloud as separate workers.

`SparkContext` can be used to create resilient distributed datasets, or RDDs. These are references to data streams that can be manipulated on the controller, and processing on the RDD can be farmed out to all the workers. `SparkContext` allows you to load up data files stored on a distributed filesystem like Hadoop Distributed File System (HDFS) or cloud buckets. By calling the `SparkContext`'s `textFile` method, we are returned a handle to an RDD. A stateless function can then be applied or mapped on the RDD to transform it from one RDD to another by repeatedly applying the function to the contents of the RDD.

For example, this program fragment loads a text file and converts all lines to lowercase by running an anonymous lambda function that converts single lines to lowercase:

```
def lower_rdd(input_file: str,
              output_file: str):
    """Takes a text file and converts it to lowercase.."""
    sc = SparkContext()
    input_rdd = sc.textFile(input_file)
    input_rdd.map(lambda line: line.lower()).saveAsTextFile(output_file)
```

In a single-machine implementation, we would simply load up each Wikipedia article, keep a running dictionary in RAM, and count each token and then add 1 to the token count in the dictionary. A *token* is an atomic element of a document that is divided into pieces. In regular English, it would be a word, but Wikipedia documents have other entities such as the document references themselves that need to be kept track of separately, so we call the division into pieces *tokenization* and the atomic elements *tokens*. The single-machine implementation would take a while to go through the thousands of documents on Wikipedia, which is why we use a distributed processing framework like Spark. In the Spark paradigm, computation is broken into maps, where a function is applied statelessly on each document in parallel. Spark also has a reduce function, where the outputs of separate maps are joined together.

For example, suppose we have a list of word counts and want to sum up the values of words that occur in different documents. The input to the reducer will be something like this:

- (apple, 10)
- (orange, 20)
- (apple, 7)

Then we call the Spark function reduceByKey(lambda a, b: a+ b), which adds all the values with the same key together and returns the following:

- (orange, 20)
- (apple, 17)

If you look at the code in *make_dictionary.py* (*https://oreil.ly/IESlx*), the *map phase* is where we take a document as input and then break it into tuples of (token, 1). In the *reduce phase*, the map outputs are joined by the key, which in this case is the token itself, and the reduce function is simply to sum up all the counts of tokens.

Note that the reduce function assumes that the reduction is associative—that is, $(a + b + c) = (a + b) + c = a + (b + c)$. This allows the Spark framework to sum up some parts of the token dictionary in memory on the map phase (in some frameworks, this is called the *combine step*, where you run part of the reduction on the output of the map phase on the mapper machine) and then sum them up over several passes on the reduce phase.

As an optimization, we use the Spark function mapPartitions. Map runs the provided function once per line (for which we have encoded an entire Wikipedia document as a protocol buffer, uuencoded as a single text line), whereas mapPartitions runs it over an entire partition, which is many documents, usually 64 MB of them. This optimization lets us construct a small Python dictionary over the entire partition so that we have many fewer token-count pairs to reduce. This saves on network bandwidth so the mapper has less data to send to the reducer, and is a good tip in general for these data processing pipelines to reduce network bandwidth (which is generally the most time-consuming part of data processing compared to computation).

Group Theory

Because we are math nerds, and also because group theory shows up a lot in reduction operations, we will briefly introduce an algebraic structure known as *groups* so that you clearly understand all the terms used in the reduction phase.

The concept of sets was mentioned in the introductory chapters; a *set* is a collection of items. The other concept you need to know is an operator. A binary *operator* takes two items and returns another item that is in the set.

Examples of sets that are commonly used are integers, real numbers, and matrices. Examples of binary operators are addition, multiplication, and composition.

An operator and a set denoted by the tuple (binary operator, a set of integers) form a group only if the group axioms are satisfied, namely:

An identity element exists.

> For every element x in the group, there exists an element e such that $x + e = e + x = e$. For the addition operation, the identity is 0, and for multiplication, the identity is called 1. This concept is important in the reduction step because in some frameworks the reduction step is initialized with the identity element. For example, sums are usually initialized with 0, and products are usually initialized with 1.

The operator is associative.

> For elements x, y, z in the set, $(x + y) + z = x + (y + z)$.

An inverse exists.

> For every element x in the group, there exists a y in the group, such that $x + y = e$.

An operator can also be commutative. This isn't a requirement to be a group, but groups that have this property are called *commutative groups*. With commutativity, for elements x, y in the group, $x + y = y + x$. This property is helpful in the reduction step because it allows the reducer to perform the operations in parallel and then reduce them together without worrying which operations occur in what order.

It is important to note that while addition over real numbers is associative and commutative, addition of floating-point numbers isn't. The reason is that floating-point approximately represents real numbers. So when you add a large number with a small number in floating-point, the small number isn't represented accurately and might simply be discarded. A more accurate and consistent way to add floating-point numbers is to sort the list of numbers to be added first and add all the small numbers up before adding them to the large numbers. Adding two small numbers together first to make a larger number ensures that they do not get lost when being absorbed into the accumulator (the sum). Thus, while addition of numbers is in theory associative and commutative with real numbers, you might get different results in practice with floating-point numbers, depending on the order of operations.

Next we show a complete Spark program that reads in documents in the protocol buffer format of TextDocument shown in the preceding code block and then counts how often the words, or tokens, occur in the entire corpus. The file in the GitHub repo is *make_dictionary.py* (*https://oreil.ly/lESlx*). The following code is presented slightly differently from the repo file in that it is broken into three chunks for readability and the order of the main and subroutines have been swapped for clarity. Here, we present first the dependencies and flags, then the main body, and then the functions being called by the main body so that the purposes of the functions are clearer.

First, let's look at the dependencies. The main ones are the protocol buffer representing the text document of the Wikipedia article, as discussed earlier. This is the input we are expecting. For the output, we have the `TokenDictionary` protocol buffer, which mainly counts the occurrences of words in the article. We will use the co-occurrences of words to form a similarity graph of articles that we can then use as the basis of a warm-start recommender system. We also have dependencies on PySpark, the data processing framework we are using to process the data, as well as a flag library that handles the options of our program. The absl flags library is pretty handy for parsing and explaining the purposes of command-line flags and also retrieving the set values of flags easily. Here are the dependencies and flags:

```python
#!/usr/bin/env python
# -*- coding: utf-8 -*-
#
#

"""
   This reads a doc.pb.b64.bz2 file and generates a dictionary.
"""
import base64
import bz2
import nlp_pb2 as nlp_pb
import re
from absl import app
from absl import flags
from pyspark import SparkContext
from token_dictionary import TokenDictionary

FLAGS = flags.FLAGS
flags.DEFINE_string("input_file", None, "Input doc.pb.b64.bz2 file.")
flags.DEFINE_string("title_output", None,
                    "The title dictionary output file.")
flags.DEFINE_string("token_output", None,
                    "The token dictionary output file.")
flags.DEFINE_integer("min_token_frequency", 20,
                     "Minimum token frequency")
flags.DEFINE_integer("max_token_dictionary_size", 500000,
                     "Maximum size of the token dictionary.")
flags.DEFINE_integer("max_title_dictionary_size", 500000,
                     "Maximum size of the title dictionary.")
flags.DEFINE_integer("min_title_frequency", 5,
                     "Titles must occur this often.")

# Required flag.
flags.mark_flag_as_required("input_file")
flags.mark_flag_as_required("token_output")
flags.mark_flag_as_required("title_output")
```

Next, we have the main body of the program, which is where all the subroutines are called. We first create SparkContext, which is the entry point into the Spark data processing system, and then call its textFile method to read in the bzipped Wikipedia articles. Please read the README on the repo to understand how it was generated. Next, we parse the text document and send the RDD to two processing pipelines, one to make a dictionary for the body of the article and another to make a dictionary of the titles. We could choose to make a single unified dictionary for both, but having them separate allows us to create a content-based recommender using the token dictionary and an article-to-article recommender using the title dictionary, as titles are identifiers for the Wikipedia article. Here's the main body:

```python
def main(argv):
    """Main function."""
    del argv  # Unused.
    sc = SparkContext()
    input_rdd = sc.textFile(FLAGS.input_file)
    text_doc = parse_document(input_rdd)
    make_token_dictionary(
        text_doc,
        FLAGS.token_output,
        FLAGS.min_token_frequency,
        FLAGS.max_token_dictionary_size
    )
    make_title_dictionary(
        text_doc,
        FLAGS.title_output,
        FLAGS.min_title_frequency,
        FLAGS.max_title_dictionary_size
    )


if __name__ == "__main__":
    app.run(main)
```

Finally, we have the subroutines called by the main function, all decomposed into smaller subroutines for counting the tokens in the article body and the titles:

```python
def update_dict_term(term, dictionary):
    """Updates a dictionary with a term."""
    if term in dictionary:
        x = dictionary[term]
    else:
        x = nlp_pb.TokenStat()
        x.token = term
        dictionary[term] = x
    x.frequency += 1


def update_dict_doc(term, dictionary):
    """Updates a dictionary with the doc frequency."""
    dictionary[term].doc_frequency += 1
```

```python
def count_titles(doc, title_dict):
    """Counts the titles."""
    # Handle the titles.
    all_titles = [doc.primary]
    all_titles.extend(doc.secondary)
    for title in all_titles:
        update_dict_term(title, title_dict)
    title_set = set(all_titles)
    for title in title_set:
        update_dict_doc(title, title_dict)


def count_tokens(doc, token_dict):
    """Counts the tokens."""
    # Handle the tokens.
    for term in doc.tokens:
        update_dict_term(term, token_dict)
    term_set = set(doc.tokens)
    for term in term_set:
        update_dict_doc(term, token_dict)


def parse_document(rdd):
    """Parses documents."""
    def parser(x):
        result = nlp_pb.TextDocument()
        try:
            result.ParseFromString(x)
        except google.protobuf.message.DecodeError:
            result = None
        return result
    output = rdd.map(base64.b64decode)\
        .map(parser)\
        .filter(lambda x: x is not None)
    return output


def process_partition_for_tokens(doc_iterator):
    """Processes a document partition for tokens."""
    token_dict = {}
    for doc in doc_iterator:
        count_tokens(doc, token_dict)
    for token_stat in token_dict.values():
        yield (token_stat.token, token_stat)


def tokenstat_reducer(x, y):
    """Combines two token stats together."""
    x.frequency += y.frequency
    x.doc_frequency += y.doc_frequency
```

```
        return x


def make_token_dictionary(
    text_doc,
    token_output,
    min_term_frequency,
    max_token_dictionary_size
):
    """Makes the token dictionary."""
    tokens = text_doc.mapPartitions(process_partition_for_tokens)
        .reduceByKey(tokenstat_reducer).values()
    filtered_tokens = tokens.filter(
        lambda x: x.frequency >= min_term_frequency)
    all_tokens = filtered_tokens.collect()
    sorted_token_dict = sorted(
        all_tokens, key=lambda x: x.frequency, reverse=True)
    count = min(max_token_dictionary_size, len(sorted_token_dict))
    for i in range(count):
        sorted_token_dict[i].index = i
    TokenDictionary.save(sorted_token_dict[:count], token_output)


def process_partition_for_titles(doc_iterator):
    """Processes a document partition for titles."""
    title_dict = {}
    for doc in doc_iterator:
        count_titles(doc, title_dict)
    for token_stat in title_dict.values():
        yield (token_stat.token, token_stat)


def make_title_dictionary(
    text_doc,
    title_output,
    min_title_frequency,
    max_title_dictionary_size
):
    """Makes the title dictionary."""
    titles = text_doc
      .mapPartitions(process_partition_for_titles)
      .reduceByKey(tokenstat_reducer).values()
    filtered_titles = titles.filter(
      lambda x: x.frequency >= min_title_frequency)
    all_titles = filtered_titles.collect()
    sorted_title_dict = sorted(
      all_titles, key=lambda x: x.frequency, reverse=True)
    count = min(max_title_dictionary_size, len(sorted_title_dict))
    for i in range(count):
        sorted_title_dict[i].index = i
    TokenDictionary.save(sorted_title_dict[:count], title_output)
```

As you can see, Spark makes it easy to scale a program from a single machine to run on a cluster of many machines! Starting from the main function, we create SparkContext, read in the input file as a text file, parse it, and then make the token and title dictionaries. The RDD is passed around as arguments of the processing function and can be used multiple times and fed to various map functions (such as the token and title dictionary methods).

The heavy lifting in the make-dictionary methods is done by the process-partitions functions, which are map functions that are applied to entire partitions at once. *Partitions* are large chunks of the input, typically about 64 MB in size and processed as one chunk so that we save on network bandwidth by doing map-side combines. This is a technique to apply the reducer repeatedly on mapped partitions as well as after joining by the key (which in this case is the token) and summing up the counts. The reason we do this is to save on network bandwidth, which is typically the slowest part of data processing pipelines after disk access.

You can view the output of the make_dictionary phase by using the utility *codex.py*, which dumps protocol buffers of different kinds registered in the program. Since all our data is serialized as bzipped and uuencoded text files, the only difference is which protocol buffer schema is used to decode the serialized data, so we can use just one program to print out the first few elements of the data for debugging. Although it might be much simpler to store data as JSON, XML, or CSV files, having a schema will save you from future grief because protocol buffers are extensible and support optional fields. They are also typed, which can save you from accidental mistakes in JSON, such as not knowing whether a value is a string or float or int, or having a field as a string in some files and as an int in others. Having an explicit typed schema saves us from a lot of these mistakes.

The next step in the pipeline is *make_cooccurrence.py*. As the name implies, this program simply counts the number of times each token occurs with another token. This is essentially a sparse way of representing a graph. In *nlp.proto*, each row of the sparse co-occurrence matrix is as follows:

```
// Co-occurrence matrix row.
message CooccurrenceRow {
    uint64 index = 1;
    repeated uint64 other_index = 2;
    repeated float count = 3;
}
```

In a *co-occurrence matrix*, each row i has an entry at column j that represents the number of times token j has co-occurred with token i. This is a handy way of associating the similarity between tokens i and j because if they co-occur a lot, they must be more related to each other than tokens that do not co-occur. In the protocol buffer format, these are stored as two parallel arrays of other_index and count. We use indices because they are smaller than storing raw words, especially with the varying encoding that protocol buffers use (i.e., the matrix of rows and columns indexed by tokens, and elements that are the co-occurrences of the indices). In this encoding, small integers take fewer bits to represent than large integers; since we reverse-sorted the dictionary by frequency, the most commonly occurring tokens have the smallest indices.

At this stage, if you wanted to make a very simple recommender based on frequent item similarity co-occurrence, you would look up the row for token i and return by count order the tokens j. The simple recommender would make a good variant on the popular item recommender as described in the earlier chapters.

Customers Also Bought

This concept of co-occurrences will be developed further in Chapter 9, but let's take a moment to reflect on this concept of the MPIR and co-occurrences. When we look at the co-occurrence matrix for items, we can take row sums or column sums to determine the number of times each item has been seen (or purchased). That was how we built the MPIR in Chapter 2. If instead we look at the MPIR for a particular row corresponding to an item the user has seen, that's simply the *conditional MPIR*—i.e., the most popular item, given that the user has seen item i.

However, here we can choose to do an embedding or low-rank representation of the co-occurrence matrix. An embedding representation of a matrix is handy because it allows us to represent each item as a vector. One way to factor the matrix is via singular value decomposition, or SVD (see "Latent Spaces" on page 167), but we won't be doing that here. Instead we will be learning GloVE embeddings, which were developed for NLP.

The objective function of GloVE embedding is to learn two vectors such that their dot product is proportional to the log count of co-occurrence between the two vectors. The reason this loss function works is that the dot product will then be proportional to the log count of co-occurrence; thus, words that frequently occur together will have a larger dot product than words that do not. To compute the embeddings, we need to have the co-occurrence matrix handy, and luckily the previous step in the pipeline has generated such a matrix for us to process.

Feature-Item Versus Item-Item

We introduce feature-item recommenders in this section via the conversion step from words to token IDs. The way we look up the embedding ID for the model is based on the index—either features or items. For the top N popular words, we have a one-to-one mapping from the dictionary index to the embedding ID. However, for long-tailed words, we want them to map to the same value of embedding_id if we can help it.

One cheap way of computing a feature from a word is called *min-hashing*: we find 4 consecutive bytes of a word, compute the hash of these bytes, and find the minimum hash of the overlapping 4 bytes. This process makes it more likely to relate *z*e*b*r*a* h*a*s*h*e*s* to zebras. This feature is then used to represent these sets of words as an equivalence class. All words that hash to the same MinHash value are in the same equivalence class. This allows us to handle any new long-tailed word naturally for the time being until a new dictionary is built. It might result in undesirable mistakes in certain applications, but for other applications where it might be safe to do so, a feature-based representation of an item might be mixed into an embedding system as we have done.

Another alternate way to get feature embeddings is to train an autoencoder or some kind of embedding representation that is learned off the features of the item so that the recommender might generalize to new, unseen items. However, for the sake of simplicity and in this word embedding case, we simply use the MinHash for ease of understanding. The MinHash implementation can be seen at *wikipedia/token_dictionary.py* (*https://oreil.ly/CSaOY*).

GloVE Model Definition

For this section, please refer to the code at *train_coccurence.py* (*https://oreil.ly/exOH2*).

Suppose we have tokens *i* and *j* from the token dictionary. We know that they have co-occurred with each other N times. We want to somehow generate an embedding space such that the vectors $x(i) * x(j)$ are proportional to $\log(N)$. The arguments for log count and the exact equation are derived in the "GloVe: Global Vectors for Word Representation" (*https://oreil.ly/cMHB3*) by Jeffrey Pennington et al. We will show just the derived result:

$$y_{\text{predicted}} = x(i)\dot{x}(j) + \text{bias}(i) + \text{bias}(j)$$

Here, x is the embedding lookup. In the code, we use 64-dimensional vectors, which are not too small as to have insufficient capacity to represent the embedding space but are not too large that it would take up too much memory when we have an embedding for the entire dictionary. The bias terms are there to soak up the large counts from very popular items such as *the*, *a*, and *and* that co-occur with many other terms.

The loss we want to minimize is the squared difference between the prediction and the actual value:

$$y_{target} = 1 + \log_{10}(N)$$

$$weight = \min(1, N/100)^{0.75}$$

$$loss = weight * \left(y_{predicted} - y_{target}\right)^2$$

The weighting term in the loss function is to prevent domination by very popular co-occurrences as well as to downweight rarer co-occurrences.

GloVE Model Specification in JAX and Flax

Let's look at the implementation of the GloVE model based on JAX and Flax. This is in the file *wikipedia/models.py* on the GitHub repository:

```python
import flax
from flax import linen as nn
from flax.training import train_state
import jax
import jax.numpy as jnp


class Glove(nn.Module):
    """A simple embedding model based on gloVe.
       https://nlp.stanford.edu/projects/glove/
    """
    num_embeddings: int = 1024
    features: int = 64

    def setup(self):
        self._token_embedding = nn.Embed(self.num_embeddings,
                                         self.features)
        self._bias = nn.Embed(
            self.num_embeddings, 1, embedding_init=flax.linen.initializers.zeros)

    def __call__(self, inputs):
        """Calculates the approximate log count between tokens 1 and 2.
        Args:
          A batch of (token1, token2) integers representing co-occurence.
        Returns:
          Approximate log count between x and y.
        """
        token1, token2 = inputs
        embed1 = self._token_embedding(token1)
        bias1 = self._bias(token1)
        embed2 = self._token_embedding(token2)
        bias2 = self._bias(token2)
        dot_vmap = jax.vmap(jnp.dot, in_axes=[0, 0], out_axes=0)
```

```
        dot = dot_vmap(embed1, embed2)
        output = dot + bias1 + bias2
        return output

    def score_all(self, token):
        """Finds the score of token vs all tokens.
        Args:
          max_count: The maximum count of tokens to return.
          token: Integer index of token to find neighbors of.
        Returns:
          Scores of nearest tokens.
        """
        embed1 = self._token_embedding(token)
        all_tokens = jnp.arange(0, self.num_embeddings, 1, dtype=jnp.int32)
        all_embeds = self._token_embedding(all_tokens)
        dot_vmap = jax.vmap(jnp.dot, in_axes=[None, 0], out_axes=0)
        scores = dot_vmap(embed1, all_embeds)
        return scores
```

Flax is rather simple to use; all networks inherit from Flax's linen neural network library and are modules. Flax modules are also Python dataclasses, so any hyperparameters for the module are defined at the start of the module as variables. We have only two for this simple model: the number of embeddings we want, which corresponds to the number of tokens in the dictionary, and the dimension of the embedding vectors. Next, in the setup of the module, we actually create the layers we want, which is just the bias term and embedding for each token.

The next part of the definition is the default method that is called when we use this module. In this case, we want to pass in a pair of tokens, i, j; convert them to embeddings, $x(i), x(j)$; and then compute the predicted $\log(count(y_{predicted}))$.

In this section of code, we encounter the first difference between JAX and NumPy—namely, a vectorized map, or vmap. A vmap takes in a function and applies it in the same way across axes of tensors; this makes coding easier because you just have to think about how the original function operates on lower-rank tensors such as vectors. In this example, since we are passing in batches of pairs of tokens and then embedding them, we actually have a batch of vectors, and so we want to run the dot product over the batch dimension. We pass in JAX's dot function, which takes vectors, run it over the batch dimension (which is axis 0), and tell vmap to return the outputs as another batch dimension as axis 0. This allows us to efficiently and simply write code for lower-dimensional tensors and obtain a function that can operate on higher-dimensional tensors by vmapping over the extra axes. Conceptually, it would be as if we looped over the first dimension and returned an array of the dot products. However, by converting this process to a function, we allow JAX to push this loop into JITable code that can be compiled to run fast on a GPU.

Finally, we also declare the helper function score_all (*https://oreil.ly/-zYon*), which takes one token and scores it against all the other tokens. Again, we use vmap to take the dot product with the particular token $x(i)$ but run it against all the other token embeddings. The difference here is that since $x(i)$ is already a vector, we don't need to vmap over it. Therefore, in in_axes, we supply [None, 0], which means don't vmap over the axes of the first argument but instead vmap over axis 0 of the second argument, which is the batch of all the embeddings of all the tokens. Then we return the result, which is an array that is the dot product of $x(i)$ against all other embeddings but without the bias terms. We don't use the bias term in scoring because it was used in part to soak up the popularity of very common tokens, and our scoring function would be more interesting if we just used the dot product part of it for scoring.

GloVE Model Training with Optax

Next, let's take a look at *wikipedia/train_coocurrence.py* (*https://oreil.ly/A1o24*). Let's look specifically at the part where the model is called to dig into some JAX specifics:

```
@jax.jit
def apply_model(state, inputs, target):
    """Computes the gradients and loss for a single batch."""

    # Define glove loss.
    def glove_loss(params):
        """The GloVe weighted loss."""
        predicted = state.apply_fn({'params': params}, inputs)
        ones = jnp.ones_like(target)
        weight = jnp.minimum(ones, target / 100.0)
        weight = jnp.power(weight, 0.75)
        log_target = jnp.log10(1.0 + target)
        loss = jnp.mean(jnp.square(log_target - predicted) * weight)
        return loss

    grad_fn = jax.value_and_grad(glove_loss)
    loss, grads = grad_fn(state.params)

    return grads, loss
```

The first point you will notice is the function decorator, `@jax.jit`. This tells JAX that everything in the function is JITable. There are some requirements for a function to be JITable—mostly that it is pure, which is a computer science term indicating that if you call a function with the same arguments, you would expect the same result. That function should not have any side effects and shouldn't rely on a cached state such as a private counter or random-number generator with implicit state. The tensors that are passed in as arguments should probably also have fixed shape, because every new shape would trigger a new JIT compilation. You can give hints to the compiler that certain parameters are constants with `static_argnums`, but these arguments shouldn't change too frequently, or else a lot of time will be spent compiling a program for each of these constants.

One consequence of this pure function philosophy is that the model structure and model parameters are separated. This way, the model functions are pure and the parameters are passed in to the model functions, allowing the model functions to be jitted. This is why we apply the model's `apply_fn` to the parameters rather than simply having the parameters as part of the model.

This `apply_model` function can then be compiled to implement the GloVE loss that we described earlier. The other new functionality that JAX provides above NumPy is automatically computing gradients of functions. The JAX function `value_and_grad` computes the gradient of the loss with respect to the parameters. Since the gradient always points in the direction in which the loss increases, we can use gradient descent to go the other way and minimize the loss. The Optax library has a few optimizers to pick from, including SGD (stochastic gradient descent with momentum) and ADAM.

When you run the training program, it will loop over the co-occurence matrix and try to generate a succinct form of it by using the GloVE loss function. After about an hour, you should be able to see the highest-scoring term.

The nearest neighbors for "democracy," for example, are as follows: democracy:1.064498, liberal:1.024733, reform:1.000746, affairs:0.961664, socialist:0.952792, organizations:0.935910, political:0.919937, policy:0.917884, policies:0.907138, and --date:0.889342.

As you can see, the query token itself is usually the highest-scoring neighbor, but this is not necessarily true, as a very popular token might actually be higher scoring to the token than the query token itself.

Summary

After reading this chapter, you should have a good overview of the basic ingredients for assembling a recommender system. You have seen how to set up a basic Python development environment; manage packages; specify inputs and outputs with flags; encode data in various ways, including using protocol buffers; and process the data with a distributed framework with PySpark. You also learned how to compress gigabytes of data into a few megabytes of a model that is able to generalize and quickly score items, given a query item.

Take some time to play with the code and read the documentation of the various packages referenced to get a good sense of the basics. These foundational examples have widespread applications, and having a firm grasp on them will make your production environments more accurate.

## PART III

Ranking

What are the appropriate candidates for a given recommendation? Which of these candidates is the best? What about the 10 best?

Sometimes the best recommender system is simply item availability, but in the majority of cases, you're hoping to capture subtle signals about user preference to deliver excellent recommendations among potentially millions of options. Personalization is the name of the game; while we previously focused on item-item similarity with respect to external meaning, we need to start attempting to infer user taste and desire.

We'd also better start making this an ML task eventually. Beyond discussions of features and architectures, we'll need to define the objective functions. At first blush, the objective for recommendations is the simple binary "Did they like it?"—so maybe we're simply predicting the outcome of a Bernoulli trial. However, as we discussed in the introduction, there are a variety of ways to get the signal about how much they liked it. Moreover, recommendation systems in most cases grant one kindness: you get multiple shots on goal. Usually you get to recommend a few options, so we are very interested in predictions of which things they'll like the most. In this part of the book, we'll take all that you've learned and start getting numbers out. We'll also talk about explicit loss functions used to train and evaluate your models.

## CHAPTER 9

Feature-Based and Counting-Based Recommendations

Consider this oversimplified problem: given a bunch of new users, predict which will like our new mega-ultra-fancy-fun-item-of-novelty, or MUFFIN for short. You may start by asking which old users like MUFFIN; do those users have any aspects in common? If so, you could build a model that predicts MUFFIN affinity from those correlated user features.

Alternatively, you could ask, "What are other items people buy with MUFFIN?" If you find that others frequently also ask for JAM (just-awesome-merch), then MUFFIN may be a good suggestion for those who already have JAM. This would be using the co-occurrence of MUFFIN and JAM as a predictor. Similarly, if your friend comes along with tastes similar to yours—you both like SCONE, JAM, BISCUIT, and TEA—but your friend hasn't yet had the MUFFIN, if you like MUFFIN, it's probably a good choice for your friend too. This is using the co-occurrence of items between you and your friend.

These item relationship features will form our first ranking methods in this chapter; so grab a tasty snack and let's dig in.

Bilinear Factor Models (Metric Learning)

As per the usual idioms about running in front of horses and walking after the cart, let's start our journey into ranking systems with what can be considered the *naive* ML approaches. Via these approaches, we will start to get a sense of where the rub lies in building recommendation systems and why some of the forthcoming efforts are necessary at all.

Let's begin again with our basic premise of recommendation problems: to estimate ratings of item x by user i written as $r_{i,x}$. *Note the slight change in notation from earlier for reasons that will become clear momentarily.* In a usual ML paradigm, we might claim that estimating this score is done via properties of the item and the user, and frequently those properties would be described as features, and thus **i** and **x** can be the user and item vectors, respectively, composed of these features.

Now, we consider user i with their collection of previously interacted-with items $\mathcal{R}_i$, and consider $\mathcal{I} = \{\mathbf{x} \mid x \in \mathcal{R}_i\}$ the set of vectors associated to those items in this feature space. We can then map this collection of vectors to a representation to yield a *content-based feature vector for i*. Figure 9-1 illustrates an example mapping.

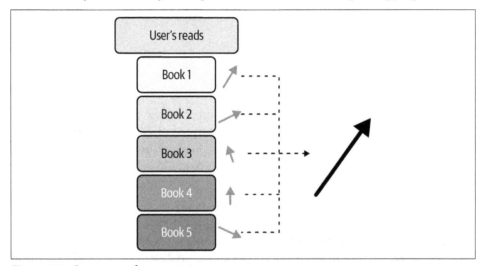

Figure 9-1. Content-to-feature vector

This extremely simple approach can turn a collection of item features and user-item interactions into features of the user. Much of the following will be increasingly rich ways of doing this. Thinking very hard about the map, the features, and the requirements for *interaction* yields many of the key insights in the rest of the book.

Let's take the preceding mapping, $\mathbf{i} := F(\mathcal{I})$, to be a simple aggregation like dimension-wise average. Then recognize that the mapping will provide a vector of the same dimension as the items. Now we have a user vector in the same "space" as the items, and we can ask a similarity question as we did in our discussion of latent space in Chapter 3.

We need to move back to the mathematical framings to set up how to use these vectors. Ultimately, we're now in a latent space with users and items, but how can we do anything with that? Well you may already remember how to compare vector similarity. Let's define the similarity to be *cosine-similarity*:

$$sim(\mathbf{i}, \mathbf{x}) = \frac{\mathbf{i} \cdot \mathbf{x}}{|\mathbf{i}| * |\mathbf{x}|}$$

If we precompose our similarity with vector normalization, this is simply the inner product—*and this is an essential first step toward recommendation systems.* For convenience, let's always assume this space we're working in is after normalization, so all similarity measures are done on the unit sphere:

$$r_{i,x} \sim sim(\mathbf{i}, \mathbf{x}) = \sum_k \mathbf{i}_k * \mathbf{x}_k$$

This now approximates our ratings. But wait, dear reader, where are the learnable parameters? Let's go ahead and make this a weighted summation, via a diagonal matrix A:

$$r_{i,x} \sim sim^A(\mathbf{i}, \mathbf{x}) = \sum_k a_k * \mathbf{i}_k * \mathbf{x}_k$$

This slight generalization already puts us in the world of statistical learning. You can probably already see how A can be used to learn which of the dimensions in this space are most important for approximating the ratings, but before we make that precise, let's generalize yet once more:

$$r_{i,x} \sim sim^A(\mathbf{i}, \mathbf{x}) = \sum_{k,l} a_{kl} * \mathbf{i}_k * \mathbf{x}_l$$

This nets us even more parameters! We see that now $sim^A(\mathbf{i}, \mathbf{x}) = \mathbf{i}A\mathbf{x}$, and we are only one step away from the familiar ground of linear regression. Currently, our model is in the form of a *bilinear regression*, so let's utilize a little linear algebra. For the sake of exposition, let $\mathbf{i} \in \mathbb{R}^n$, $\mathbf{x} \in \mathbb{R}^m$, and $A \in \mathbb{R}^{n \times m}$, and then we have this:

$$\mathbf{vect}(\mathbf{i} * \mathbf{x}^T) \in \mathbb{R}^{n*m}$$

We can simplify to the following:

$$sim^A(\mathbf{i}, \mathbf{x}) = \mathbf{i}A\mathbf{x} = \mathbf{vect}(\mathbf{i} * \mathbf{x}^T) * \mathbf{vect}(A)$$

If we make up notation for the right-hand side, you'll find your friend linear regression waiting for you:

$$\mathbf{v}_{ix} := \mathbf{vect}(\mathbf{i} * \mathbf{x}^T), \beta := \mathbf{vect}(A)$$

Thus:

$$r_{i,x} \sim sim^A(\mathbf{i}, \mathbf{x}) = \mathbf{v}_{ix}\beta$$

With this computation behind us, we see that whether we wish to compute binary ratings, ordinal ratings, or likelihood estimation, the tools in our linear models toolbox can enter the party. We have available to us regularization and optimizers and any other fun we're interested in from the linear models world.

If these equations feel frustrating or painful, let me try to offer you a geometric mental model. Each item and user is in a high-dimensional space, and ultimately we're trying to figure out which ones are closest to one another. People frequently misunderstand these geometries by imagining the tips of the vectors being near one another; this is not the case. These spaces are extremely high-dimensional, which results in the analogy being far from the truth. Instead, ask if *the values are similarly large in some of the vector indices*. This is a much simpler, but also more accurate, geometric view: there are some subspaces in the extremely high-dimensional space where the vectors point in the same direction.

This forms the foundation for where we are going but has serious limitations for large-scale recommender problems. You will see, however, that the feature-based learning still has its place in the cold-start regime.

Note that in addition to the preceding approach of building content-based features for a user, we may also have obvious user features that are obtained via queries to the user, or implicitly via other data collection; examples of these features include location, age range, and height.

Is User Space the Same as Item Space?

In this section, we've discussed ways to put users and items in the same latent spaces. We claim that we can make comparisons between users and items by vector operations. In mathematics, vectors are elements of vector spaces, and (finite dimensional) vector spaces are defined by their number of dimensions and the values that the vectors have as elements. For example, if we say it's a three-dimensional vector space with 8-bit integers, that's sufficient to specify a vector space.

However, devilish details are lurking around. First, what does *distance* mean in a specified vector space? We have many conventional measures, but it's important to ensure that comparisons between two spaces are utilizing the same definitions of distance. Another consideration is the process by which you define the vectors of the space; if you arrive at your vectors via a dimension reduction from a larger space, there are likely density properties that you can expect not to be present naively. Where this is most relevant for ranking models and recommendation systems is that we frequently arrive at user space and item space separately, and often compute distance between user and item vectors.

Is this OK? In many cases, it lacks firm theoretical footing but works well. One particular case where this *does* have a firm theoretical footing is MF. Rather than a long digression on geometric algebra, we will give the following guidance: if you're interested in comparing two vectors that aren't in the same space, ask yourself if they're of the same dimension, if distance is defined the same in both spaces, and if the density priors are similar. In fact, at times, none of these is true and you can *still* get away with a comparison. But for each of these potential risks, it's worth a stop-and-think.

One explicit example of a troubling difference in two latent spaces is found in "Poincaré Embeddings for Learning Hierarchical Representations" (*https://oreil.ly/ReDF6*) by Maximilian Nickel and Douwe Kiela; this paper provides an interesting way to encode relationships between items in your latent space via the implicit geometry. However, your users may not be encoded in a hyperbolic space. Tread carefully if you compute inner products between these and Euclidean embedded vectors!

Feature-Based Warm Starting

As you saw in Chapter 7, there are a variety of ways to use features alongside some of the collaborative filtering (CF) and MF approaches we've presented. In particular, you saw how encoders built via a two-towers architecture can be used for fast feature-based recommendations in the cold-start scenario. Let's look into this deeper and think carefully about features for new users or items.

In Chapter 9, we built our bilinear factor model as a simple regression and, in fact, saw that all the standard ML modeling approaches would apply. However, we took the user embedding to be features learned from item interactions: that is, the content-based feature vector. If our goal is to build a recommendation algorithm that does not need a history of user ratings, obviously this construction will not suffice.

We might begin by asking if the preceding factor regression approach could work in the pure user-feature setting—leave aside worries about the inner product that depended on a mutual embedding and just take everything to be pure matrices. While this is a reasonable idea that can yield some results, we may quickly identify the coarseness of this model: each user would then need to provide answers to queries q_k such that $\mathbf{i} \in \mathbb{R}^k$. Because the dimensionality of these user vectors scales linearly with the number of questions we're willing and able to ask the user, we are passing along the difficulty of the problem to our user experience.

Because we intend on using CF via MF as our core model, we'd really like to find a way to smoothly transition from the feature-based model into this MF, ensuring we take advantage of user/item ratings as they emerge. In "The Evaluation Flywheel" on page 117, we discussed using inference results and their subsequent outcomes in real time to update the model, but how do we account for that in the modeling paradigm?

In a latent-factor model obtained via MF, we have the following:

$$\mathbf{u}_i \mathbf{v}_x$$

Here, $\mathbf{u}_i$ has a Gaussian prior with zero mean; this is why new users won't yield useful ratings before they have interaction data. We thus say that the *user-matrix* has *zero-concentrated priors*. Our first strategy to including features in our MF is to simply build a better priors distribution.

More mathematically: we learn a regression model $G(\mathbf{i}) \sim \mathbf{u}_i$ for initialization of our learned factor matrix, and this means we're learning the following:

$$s(i, x) \sim \mathbf{w}_{ix}\gamma + \alpha_i + \beta_x + \mathbf{u}_i \mathbf{v}_x$$

Here, our $\mathbf{w}_{ix}\gamma$ is now a standard bilinear feature regression from user and item features, the bias terms are learned to estimate popularity or *rank inflation*, and our familiar MF terms are $\mathbf{u}_i \mathbf{v}_x$.

Note that this approach provides a general strategy for including features into an MF model. How we fit the factors-features model is totally up to us, as are the optimization methods we wish to employ.

Also note that instead of regression-based approaches, priors can be established via *k*-nearest neighbors in a purely feature-based embedding space. This modeling strategy is explored in great detail in "Eliciting Auxiliary Information for Cold Start User Recommendation: A Survey" (*https://oreil.ly/N4Ast*) by Nor Aniza Abdullah et al. Compare this with the item-item content-based recommender from Chapter 5, where the query is an item and similarity in item space is the link between the last item and the next.

We have established a strategy and a collection of approaches to building our models via features. We've even seen how our MF will fall over for new users, only to be saved by a feature-based model. So why not stick to features? Why introduce factors at all?

Segmentation Models and Hybrids

Similar to our preceding discussion of warm-starting via features is the closely related concept of *demographic-based systems*. Note that *demographic* in this context need not refer explicitly to personally identifiable information and can refer to the user data collected during the sign-up process. Simple examples from book recommendations might include a user's favorite genres, self-identified price preference, book-length preferences, and favorite author. Standard methods of clustering-based regression can be helpful in converting a small set of user features into recommendations for new users. For these coarse user features, building simple feature-based models like naive Bayes, can be especially effective.

More generally, given user feature vectors, we can formulate a similarity measure and then user segments to make new-user recommendations. This should feel similar to feature-based recommenders, but instead of requiring usage of user features, we model the user's containment in a segment and then build our factor model from the segment to different items.

One way to imagine this approach is to consider the modeling problem as estimating the following for C, a user cluster:

$$r_{C,x} := \mathrm{Avg}\big(r_{\mathbf{i},x} \mid \mathbf{i} \in C\big)$$

Then we estimate $P(\mathbf{j} \in C)$, the probability a user $\mathbf{j}$ is a member of C. We can easily imagine that we instead wish to use the probability associated with each cluster to build a bagging model, and have each cluster contributed to a weighted average rating.

While these ideas may not seem like interesting extensions to what we've built previously, in practice they can be enormously useful for fast, explainable recommendations for new users.

Also note that nothing in this construction is particular to the users; we can consider the *dual model* that takes the clustering to be at the level of the items and performs a similar process. Combining these models can provide the coarsest model of simply user segments to item groups, and utilizing several of these modeling approaches simultaneously can provide important and flexible models.

Tag-Based Recommenders

One special case of the segmentation model for item-based recommenders is a *tag-based recommender*. This is a quite common first recommender to try when you have some human labels and need to quickly turn it into a working recommender.

Let's talk through a toy example: you have a personal digital wardrobe, where you've logged many features about each article of clothing in your personal closet. You want your fashion recommender to give you suggestions for what else to wear, given that you've selected one piece for the day. You wake up and see that it's rainy outside, so you start by choosing a cozy cardigan. The model you've trained has found that cardigan has tags *outerwear* and *cozy*, which it knows correlate well with *bottoms* and *warm*—so it's likely to recommend heavier jeans today.

The upside of a tag recommender is how explainable and understandable the recommendations are. The downside is that performance is directly tied to the amount of effort that's put into tagging items.

Let's discuss a slightly more involved example of a tag-based recommender that one of the authors built in collaboration with Ashraf Shaik and Eric Bunch for recommending blog posts.

The goal was to warm-start the blog-post recommender by utilizing high-quality tags that classified the blogs into themes. One special aspect of this system was its rich hierarchical tagging maintained by the marketing team. In particular, each *tag type* had several values, and there were 11 tag types with up to 10 values each. Blogs had values for each tag type and sometimes had multiple tags in a single tag type for the blog. This may sound a bit complicated, but suffice it to say that each blog post could have some of the 47 tags, and the tags were further grouped into types.

One of the first potential tasks is to use those tags to build a simple recommender, and we did, but doing so would mean missing a significant additional opportunity when afforded such high-quality tag data: evaluating our embeddings.

First, we needed to understand how we could build user embeddings. Our plan was to average the blog embeddings a user had seen, a simple CF approach when you have a clear item embedding. Thus we wanted to train the best embedding model possible for these blogs. We started by considering models like BERT but were unsure whether the highly technical content would be meaningfully captured by our embedding model. This led us to realize that we could use the tags as a classifier dataset for our embedding. If we could test several embedding models by training a simple multilayer perceptron (MLP) to perform multilabel multiclassification for each tag type, where the input features were the embedding dimensions, then our embedding space would capture the content well.

Some of the embedding models were of varying dimensions, and some were quite large, so we also first used a dimension reduction (UMAP) to a standard size before we trained the MLP. We used F1 scores (*https://oreil.ly/rYGsU*) to determine which of the embedding models led to the best classification model for tags, and we used visual inspection to ensure the groups were as we'd hoped. This worked quite well and showed that some embeddings were much better than others.

Hybridization

You saw in the previous section how to blend our MF with simpler models by taking priors from the simpler models and learning how to transition away. Coarser approaches to this process of *hybridization* exist:

Weighted combinations of models
> This approach is incredibly powerful, and the weights can be learned in a standard Bayesian framework.

Multilevel modeling
> This approach can include learning a model to select which recommendation model should be used, and then learning models in each regime. For example, we could use a tree-based model on user features when the user has fewer than 10 historical ratings and then use MF after that. A variety of multilevel approaches exist, including *switching* and *cascading*, which correspond roughly to voting and boosting, respectively.

Feature augmentation
> This allows multiple vectors of features to be concatenated and a larger model to be learned. By definition, if we wish to combine feature vectors with factor vectors, like those coming from a CF, we will expect substantial nullity. Learning despite that nullity allows a somewhat naive combination of the different kinds of features to be fed into the model and operated on in all regimes of user activity.

We can combine these models in a variety of useful ways. However, we take the position that instead of more complicated combinations of several models that work well in different paradigms, we will attempt to stick to a relatively straightforward model-service architecture by doing the following:

- Training the best model we can by using MF-based CF
- Using user and item feature-based models for cold start

Let's see why we think feature-based modeling might not be the best strategy, even if we do it via neural networks and latent factor models.

Limitations of Bilinear Models

We started this chapter by describing *bilinear modeling* approaches, and immediately you should take warning—they're linear relationships. You can immediately wonder, "Are there really linear relationships between the features of my users and items and the pairwise affinity?"

The answer to this question might depend on the number of features, or it might not. Either way, skepticism is appropriate, and in practice the answer is overwhelmingly *no*. You might think, "Well then, as it is a linear approximation, MF also cannot succeed," but that's not so clear-cut. In fact, MF suggests that the linear relationship is *between the latent factors*, not the actual features. This subtle difference makes a world of difference.

One important callout before we move on to simpler ideas is that neural networks with nonlinear activation functions can be used to build feature-based methods. This domain has had some successes, but ultimately a surprising and important result is that neural CF does not outperform matrix factorization (*https://oreil.ly/rFWaS*). This doesn't suggest that there are no useful approaches for feature-based models utilizing MLPs, but it **does defray some of our worries** about MF being *too linear*. So why not use more feature-based approaches?

The first most obvious challenge for content-based, demographic-based, and any other feature-based method is *getting the features*. Let's consider the dual problems:

Features for users
> If we want to collect features for users, we need to either ask them a series of queries or infer those features implicitly. Inferring these via exogenous signals is noisy and limited, but each query that we ask the user increases the likelihood of onboarding drop-off. When we think of user-onboarding funnels, we know that each additional prompt or question incurs another chance that the user will not complete the onboarding. This effect accumulates quickly, and without users making it through the funnel, the recommendation system won't be very useful.

Features for items
> On the flip side, creating features for items is a heavily manual task. While many businesses need to do this task to serve other purposes as well, it still incurs a significant cost in many cases. If the features are to be useful, they need to be of high quality, which incurs more debt. But most importantly, if the number of items is extremely large, the cost may quickly get out of reach. For large-scale recommendation problems, manually adding features is simply infeasible. This is where automatic feature-engineering models can help.

Another significant issue in these feature-based models is *separability* or *distinguishability*. These models are not useful if the features cannot separate the items or users well. This leads to compounding problems as the cardinality increases.

Finally, in many recommendation problems, we start with the assumption that taste or preference is extremely personal. We fundamentally believe that our interest in a book will have less to do with the number of pages and publication date than how it connects with us and our personal experience (*our deepest apologies to anyone who bought this book based on page number and publication date*). CF—while simple in concept—speaks better to these connections via a *shared experience network*.

Counting Recommenders

Here we will use the simplest feature type, simple counting. Counting the frequency and pairwise frequencies will provide a simple but useful set of initial models.

Return to the Most-Popular-Item Recommender

Our super simple scheme from before, implementing the MPIR, provided us with a convenient toy model, but what are the practical considerations of deploying an MPIR? It turns out that the MPIR provides an excellent framework for getting started on a Bayesian approximation approach to recommendations. Note that in this section, we're not even considering a personalized recommender; everything here is reward maximization across the entire user population. We follow the treatment in *Statistical Methods for Recommender Systems* by Deepak K. Agarwal and Bee-Chung Chen (Cambridge University Press).

For the sake of simplicity, let's consider *click-through rate (CTR)* as our simple metric to optimize. Our formulation is as follows: we have $\mathscr{I} = \{i\}$ items available to recommend and initially *only one time period* in which to do it, and we're interested in an *allocation plan*, or a set of proportions x_i, $\Sigma_{i \in \mathscr{I}} x_i = 1$, for how to recommend items. This can be seen as a very simple multiarmed bandit problem with the reward given by the following:

$$R(\mathbf{x}, \mathbf{c}) = \sum_{i \in \mathscr{I}} c_i * (N * x_i)$$

Here, c_i represents prior distributions of CTR for each item. It's plain to see that maximizing this reward is achieved by allocating all recommendations to the item with greatest p_i, i.e., picking the most popular item in terms of CTR.

This setup makes it obvious that if we have strong confidence in our priors, this problem seems trivial. So let's move to a case where we have a mismatch in confidence.

Let's consider *two time periods*, N_0 and N_1, as indicating the number of user visits. Note that we think of 0 as the past and 1 as the future in this model. Let's assume that we offer *only two items* and that, somewhat mysteriously, for one item we have 100% confidence in its CTR in each time period: q_0 and q_1 will denote these rates, respectively. In contrast, we have only priors for our second item: $p_0 \sim \mathscr{P}(\theta_0)$ and $p_1 \sim \mathscr{P}(\theta_1)$ will denote these rates, respectively, and we regard θ_i as a state vector. We again notate the allocations with $x_{i,t}$, where now the second index refers to time period. Then we can simply compute the expected number of clicks as follows:

$$\mathbb{E}[N_0 * x_0(p_0 - q_0) + N_1 * x_1(p_1 - q_1)] + q_0 N_0 + q_1 N_1$$

This is maximized by assuming a distribution for p_1 as a function of x_0 and p_0. With distributional assumptions that p_0 is gamma distributed and p_1 is normally distributed, we can treat this as a convex optimization problem to maximize the clicks. See *Statistical Methods for Recommender Systems* for a full treatment of the statistics.

This toy example extends in both dimensions to model larger item sets and more time windows and provides us with relatively straightforward intuition about the relationship between our priors for each item and time step during this step-forward optimization.

Let's put this recommender in context: we've started with item popularity and generalized to a Bayesian recommender that learns with respect to user feedback. You might consider a recommender like this for a very trend-based recommendations context like news; popular stories are often important, but that can change rapidly, and we want to be learning from user behavior.

Correlation Mining

We've seen ways to use correlations between features of items and recommendations, but we should not forget to use correlations between items themselves. Think back to our early discussions of cheese in Chapter 2 (Figure 2-1); we said that our CF gave us a way to find mutual cheese tastes to recommend new cheeses. This was built on the notion of ratings, but we can abstract away from the ratings and simply look at the correlations of items a user chooses. You can imagine for an ecommerce bookseller that a user's choice of one book to read may be useful in recommending others— even if that user chooses not to rate the first book. We also saw this phenomena in Chapter 8 as we used the co-occurrence of tokens in Wikipedia entries.

We introduced the co-occurrence matrix as the multidimensional array of counts where two items, i and j, co-occur. Let's take a moment to discuss co-occurrence a bit more deeply.

Co-occurrence is context dependent; for our Wikipedia articles, we considered co-occurrence of tokens in an article. In the case of ecommerce, co-occurrence can be two items purchased by the same user. For ads, co-occurrence can be two things that the user clicked, and so on. Mathematically, given users and items, we construct an *incidence vector* for each user, the binary vector of one-hot encoded features for each item that they interacted with. Those vectors are stacked into a vector to yield a # $(users) \times$ # $(items)$ matrix in which each row is a user, each column is an item, and the elements equal 1 when a user-item pair has interacted.

To be mathematically precise, a *user-item incidence structure* is a collection of sets of user interactions, $\{y_u\}_{u \in U}$, with items $\{x_i\}_{i \in I}$, where U indexes users and I indexes items.

The associated *user-item incidence matrix*, $\mathcal{U}$, is the binary matrix with rows indexed by sets, and columns indexed by nodes, such that elements are as follows:

$$e_{y_u, x_i} = \begin{cases} 1 & x_i \in y_u \\ 0 & \text{otherwise} \end{cases}$$

The *co-occurrence of x_a and x_b* is the order of the set $\{y_u \mid x_a \in y_u \text{ and } x_b \in y_u\}$. We can also write that as a matrix that can be computed via a simple formula; let $C_{\mathcal{G}}$ be the co-occurrences matrix—i.e., the matrix with rows and columns indexed by $\{x_i\}_{i \in I}$ and with elements that are the co-occurrences of the indices. Then we use the following:

$$C_{\mathcal{G}} = \mathcal{I}^T \star \mathcal{I}$$

Higher-Order Co-occurrences

You could imagine further generalizing this recommender to aggregate across several items the user has seen. In practice, you could consider the last five items the user has interacted with and then compute the conditional-MPIR recommendations for each and union them together.

Alternatively, you could generalize to *higher-order* co-occurrences. In other words, instead of pairs of items that co-occur, look at triples, quadruples, or more. To read one approach to this generalization, check out "Higher Order Co-occurrence Tensors for Hypergraphs via Face-Splitting" (*https://oreil.ly/ta8HU*) by one of the authors.

As mentioned in "Customers Also Bought" on page 141, we can build a new variant of our MPIR by considering the rows or columns of the co-occurence matrix. The *conditional MPIR* is the recommender that returns the max of the elements in the row corresponding to x_i, given the user's last interaction was the item x_i.

In practice, we often think of the row corresponding to x_i as a *basis vector*, i.e., a vector q_{x_i} with one nonzero element in the x_ith position:

$$q_{x_i, j} = \begin{cases} 1 & j = x_i \\ 0 & \text{otherwise} \end{cases} = \begin{bmatrix} 0 \\ \vdots \\ 1 \\ \vdots \\ 0 \end{bmatrix}$$

Then we can consider max—or even softmax—of the preceding dot products:

$$C_{\mathscr{I}} = \mathscr{I}^T \cdot \mathscr{I} * q_{x_i}$$

This yields the vector of co-occurrence counts between x_i and each other item. Here we frequently will call q_{x_i} a *query* to indicate that it's the input to our co-occurrence recommendation model.

How Do You Store This Data?

We can think about co-occurrence data in a *lot* of ways. The main reason is because we expect that co-occurrences for recommendation systems are incredibly sparse. This means that the preceding method of matrix multiplication—which is approximately $O(n^3)$—is going to be relatively slow to compute fewer nonzero entries. Because of this and concerns about storing huge matrices full of zeros, computer scientists have taken seriously the problem of representing sparse matrices.

Max Grossman (*https://oreil.ly/c3Gif*) claims there are 101 ways, but in practice there are only a few. JAX supports BCOO (*https://oreil.ly/AB5vk*), or *batched coordinate format*, which is essentially a list of coordinates for nonzero elements, and then what those elements are.

In our binary case of interactions, those are 1s, and for the co-occurrence matrix, those are the counts. The structure of these matrices can be written as follows:

```
{
  'indices': indices,
  'values': values,
  'shape': [user_dim, items_dim]
}
```

Pointwise Mutual Information via Co-occurrences

An early recommendation system for articles used *pointwise mutual information*, or PMI, which is closely related to co-occurrences. In the context of NLP, PMI attempts to express how much more frequent co-occurrence is than random chance. Given what we've seen before, you can think of this as a normalized co-occurrences model. Computational linguists frequently use PMI as an estimator for word similarity or word meaning following from the distributional hypothesis:

> You shall know a word by the company it keeps.
>
> —John R. Firth, British linguist

In the context of recommendation ranking, items with very high PMI are said to have a highly meaningful co-occurrence. This can thus be used as an estimator for *complementary* items: given you've interacted with one of them, you should interact with the other.

PMI is computed for two items, x_i, x_j, via the following:

$$\frac{p(x_i, x_j)}{p(x_i) * p(x_j)} = \frac{(C_{\mathscr{I}})_{x_i, x_j} * \text{\# (total interactions)}}{\text{\# } (x_i) * \text{\# } (x_j)}$$

The PMI calculation allows us to modify all our work on co-occurrence to a more normalized computation, and thus is a bit more meaningful. This process is related to the GloVE model we learned in "GloVE Model Definition" on page 142. The negative PMI values allow us to understand when two things are not often witnessed together.

These PMI calculations can be used to recommend *another item in a cart* when an item has been added and you find those with very high PMI. It can be used as a retrieval method by looking at the set of items a user has already interacted with and finding items that have high PMI with several of them.

Let's look at how to turn co-occurrences into other similarity measures.

Is PMI a Distance Measurement?

A good question to consider at this point is "Is PMI between two objects a measurement of distance? Can I define similarity directly as the PMI between two items, and thus yield a convenient geometry in which to consider distances?" The answer is no. Recall that one of the axioms of a distance function is the triangle inequality; a useful exercise is to consider why the triangle inequality would not be true for PMI.

But all is not lost. In the next section, we'll show you how to formulate some important similarity measurements from co-occurrence structures. Further, in the next chapter, we'll discuss Wasserstein distance, which allows you to turn the co-occurrence counts into a distance metric directly. The key difference will be considering the co-occurrence counts of all other items simultaneously as a distribution.

Similarity from Co-occurrence

Earlier, we discussed similarity measures and how they come from the Pearson correlation. The Pearson correlation is a special case of similarity when we have explicit ratings, so let's instead look at when we don't.

Consider incidence sets associated to users, $\{y_u\}_{u \in U}$, as we define three distance metrics:

Jaccard similarity, $Jac(\, - \,)$

The ratio of shared items by two users to the total items those users have interacted with

Sørensen-Dice similarity, $DSC(\, - \,)$

Twice the ratio of shared items by two users to the sum of total items each user has interacted with

Cosine similarity, $Cosim(\, - \,)$

The ratio of shared items by two users to the product of total items each user has interacted with

These are all very related metrics with slightly different strengths. Here are some points to consider:

- Jaccard similarity is a real distance metric that has some nice properties for geometry; neither of the other two is.
- All three are on the interval $(0, 1)$, but you'll often see cosine extended to $(\, - \, 1, 1)$ by including negative ratings.
- Cosine can accommodate "thumbs-up/thumbs-down" by merely extending all interactions to have a polarity of ± 1.
- Cosine can accommodate "multiple interactions" if you allow the vectors to be nonbinary and count the number of times a user interacts with an item.
- Jaccard and Dice are related by the simple equation $S = 2J/(1 + J)$, and you can easily compute one from the other.

Notice that we've defined all these similarity measures between users. We'll show in the next section how to extend these definitions to items and how to turn these into recommendations.

Similarity-Based Recommendations

In each of the preceding distance metrics, we've defined a similarity measure, but we haven't yet discussed how similarity measures turn into recommendations. As we discussed in "Nearest Neighbors" on page 35, we utilize similarity measures in our retrieval step; we wish to find a space in that items that are *close* to one another are good recommendations. In the context of ranking, our similarity measure can be used directly to order the recommendations in terms of how likely the recommendation is relevant. In the next chapter, we'll talk more about metrics of relevance.

In the preceding section, we looked at three similarity scores, but we need to expand our notion of the relevant sets for these measures. Let's consider Jaccard similarity as a prototype.

Given a user y_u and an unseen item x_i, let's ask, "What is the Jaccard similarity between this user and item?" Let's remember that Jaccard similarity is the similarity between two sets, and in the definition those sets were both *incidence sets of users' interactions*. Here are three ways to use this approach for recommendations:

User-user

Using our preceding definition, find the k users with maximum Jaccard similarity. Compute the percentage of these users who have interacted with x_i. You may also wish to normalize this by popularity of the item x_i.

Item-item

Compute the set of users that each item has interacted with, and compute the k items most similar to x_i with respect to Jaccard similarity of these item-user incidence sets. Compute the percentage of these items that are in y_u's set of interactions. You may also wish to normalize this by total interactions of y_u or the popularity of the similar items.

User-item

Compute the user y_u's set of items they've interacted with, and the set of items co-occurring with x_i in any user's incidence set of interaction. Compute the Jaccard similarity between these two sets.

Frequently in designing ranking systems, we specify the *query*, which refers to which nearest neighbors you're looking for. We then specify how you use those neighbors to yield a recommendation. The items that may become the recommendation are the candidates, but as you saw in the preceding example, the neighbors may not be the candidates themselves. An additional complication is that you usually need to compute many candidate scores simultaneously, which requires optimized computations that we'll see in Chapter 16.

Summary

In this chapter, we've begun to dig deeper into notions of similarity—building on our intuition from retrieval that users' preferences might be captured by the interactions they've already demonstrated.

We started out with simple models based on features about users and built linear models relating them to our target outcomes. We then combined those simple models with other aspects of feature modeling and hybrid systems.

Next, we moved into discussing counting—in particular, counting the co-occurrence of items, users, or baskets. By looking at frequent co-occurrence, we can build models that capture "If you liked *a*, you may like *b*." These models are simple to understand, but we can use these basic correlation structures to build similarity measures, and thus latent spaces where ANN-based retrieval can yield good candidates for recommendations.

One point that you may have noticed about the featurization of all the items and the building of our co-occurrence matrices is that the number of features is astronomically large—one dimension for each item! This is the area of investigation we'll tackle in the next chapter: how to reduce the dimensionality of your *latent space*.

## CHAPTER 10

Low-Rank Methods

In the preceding chapter, we lamented at the challenge of working with so many features. By letting each item be its own feature, we were able to express a lot of information about user preference and item-affinity correlations, but we were in big trouble in terms of the curse of dimensionality. Combine this with the reality of very sparse features, and you're in danger. In this chapter, we'll turn to smaller feature spaces. By representing users and items as low-dimensional vectors, we can capture the complex relationships between them in a more efficient and effective way. This allows us to generate more personalized and relevant recommendations for users while also reducing the computational complexity of the recommendation process.

We will explore the use of low-dimensional embeddings and discuss the benefits and some of the implementation details of this approach. We will also look at code in JAX that uses modern gradient-based optimization to reduce the dimension of your item or user representations.

Latent Spaces

You are already familiar with feature spaces, which are usually categorical or vector-valued direct representations of the data. This can be the raw red, green, and blue values of an image, counts of items in a histogram, or attributes of an object like length, width, and height. Latent features, on the other hand, do not represent any specific real value feature of the items but are initialized randomly and then learned to suit a task. The GloVe embeddings we discussed in Chapter 8 are one such example of a latent vector that was learned to represent the log count of words. Here we will cover more ways to generate these latent features or embeddings.

Focus on Your "Strangths"

This chapter relies heavily on linear algebra, so it's good to read up on vectors, dot products, and norms of vectors before proceeding. Having an understanding of matrices and the rank of matrices will also be useful. Consider *Linear Algebra and Its Applications* (*https://oreil.ly/8MBN8*) by Gilbert Strang.

One of the reasons latent spaces are so popular is that they are usually lower in dimension than the features they represent. For example, if the user-item rating matrix or interaction matrix (where the matrix entries are 1 if a user has interacted with an item) is $N \times M$ dimensional, then factorizing the matrix into latent factors of $N \times K$ and $K \times M$, where K is much smaller than N or M is an approximation of the missing entries because we're relaxing the factorization. K being smaller than N or M is usually called an *information bottleneck*—that is, we are forcing the matrix to be made up of a much smaller matrix. This means the ML model has to make up missing entries, which might be good for recommender systems. As long as users have interacted with enough similar items, by forcing the system to have a lot less capacity in terms of degrees of freedom, then factorization can completely reconstruct the matrix, and the missing entries tend to get filled by similar items.

Let's see what happens, for example, when we factor a user-item matrix of 4×4 into a 4×2 and a 2×4 vector using SVD.

We are supplying a matrix whose rows are users and whose columns are items. For example, row 0 is [1, 0, 0, 1], which means user 0 has selected item 0 and item 3. These can be ratings or purchases. Now let's look at some code:

```
import numpy as np

a = np.array([
    [1, 0, 0 ,1],
    [1, 0, 0 ,0],
    [0, 1, 1, 0],
    [0, 1, 0, 0]]
)

u, s, v = np.linalg.svd(a, full_matrices=False)

# Set the last two eigenvalues to 0.
s[2:4] = 0
print(s)
b = np.dot(u * s, v)
print(b)

# These are the eigenvalues with the smallest two set to 0.
s = [1.61803399 1.61803399 0.         0.        ]

# This is the newly reconstructed matrix.
```

```
b = [[1.17082039 0.         0.         0.7236068 ]
     [0.7236068  0.         0.         0.4472136 ]
     [0.         1.17082039 0.7236068  0.        ]
     [0.         0.7236068  0.4472136  0.        ]]
```

Notice that the user in row 1 now has a score for an item in column 3, and the user in row 3 now has a positive score for the item in column 2. This phenomenon is generally known as *matrix completion* and is a good property for recommender systems to have because now we get to recommend new items to users. The general method of forcing the ML to go through a bottleneck that is smaller than the size of the matrix that it is trying to reconstruct is known as a *low-rank approximation* because the rank of the approximation is 2 but the rank of the original user-item matrix is 4.

What Is the Rank of a Matrix?

An $N \times M$ matrix may be considered as N row vectors (corresponding to users) and M column vectors (corresponding to items). When you consider the N vectors of dimension M, the *rank of the matrix* is the volume of the polyhedron defined by the N vectors in M dimensions. This is often different from the way we talk about the rank of matrices, however. While it's the most natural and precise definition, we instead say it's the "minimum number of dimensions necessary to represent the vectors of the matrix."

We will cover SVD in more detail later in the chapter. This was just to whet your appetite to understand how latent spaces are related to recommender systems.

Dot Product Similarity

In Chapter 3 we introduced similarity measures, but now we return to the dot product in the context of similarity because of their increased importance in latent spaces. After all, latent spaces are built on the assumption that distance is similarity.

The dot-product similarity is meaningful in recommendation systems because it provides a geometric interpretation of the relationship between users and items in the latent space (or potentially items and items, users and users, etc.). In the context of recommendation systems, the dot product can be seen as a projection of one vector onto another, indicating the degree of similarity or alignment between the user's preferences and the item's characteristics.

To understand the geometric significance of the dot product, consider two vectors, u and p, representing the user and the product in the latent space, respectively. The dot product of these two vectors can be defined as follows:

$$u \times p = ||u|| \, ||p|| \, cos(\theta)$$

Here, $||u||$ and $||p||$ represent the magnitudes of the user and product vectors, and θ is the angle between them. The dot product is thus a measure of the projection of one vector onto another, which is scaled by the magnitudes of both vectors.

The cosine similarity, which is another popular similarity measure in recommendation systems, is derived directly from the dot product:

$$cosine\ similarity(u, p) = \frac{(u \times p)}{(||u|| \, ||p||)}$$

The cosine similarity ranges from -1 to 1, where -1 indicates completely dissimilar preferences and characteristics. A 0 indicates no similarity, and 1 indicates perfect alignment between the user's preferences and the product's characteristics. In the context of recommendation systems, cosine similarity provides a normalized measure of similarity that is invariant to the magnitudes of the user and product vectors. Note that the choice of using cosine similarity versus L2 distance depends on the type of embeddings you're using and the way you optimize the computations. In practice, the only important feature is often the relative values.

The geometric interpretation of the dot product (and cosine similarity) in recommendation systems is that it captures the alignment between user preferences and product characteristics. If the angle between the user and product vectors is small, the user's preferences align well with the product's characteristics, leading to a higher similarity score. Conversely, if the angle is large, the user's preferences and product's characteristics are dissimilar, resulting in a lower similarity score. By projecting user and item vectors onto each other, the dot-product similarity can capture the degree of alignment between user preferences and item characteristics, allowing the recommendation system to identify items that are most likely to be relevant and appealing to the user.

Anecdotally, the dot product seems to capture popularity, as very long vectors tend to be easy to project on anything that isn't completely perpendicular or pointing away from them. As a result, a trade-off exists between frequently recommending popular items with a large vector length and longer-tail items that have smaller angular difference with cosine distance.

Figure 10-1 considers two vectors, a and b. With cosine similarity, the vectors are unit length, so the angle is just the measure of similarity. However, with dot product, a very long vector like c might be considered more similar to a than b even though the angle between a and b is smaller because of the longer length of c. These long vectors tend to be very popular items that co-occur with many other items.

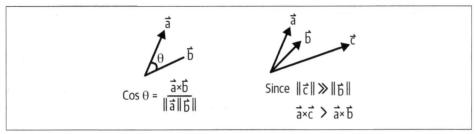

$$\text{Cos } \theta = \frac{\vec{a} \times \vec{b}}{\|\vec{a}\| \|\vec{b}\|}$$

Since $\|\vec{c}\| \gg \|\vec{b}\|$

$$\vec{a} \times \vec{c} > \vec{a} \times \vec{b}$$

Figure 10-1. Cosine versus dot-product similarity

Co-occurrence Models

In our Wikipedia co-occurrences examples, we determined that the co-occurrence structure between two items could be used to generate measures of similarity. We covered how PMI can take the counts of co-occurrence and make recommendations based on very high mutual information between an item in the cart and others.

As we've discussed, PMI is not a distance metric but still has important similarity measures based on co-occurrence. Let's return to this topic.

Recall from earlier that PMI is defined as follows:

$$\frac{p(x_i, x_j)}{p(x_i) * p(x_j)} = \frac{(C_g)_{x_i, x_j} * \text{# (total interactions)}}{\text{# } (x_i) * \text{# } (x_j)}$$

Now let's consider the *discrete co-occurrence distribution*, CD_{x_i}, defined as the collection of co-occurrences over all other x_j:

$$CD_{x_i} = (C_g)_{x_i, x_1}, \dots, (C_g)_{x_i, x_j}, \dots, (C_g)_{x_i, x_N}$$

Here, $j \in 1\dots N$, and N is the total number of items. This represents the co-occurrence histogram between x_i and all other items. By introducing this discrete distribution, we can utilize another tool: the Hellinger distance.

We can measure distributional distance in a few ways, each with different advantages. For our discussion, we will not go deeply into the differences and will stick to the simplest but most appropriate. Hellinger distance is defined as follows:

$$H(P, Q) = \sqrt{1 - \sum_i^n \sqrt{p_i q_i}} = \frac{1}{\sqrt{2}} \| \sqrt{P} - \sqrt{Q} \|_2$$

$P = \langle p_i \rangle$ and $Q = \langle q_i \rangle$ are two probability density vectors. In our setting, P and Q can be CD_{x_i} and CD_{x_j}.

The motivation behind this process is that we now have a proper distance between items purely based on co-occurrences. We can use any dimension transformation or reduction on this geometry. Later we will show dimension-reduction techniques that can use an arbitrary distance matrix and reduce the space to a lower-dimensional embedding that approximates it.

What About Measure Spaces and Information Theory?

While we're discussing distributions, you may find yourself wondering, "Is there a distance between distributions such that distributions are points in a latent space?" Oh, you weren't wondering that? Well, OK. We'll address it anyway.

The short answer is that we can measure the differences between distributions. The most popular is Kullback–Leibler (KL) divergence, which is usually described in a Bayesian sense as the amount of surprise in seeing the distribution P, when expecting the distribution Q. However, KL is not a proper distance metric because it is asymmetric.

Another symmetric distance metric that has some nice properties is the Hellinger distance. Hellinger distance is effectively the 2-norm measure theoretic distance. Additionally, Hellinger distance naturally generalizes to discrete distributions.

If this still hasn't scratched your itch for abstraction, we can also consider the total variation distance, which is the limit in the space of Fisher's exact distance measures, which really means that it has all the nice properties of a distance of two distributions and no measure would ever consider them more dissimilar. Well, all the nice properties except for one: it's not smooth. If you also want smoothness for differentiability, you'll need to approximate it via an offset.

If you ever need a distance between distributions, just use Hellinger.

Reducing the Rank of a Recommender Problem

We've shown that as the number of items and users grows, we rapidly increase the dimensionality of our recommender problem. Because we're representing each item and user as a column or vector, this scales like n^2. One way to push back against this difficulty is by rank reduction; recall our previous discussions about rank reduction via factorization.

Like many integers, many matrices can be *factored* into smaller matrices; for integers, *smaller* means of smaller value, and for matrices, *smaller* means of smaller dimensions. When we factor an $N \times M$ matrix, we will be looking for two matrices $U_{N \times d}$ and $V_{d \times M}$; note that when you multiply matrices together, they must share a dimension, and that dimension is eliminated, leaving the other two. Here, we'll consider MFs when $d \leq N$ and $d \leq M$. By factorizing a matrix, we ask for two matrices that together equal, or approximate, the original matrix:

$$A_{i,j} \simeq \left\langle U_i, V_j \right\rangle$$

We seek a small value for d to reduce the number of latent dimensions. As you may have already noticed, each of the matrices $U_{N \times d}$ and $V_{d \times M}$ will correspond to rows or columns of the original ratings matrix. However, they're expressed in fewer dimensions. This utilizes the idea of a *low-dimensional latent space*. Intuitively, a latent space seeks to represent the same relationships as the full $N \times M$ dimensional relationships in two sets of relationships: items versus latent features, and users versus latent features.

These methods are also popular in other kinds of ML, but for our case, we'll primarily be looking at factorizing ratings or interaction matrices.

MF via SVD

SVD and MF are closely related, but SVD is an important special case. The key difference is in how the factorization is done and the types of matrices that each can be applied to.

Figure 10-2 shows how SVD works. The eigenvectors $e1$ and $e2$ correspond to the largest two eigenvalues. $e1$ explains more of the data than $e2$ and lies along the direction of the largest spread of points. Eigenvectors are always perpendicular to each other, so their dot product is always 0.

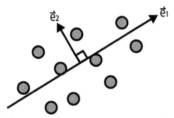

$\vec{e}_1$ explains more of the data than $\vec{e}_2$

$\vec{e}_1$ is perpendicular to $\vec{e}_2$

Figure 10-2. Singular value decomposition

SVD is a specific type of MF that decomposes a matrix into three separate matrices: a left singular matrix, a diagonal matrix, and a right singular matrix. SVD can be applied to any real-valued matrix, but it is particularly well suited to dense matrices with many nonzero entries; additionally, SVD matrices have properties useful for extracting particular kinds of relationships between latent features. The columns and rows of the singular matrices are the eigenvectors, and the values in the diagonal matrix are the eigenvalues. This decomposition is handy in seeing how much information in the original space is explained by the eigenvectors and corresponds to the magnitude of the eigenvalue, so an eigenvector with a larger eigenvalue explains more of the original data than an eigenvector with a correspondingly smaller eigenvalue.

MF decomposes a user-item matrix into two matrices that represent the preferences of users and the characteristics of items. This allows the recommendation system to generate personalized recommendations by matching the preferences of users with the characteristics of items.

Frequently, you must overcome a few challenges when considering MF:

- The matrix you wish to factor is sparse and often non-negative and/or binary.
- The number of nonzero elements in each item vector can vary wildly, as we saw in the Matthew effect.
- Factorizing matrices is cubic in complexity.
- SVD and other full-rank methods don't work without imputation, which itself is complicated.

We'll address these with some alternative optimization methods.

Optimizing for MF with ALS

The basic optimization we wish to execute is to approximate as follows:

$$A_{i,j} \simeq \langle U_i, V_j \rangle$$

Notably, if you wish to optimize matrix entries directly, you'll need to optimize $d^2 * N * M$ elements simultaneously corresponding to the numbers of parameters in these factorizations. We can easily achieve a significant speedup, however, by alternating between tuning one matrix or the other. This is called *alternating least squares*, commonly *ALS*, and it is a common approach to this problem. Instead of back-propagating updates to all terms in both matrices on each pass, you may update only one of the two matrices, which dramatically reduces the number of computations that need to take place.

ALS seeks to switch back and forth between U and V, evaluating on the same loss function but updating the weights in only one matrix at a time:

$$U \leftarrow U - \eta * U * \nabla U * \mathcal{D}(A, UV)$$
$$V \leftarrow V - \eta * V * \nabla V * \mathcal{D}(A, UV)$$

Here, η is the learning rate and $\mathcal{D}$ is our chosen distance function. We'll present more details of this distance function momentarily. Before we move on, let's consider a few of the intricacies here:

- Each of these update rules requires the gradient with respect to the relevant factor matrix.
- We update an entire factor matrix at a time, but we evaluate loss on the product of the factor matrices versus the original matrix.
- We have a mysterious distance function.
- By the way that we've constructed this optimization, we're implicitly assuming that we'll use this process to converge two well-approximating matrices (we often also impose a limit on the number of iterations).

In JAX, these optimizations will be straightforward to implement, and we'll see how similar the equational forms and the JAX code look.

Distance Between Matrices

We can determine the distance between two matrices in a variety of ways. As we've seen before, different distance measurements for vectors yield different interpretations from the underlying space. We won't have as many complications for these computations, but it's worth a short observation. The most obvious approach is one you've already seen, *observed mean squared error*:

$$\frac{\Sigma_\Omega \left(A_{i,j} - \langle U_i, V_j \rangle \right)^2}{1\Omega|}$$

One useful alternative to the observed mean squared error can be used when you have a single nonzero entry for a user vector (alternatively, a max rating). In that case, you could instead use a cross-entropy loss, which provides a *logistic MF*, and thus a probability estimate. For more details on how to implement this, see the "Matrix Factorization for Recommender Systems" tutorial (*https://oreil.ly/7qWy6*) by Kyle Chung.

In our observed ratings, we expect (and see!) a large number of missing values and some item vectors with an overrepresented number of ratings. This suggests that we should consider nonuniformly weighted matrices. Next we'll discuss how to account for this and other variants with regularization.

Regularization for MF

Weighted alternating least squares (WALS) is similar to ALS but attempts to resolve these two data issues more gracefully. In WALS, the weight assigned to each observed rating is inversely proportional to the number of observed ratings for the user or item. Therefore, observed ratings for users or items with few ratings are given more weight in the optimization process.

We can apply these weights as a regularization parameter in our eventual loss function:

$$\frac{\Sigma_\Omega \left(A_{i,j} - \,<U_i, V_j> \right)^2}{|\Omega|} + \frac{1}{N} \Sigma |U|$$

Other regularization methods are important, and also popular, for MF. We'll discuss these two powerful regularization techniques:

- Weight decay
- Gramian regularization

As is often the case, *weight decay* is our l^2 regularization, which in this case is at the level of the Frobenius norm, i.e., the magnitude of the weight matrix. An elegant way to view this weight decay is that it's minimizing the magnitude of the *singular values*.

Similarly, MF has another regularization technique that looks very standard but is quite different in calculation. This is via the *Gramians*—essentially regularizing the size of the individual matrix entries, but there's an elegant trick for the optimization. In particular, a Gramian of a matrix U is the product $U^T U$. The eagle-eyed among you may recognize this term as the same term we previously used to calculate co-occurrences for binary matrices. The connection is that both are simply trying to find efficient representations of dot products between a matrix's rows and columns.

These regularizations are the Frobenius terms:

$$R(U, V) = \frac{1}{N} \sum_i^N \left| U_i \right|_2^2 + \frac{1}{M} \sum_j^M |V_j|_2^2$$

Or expanded, the equation looks like this:

$$R(U, V) = \frac{1}{N} \sum_{i}^{N} \sum_{k}^{d} U_{i,k}^2 + \frac{1}{M} \sum_{j}^{M} \sum_{l}^{d} V_{j,l}^2$$

And here are the Gramian terms:

$$G(U, V) := \frac{1}{N \cdot M} \sum_{i}^{N} \sum_{j}^{M} \langle U_i, V_j \rangle^2$$

$$= \frac{1}{N \cdot M} * \sum_{k,l}^{d} \left(U^T U * V^T V \right)_{k,l}$$

Finally, we have our loss function:

$$\frac{1}{|\Omega|} \sum_{(i,j) \in \Omega} \left(A_{ij} - \langle U_i, V_j \rangle \right)^2 + \lambda_R \left(\frac{1}{N} \sum_{i}^{N} \sum_{k}^{d} U_{i,k}^2 + \frac{1}{M} \sum_{j}^{M} \sum_{l}^{d} V_{j,l}^2 \right) + \lambda_G \left(\frac{1}{N \cdot M} * \sum_{k,l}^{d} \left(U^T U * V^T V \right)_{k,l} \right)$$

Regularized MF Implementation

So far, we've written a *lot* of math symbols, but all of those symbols have allowed us to arrive at a model that is extremely powerful. *Regularized matrix factorization* is an effective model for medium-sized recommender problems. This model type is still in production for many serious businesses. One classic issue with MF implementations is performance, but because we're working in JAX, which has extremely native GPU support, our implementation can actually be much more compact than what you may find in something like a PyTorch example (*https://oreil.ly/U-K-V*).

Let's work through how this model would look to predict ratings for a user-item matrix via this doubly regularized model with Gramians.

First we'll do the simple setup. This will assume your ratings matrix is already on wandb:

```
import jax
import jax.numpy as jnp
import numpy as np
import pandas as pd
import os, json, wandb, math

from jax import grad, jit
from jax import random
```

```
from jax.experimental import sparse

key = random.PRNGKey(0)

wandb.login()
run = wandb.init(
    # Set entity to specify your username or team name
    entity="wandb-un",
    # Set the project where this run will be logged
    project="jax-mf",
    # associate the runs to the right dataset
    config={
        "dataset": "MF-Dataset",
    }
)

# note that we assume the dataset is a ratings table stored in wandb
artifact = run.use_artifact('stored-dataset:latest')
ratings_artifact = artifact.download()
ratings_artifact_blob = json.load(
    open(
        os.path.join(
            ratings_artifact,
            'ratings.table.json'
        )
    )
)

ratings_artifact_blob.keys()
# ['_type', 'column_types', 'columns', 'data', 'ncols', 'nrows']

ratings = pd.DataFrame( # user_id, item_id, rating, unix_timestamp
    data=ratings_artifact_blob['data'],
    columns=ratings_artifact_blob['columns']
)

def start_pipeline(df):
    return df.copy()

def column_as_type(df, column: str, cast_type):
    df[column] = df[column].astype(cast_type)
    return df

def rename_column_value(df, target_column, prior_val, post_val):
    df[target_column] = df[target_column].replace({prior_val: post_val})
    return df

def split_dataframe(df, holdout_fraction=0.1):
    """Splits a DataFrame into training and test sets.
    Args:
      df: a dataframe.
      holdout_fraction: fraction of dataframe rows to use in the test set.
```

```
        Returns:
          train: dataframe for training
          test: dataframe for testing
        """
        test = df.sample(frac=holdout_fraction, replace=False)
        train = df[~df.index.isin(test.index)]
        return train, test

all_rat = (ratings
    .pipe(start_pipeline)
    .pipe(column_as_type, column='user_id', cast_type=int)
    .pipe(column_as_type, column='item_id', cast_type=int)
)

def ratings_to_sparse_array(ratings_df, user_dim, item_dim):
    indices = (np.array(ratings_df['user_id']), np.array(ratings_df['item_id']))
    values = jnp.array(ratings_df['rating'])

    return {
        'indices': indices,
        'values': values,
        'shape': [user_dim, item_dim]
    }

def random_normal(pr_key, shape, mu=0, sigma=1, ):
    return (mu + sigma * random.normal(pr_key, shape=shape))

x = random_normal(
    pr_key = random.PRNGKey(1701),
    shape=(10000,),
    mu = 1.0,
    sigma = 3.0,
) # these hyperparameters are pretty meaningless

def sp_mse_loss(A, params):
    U, V = params['users'], params['items']
    rows, columns = A['indices']
    estimator = -(U @ V.T)[(rows, columns)]
    square_err = jax.tree_map(
        lambda x: x**2,
        A['values']+estimator
    )
    return jnp.mean(square_err)

omse_loss = jit(sp_mse_loss)
```

Note that we've had to implement our own loss function here. This is a relatively straightforward mean square error (MSE) loss, but it's taking advantage of the sparse nature of our matrix. You may notice in the code that we've converted the matrix to a sparse representation, so it's important that our loss function cannot only take advantage of that representation, but also be written to utilize the JAX device arrays and mapping/jitting.

Is That Loss Function Really Right?

If you're curious about this loss function that appeared like magic, we understand. While writing this book, we were extremely uncertain about what the best implementation of this loss function that leverages JAX would look like. There are actually many reasonable approaches to this kind of optimization. To that end, we wrote a public experiment to benchmark several approaches on Colab (*https://oreil.ly/6zwEX*).

Next, we need to build model objects to handle our MF state as we train. This code, while essentially mostly template code, will set us up well to feed the model into a training loop in a relatively memory-efficient way. This model was trained on 100 million entries for a few thousand epochs on a MacBook Pro in less than a day:

```
class CFModel(object):
    """Simple class that represents a collaborative filtering model"""
    def __init__(
        self,
        metrics: dict,
        embeddings: dict,
        ground_truth: dict,
        embeddings_parameters: dict,
        prng_key=None
    ):
        """Initializes a CFModel.
        Args:
        """
        self._metrics = metrics
        self._embeddings = embeddings
        self._ground_truth = ground_truth
        self._embeddings_parameters = embeddings_parameters

        if prng_key is None:
            prng_key = random.PRNGKey(0)
        self._prng_key = prng_key


    @property
    def embeddings(self):
        """The embeddings dictionary."""
        return self._embeddings

    @embeddings.setter
    def embeddings(self, value):
        self._embeddings = value
```

```python
    @property
    def metrics(self):
        """The metrics dictionary."""
        return self._metrics

    @property
    def ground_truth(self):
        """The train/test dictionary."""
        return self._ground_truth

    def reset_embeddings(self):
        """Clear out embeddings state."""

        prng_key1, prng_key2 = random.split(self._prng_key, 2)

        self._embeddings['users'] = random_normal(
            prng_key1,
            [
              self._embeddings_parameters['user_dim'],
              self._embeddings_parameters['embedding_dim']
            ],
            mu=0,
            sigma=self._embeddings_parameters['init_stddev'],
        )
        self._embeddings['items'] = random_normal(
            prng_key2,
            [
              self._embeddings_parameters['item_dim'],
              self._embeddings_parameters['embedding_dim']],
            mu=0,
            sigma=self._embeddings_parameters['init_stddev'],
        )

def model_constructor(
    ratings_df,
    user_dim,
    item_dim,
    embedding_dim=3,
    init_stddev=1.,
    holdout_fraction=0.2,
    prng_key=None,
    train_set=None,
    test_set=None,
):
    if prng_key is None:
      prng_key = random.PRNGKey(0)

    prng_key1, prng_key2 = random.split(prng_key, 2)

    if (train_set is None) and (test_set is None):
        train, test = (ratings_df
            .pipe(start_pipeline)
```

```
                .pipe(split_dataframe, holdout_fraction=holdout_fraction)
        )

        A_train = (train
            .pipe(start_pipeline)
            .pipe(ratings_to_sparse_array, user_dim=user_dim, item_dim=item_dim)
        )
        A_test = (test
            .pipe(start_pipeline)
            .pipe(ratings_to_sparse_array, user_dim=user_dim, item_dim=item_dim)
        )
    elif (train_set is None) ^ (test_set is None):
        raise('Must send train and test if sending one')
    else:
        A_train, A_test = train_set, test_set

    U = random_normal(
        prng_key1,
        [user_dim, embedding_dim],
        mu=0,
        sigma=init_stddev,
    )
    V = random_normal(
        prng_key2,
        [item_dim, embedding_dim],
        mu=0,
        sigma=init_stddev,
    )


    train_loss = omse_loss(A_train, {'users': U, 'items': V})
    test_loss = omse_loss(A_test, {'users': U, 'items': V})

    metrics = {
        'train_error': train_loss,
        'test_error': test_loss
    }
    embeddings = {'users': U, 'items': V}
    ground_truth = {
        "A_train": A_train,
        "A_test": A_test
    }
    return CFModel(
        metrics=metrics,
        embeddings=embeddings,
        ground_truth=ground_truth,
        embeddings_parameters={
            'user_dim': user_dim,
            'item_dim': item_dim,
            'embedding_dim': embedding_dim,
            'init_stddev': init_stddev,
        },
```

```
            prng_key=prng_key,
    )

    mf_model = model_constructor(all_rat, user_count, item_count)
```

We should also set this up to log nicely to wandb so it's easy to understand what is happening during training:

```
def train():
    run_config = { # These will be hyperparameters we will tune via wandb
        'emb_dim': 10, # Latent dimension
        'prior_std': 0.1, # Std dev around 0 for weights initialization
        'alpha': 1.0, # Learning rate
        'steps': 1500, # Number of training steps
    }

    with wandb.init() as run:
        run_config.update(run.config)
        model_object = model_constructor(
            ratings_df=all_rat,
            user_dim=user_count,
            item_dim=item_count,
            embedding_dim=run_config['emb_dim'],
            init_stddev=run_config['prior_std'],
            prng_key=random.PRNGKey(0),
            train_set=mf_model.ground_truth['A_train'],
            test_set=mf_model.ground_truth['A_test']
        )
        model_object.reset_embeddings() # Ensure we are starting from priors
        alpha, steps = run_config['alpha'], run_config['steps']
        print(run_config)
        grad_fn = jax.value_and_grad(omse_loss, 1)
        for i in range(steps):
            # We perform one gradient update
            loss_val, grads = grad_fn(
                model_object.ground_truth['A_train'],
                model_object.embeddings
            )
            model_object.embeddings = jax.tree_multimap(
                lambda p, g: p - alpha * g,
                # Basic update rule; JAX handles broadcasting for us
                model_object.embeddings,
                grads
            )
            if i % 1000 == 0: # Most output in wandb; little bit of logging
                print(f'Loss step {i}: ', loss_val)
                print(f"""Test loss: {
                    omse_loss(
                        model_object.ground_truth['A_train'],
                        model_object.embeddings
                    )}""")

        wandb.log({
```

```
            "Train omse": loss_val,
            "Test omse": omse_loss(
                model_object.ground_truth['A_test'],
                model_object.embeddings
            )
    })
```

Note that this code is using `tree_multimap` to handle broadcasting our update rule, and we're using the jitted loss from before in the `omse_loss` call. Also, we're calling `value_and_grad` so we can log the loss to wandb as we go. This is a common trick you'll see for efficiently doing both without a callback.

You can finish this off and start the training with a sweep:

```
sweep_config = {
    "name" : "mf-test-sweep",
    "method" : "random",
    "parameters" : {
        "steps" : {
            "min": 1000,
            "max": 3000,
        },
        "alpha" :{
            "min": 0.6,
            "max": 1.75
        },
        "emb_dim" :{
            "min": 3,
            "max": 10
        },
        "prior_std" :{
            "min": .5,
            "max": 2.0
        },
    },
    "metric" : {
        'name': 'Test omse',
        'goal': 'minimize'
    }
}

sweep_id = wandb.sweep(sweep_config, project="jax-mf", entity="wandb-un")

wandb.init()
train()

count = 50
wandb.agent(sweep_id, function=train, count=count)
```

In this case, the hyperparameter optimization (HPO) is over our hyperparameters like embedding dimension and the priors (randomized matrices). Up until now, we have trained some MF models on our ratings matrix. Let's now add regularization and cross-validation.

Let's translate the preceding math equations directly into code:

```
def ell_two_regularization_term(params, dimensions):
    U, V = params['users'], params['items']
    N, M = dimensions['users'], dimensions['items']
    user_sq = jnp.multiply(U, U)
    item_sq = jnp.multiply(V, V)
    return (jnp.sum(user_sq)/N + jnp.sum(item_sq)/M)

l2_loss = jit(ell_two_regularization_term)

def gramian_regularization_term(params, dimensions):
    U, V = params['users'], params['items']
    N, M = dimensions['users'], dimensions['items']
    gr_user = U.T @ U
    gr_item = V.T @ V
    gr_square = jnp.multiply(gr_user, gr_item)
    return (jnp.sum(gr_square)/(N*M))

gr_loss = jit(gramian_regularization_term)

def regularized_omse(A, params, dimensions, hyperparams):
    lr, lg = hyperparams['ell_2'], hyperparams['gram']
    losses = {
        'omse': sp_mse_loss(A, params),
        'l2_loss': l2_loss(params, dimensions),
        'gr_loss': gr_loss(params, dimensions),
    }
    losses.update({
        'total_loss': losses['omse'] + lr*losses['l2_loss'] + lg*losses['gr_loss']
    })
    return losses['total_loss'], losses

reg_loss_observed = jit(regularized_omse)
```

We won't dive super deep into learning rate schedulers, but we will do a simple decay:

```
def lr_decay(
    step_num,
    base_learning_rate,
    decay_pct = 0.5,
    period_length = 100.0
):
    return base_learning_rate * math.pow(
        decay_pct,
        math.floor((1+step_num)/period_length)
    )
```

Our updated train function will incorporate our new regularizations—which come with some hyperparameters—and a bit of additional logging setup. This code makes it easy to log our experiment as it trains and configures the hyperparameters to work with regularization:

```
def train_with_reg_loss():
    run_config = { # These will be hyperparameters we will tune via wandb
        'emb_dim': None,
        'prior_std': None,
        'alpha': None, # Learning rate
        'steps': None,
        'ell_2': 1, #l2 regularization penalization weight
        'gram': 1, #gramian regularization penalization weight
        'decay_pct': 0.5,
        'period_length': 100.0
    }

    with wandb.init() as run:
        run_config.update(run.config)
        model_object = model_constructor(
            ratings_df=all_rat,
            user_dim=942,
            item_dim=1681,
            embedding_dim=run_config['emb_dim'],
            init_stddev=run_config['prior_std'],
            prng_key=random.PRNGKey(0),
            train_set=mf_model.ground_truth['A_train'],
            test_set=mf_model.ground_truth['A_test']
        )
        model_object.reset_embeddings() # Ensure we start from priors

        alpha, steps = run_config['alpha'], run_config['steps']
        print(run_config)

        grad_fn = jax.value_and_grad(
            reg_loss_observed,
            1,
            has_aux=True
        ) # Tell JAX to expect an aux dict as output

        for i in range(steps):
            (total_loss_val, loss_dict), grads = grad_fn(
                model_object.ground_truth['A_train'],
                model_object.embeddings,
                dimensions={'users': user_count, 'items': item_count},
                hyperparams={
                    'ell_2': run_config['ell_2'],
                    'gram': run_config['gram']
                } # JAX carries our loss dict along for logging
            )
```

```python
            model_object.embeddings = jax.tree_multimap(
                lambda p, g: p - lr_decay(
                    i,
                    alpha,
                    run_config['decay_pct'],
                    run_config['period_length']
                ) * g, # update with decay
                model_object.embeddings,
                grads
            )
            if i % 1000 == 0:
                print(f'Loss step {i}:')
                print(loss_dict)
                print(f"""Test loss: {
                    omse_loss(model_object.ground_truth['A_test'],
                    model_object.embeddings)}""")

            loss_dict.update( # wandb takes the entire loss dictionary
                {
                    "Test omse": omse_loss(
                        model_object.ground_truth['A_test'],
                        model_object.embeddings
                    ),
                    "learning_rate": lr_decay(i, alpha),
                }
            )
            wandb.log(loss_dict)

sweep_config = {
    "name" : "mf-HPO-with-reg",
    "method" : "random",
    "parameters" : {
      "steps": {
        "value": 2000
      },
      "alpha" :{
        "min": 0.6,
        "max": 2.25
      },
      "emb_dim" :{
        "min": 15,
        "max": 80
      },
      "prior_std" :{
        "min": .5,
        "max": 2.0
      },
      "ell_2" :{
        "min": .05,
        "max": 0.5
      },
      "gram" :{
```

```
            "min": .1,
            "max": .75
        },
        "decay_pct" :{
            "min": .2,
            "max": .8
        },
        "period_length" :{
            "min": 50,
            "max": 500
        }
    },
    "metric" : {
        'name': 'Test omse',
        'goal': 'minimize'
    }
}

sweep_id = wandb.sweep(
    sweep_config,
    project="jax-mf",
    entity="wandb-un"
)

run_config = { # These will be hyperparameters we will tune via wandb
    'emb_dim': 10, # Latent dimension
    'prior_std': 0.1,
    'alpha': 1.0, # Learning rate
    'steps': 1000, # Number of training steps
    'ell_2': 1, #l2 regularization penalization weight
    'gram': 1, #gramian regularization penalization weight
    'decay_pct': 0.5,
    'period_length': 100.0
}

train_with_reg_loss()
```

The last step is to do this in a way that gives us confidence in the models we're seeing. Unfortunately, setting up cross-validation for MF problems can be tricky, so we'll need to make a few modifications to our data structures:

```
def sparse_array_concatenate(sparse_array_iterable):
    return {
        'indices': tuple(
            map(
                jnp.concatenate,
                zip(*(x['indices'] for x in sparse_array_iterable)))
            ),
        'values': jnp.concatenate(
            [x['values'] for x in sparse_array_iterable]
        ),
    }
```

```python
class jax_df_Kfold(object):
    """Simple class that handles Kfold
    splitting of a matrix as a dataframe and stores as sparse jarrays"""
    def __init__(
        self,
        df: pd.DataFrame,
        user_dim: int,
        item_dim: int,
        k: int = 5,
        prng_key=random.PRNGKey(0)
    ):
        self._df = df
        self._num_folds = k
        self._split_idxes = jnp.array_split(
            random.permutation(
                prng_key,
                df.index.to_numpy(),
                axis=0,
                independent=True
            ),
            self._num_folds
        )

        self._fold_arrays = dict()

        for fold_index in range(self._num_folds):
        # let's create sparse jax arrays for each fold piece
            self._fold_arrays[fold_index] = (
                self._df[
                    self._df.index.isin(self._split_idxes[fold_index])
                ].pipe(start_pipeline)
                .pipe(
                    ratings_to_sparse_array,
                    user_dim=user_dim,
                    item_dim=item_dim
                )
            )

    def get_fold(self, fold_index: int):
        assert(self._num_folds > fold_index)
        test = self._fold_arrays[fold_index]
        train = sparse_array_concatenate(
            [v for k,v in self._fold_arrays.items() if k != fold_index]
        )
        return train, test
```

Each hyperparameter setup should yield loss for each fold, so within *wandb.init*, we build a model with each fold:

```python
for j in num_folds:
    train, test = folder.get_fold(j)
    model_object_dict[j] = model_constructor(
```

```
        ratings_df=all_rat,
        user_dim=user_count,
        item_dim=item_count,
        embedding_dim=run_config['emb_dim'],
        init_stddev=run_config['prior_std'],
        prng_key=random.PRNGKey(0),
        train_set=train,
        test_set=test
    )
```

At each step, we'd like to not only compute the gradient for the training and evaluate on the test but also compute gradients for all folds, evaluate on all the tests, and produce the relevant errors:

```
for i in range(steps):
    loss_dict = {"learning_rate": step_decay(i)}
    for j, M in model_object_dict.items():
        (total_loss_val, fold_loss_dict), grads = grad_fn(
            M.ground_truth['A_train'],
            M.embeddings,
            dimensions={'users': 942, 'items': 1681},
            hyperparams={'ell_2': run_config['ell_2'], 'gram': run_config['gram']}
        )

        M.embeddings = jax.tree_multimap(
            lambda p, g: p - step_decay(i) * g,
            M.embeddings,
            grads
        )
```

Logging should be losses per fold, and the aggregate loss should be the target metric. This is because each fold is an independent optimization of the model parameters; however, we wish to see aggregate behavior across the folds:

```
        fold_loss_dict = {f'{k}_fold-{j}': v for k, v in fold_loss_dict.items()}
        fold_loss_dict.update(
            {
                f"Test omse_fold-{j}": omse_loss(
                    M.ground_truth['A_test'],
                    M.embeddings
                ),
            }
        )

        loss_dict.update(fold_loss_dict)

    loss_dict.update({
        "Test omse_mean": jnp.mean(
            [v for k,v in loss_dict.items() if k.startswith('Test omse_fold-')]
        )
    })
    wandb.log(loss_dict)
```

We wrap up into one big training method:

```python
def train_with_reg_loss_CV():
    run_config = { # These will be hyperparameters we will tune via wandb
        'emb_dim': None, # Latent dimension
        'prior_std': None,
        # Standard deviation around 0 that our weights are initialized to
        'alpha': None, # Learning rate
        'steps': None, # Number of training steps
        'num_folds': None, # Number of CV Folds
        'ell_2': 1, #hyperparameter for l2 regularization penalization weight
        'gram': 1, #hyperparameter for gramian regularization penalization weight
    }

    with wandb.init() as run:
        run_config.update(run.config) # This is how the wandb agent passes params
        model_object_dict = dict()

        for j in range(run_config['num_folds']):
            train, test = folder.get_fold(j)
            model_object_dict[j] = model_constructor(
                ratings_df=all_rat,
                user_dim=942,
                item_dim=1681,
                embedding_dim=run_config['emb_dim'],
                init_stddev=run_config['prior_std'],
                prng_key=random.PRNGKey(0),
                train_set=train,
                test_set=test
            )
            model_object_dict[j].reset_embeddings()
            # Ensure we are starting from priors

        alpha, steps = run_config['alpha'], run_config['steps']
        print(run_config)

        grad_fn = jax.value_and_grad(reg_loss_observed, 1, has_aux=True)
        # Tell JAX to expect an aux dict as output

        for i in range(steps):
            loss_dict = {
              "learning_rate": lr_decay(
                i,
                alpha,
                decay_pct=.75,
                period_length=250
              )
            }
            for j, M in model_object_dict.items():
            # Iterate through folds

                (total_loss_val, fold_loss_dict), grads = grad_fn(
                # compute gradients for one fold
```

```
                M.ground_truth['A_train'],
                M.embeddings,
                dimensions={'users': 942, 'items': 1681},
                hyperparams={
                    'ell_2': run_config['ell_2'],
                    'gram': run_config['gram']
                }
            )

            M.embeddings = jax.tree_multimap(
            # update weights for one fold
                lambda p, g: p - lr_decay(
                    i,
                    alpha,
                    decay_pct=.75,
                    period_length=250
                ) * g,
                M.embeddings,
                grads
            )

            fold_loss_dict = {
                f'{k}_fold-{j}':
                v for k, v in fold_loss_dict.items()
            }
            fold_loss_dict.update( # loss calculation within fold
                {
                    f"Test omse_fold-{j}": omse_loss(
                        M.ground_truth['A_test'],
                        M.embeddings
                    ),
                }
            )

            loss_dict.update(fold_loss_dict)

        loss_dict.update({ # average loss over all folds
            "Test omse_mean": np.mean(
                [v for k,v in loss_dict.items()
                if k.startswith('Test omse_fold-')]
            ),
            "test omse_max": np.max(
                [v for k,v in loss_dict.items()
                if k.startswith('Test omse_fold-')]
            ),
            "test omse_min": np.min(
                [v for k,v in loss_dict.items()
                if k.startswith('Test omse_fold-')]
            )
        })
        wandb.log(loss_dict)
```

```
            if i % 1000 == 0:
                print(f'Loss step {i}:')
                print(loss_dict)
```

Here's our final sweeps configuration:

```
sweep_config = {
    "name" : "mf-HPO-CV",
    "method" : "random",
    "parameters" : {
      "steps": {
        "value": 2000
      },
      "num_folds": {
        "value": 5
      },
      "alpha" :{
        "min": 2.0,
        "max": 3.0
      },
      "emb_dim" :{
        "min": 15,
        "max": 70
      },
      "prior_std" :{
        "min": .75,
        "max": 1.0
      },
      "ell_2" :{
        "min": .05,
        "max": 0.5
      },
      "gram" :{
        "min": .1,
        "max": .6
      },
    },
    "metric" : {
      'name': 'Test omse_mean',
      'goal': 'minimize'
    }
}

  sweep_id = wandb.sweep(sweep_config, project="jax-mf", entity="wandb-un")


wandb.agent(sweep_id, function=train_with_reg_loss_CV, count=count)
```

That may seem like a lot of setup, but we've really achieved a lot here. We've initialized the model to optimize the two matrix factors while simultaneously keeping the matrix elements and the Gramians small.

This brings us to our lovely images.

Output from HPO MF

Let's have a quick look at what the prior work has produced. First, Figure 10-3 shows that our primary loss function, observed mean square error (OMSE), is rapidly decreasing. This is great, but we should take a deeper look.

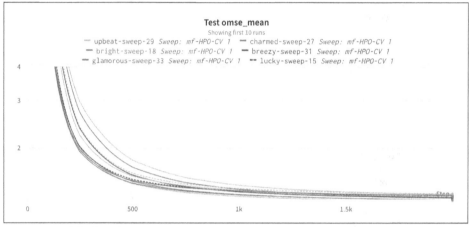

Figure 10-3. The loss during training

Let's also have a quick look to ensure that our regularization parameters (Figure 10-4) are converging. We can see that our L2 regularization could probably still decrease if we were to continue for more epochs.

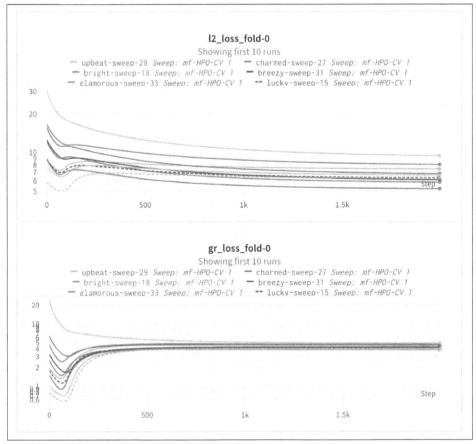

Figure 10-4. Regularization parameters

We'd like to see our cross-validation laid out by fold and corresponding loss (Figure 10-5). This is a *parallel coordinates chart*; its lines correspond to different runs that are in correspondence with different choices of parameters, and its vertical axes are different metrics. The far-right heatmap axis corresponds to the overall total loss that we're trying to minimize. In this case, we alternate test loss on a fold and total loss on that fold. Lower numbers are better, and we hope to see individual lines consistent across their loss per fold (otherwise, we may have a skewed dataset). We see that choices of hyperparameters can interact with fold behavior, but in all the low-loss scenarios (at the bottom), we see a high correlation between performance on different folds (the vertical axes in the plot).

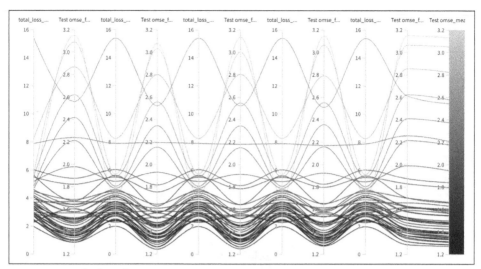

Figure 10-5. The loss during training

Next up, which choices of hyperparameters have a strong effect on performance? Figure 10-6 is another parallel coordinates plot with the vertical axes corresponding to different hyperparameters. Generally, we're looking for which domains on the vertical axes correspond to low loss on the far-right heatmap. We see that some of our hyperparameters like priors distribution and, somewhat surprisingly, `ell_2` have virtually no effect. However, small embedding dimension and small Gramian weight definitely do. A larger alpha also seems to correlate well with good performance.

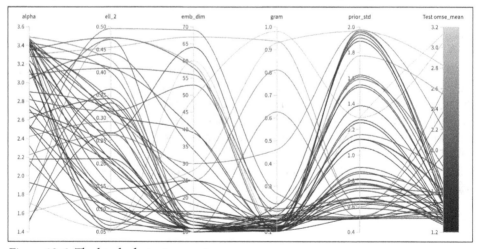

Figure 10-6. The loss by hyperparameter

Finally, we see that as we do a Bayesian hyperparameter search, we really do improve our performance over time. Figure 10-7 is a Pareto plot in which each dot in the scatterplot represents one run, and left to right is a time axis. The vertical axis is overall total loss, so lower is better, and it means that generally we're converging toward better performance. The line inscribed along the bottom of the convex hull of the scatter points is the *Pareto frontier*, or the best performance at that x value. Since this is a time-series Pareto plot, it merely tracks the best performance in time.

You may be wondering how and why we're able to converge to better loss values in time. This is because we've conducted a Bayesian hyperparameter search, which means we selected our hyperparameters from independent Gaussians, and we updated our priors for each parameter based on performance of previous runs. For an introduction to this method, see "Bayesian Hyperparameter Optimization—A Primer" (*https://oreil.ly/4nd3D*) by Robert Mitson. In a real setting, we'd see less monotonic behavior in this plot, but we'd always be hoping to improve.

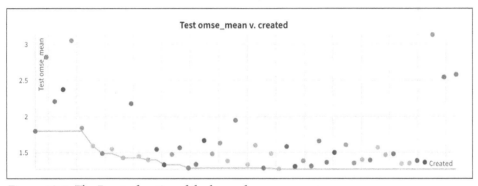

Figure 10-7. The Pareto frontier of the loss values

Prequential validation

If we were to put the preceding approach into practice, we would need to capture our trained models in a model registry for use in production. Best practice is to establish a set of explicit evaluations against which to test a selection of models. In your basic ML training, you've likely been encouraged to think about validation datasets; these may take many forms, testing particular subsets of instances or features or even distributed across covariates in a known way.

One useful framing for recommendation systems is to remember that they're a fundamentally sequential dataset. With this in mind, let's take another look at our ratings data. Later we will talk more about sequential recommenders, but while we're talking about validation, it's useful to mention how to take proper care.

Notice that all our ratings have an associated timestamp. To build a proper validation set, it's a good idea to take that timestamp from the end of our data.

However, you might be wondering, "When are different users active?" and "Is it possible that the later timestamps are a biased selection of the ratings?" These are important questions. To account for these questions, we should do a holdout by user.

To create this *prequential dataset*, where the test set follows directly after the training set in a chronological sequence, start by deciding on a desired size for validation, like 10%. Next, group the data by user. Finally, employ rejection sampling, ensuring you don't use the most recent timestamp as the rejection criterion.

Here's a simple implementation for pandas using rejection sampling. This is not the most computationally efficient implementation, but it will get the job done:

```python
def prequential_validation_set(df, holdout_perc=0.1):
    '''
    We utilize rejection sampling.

    Assign a probability to all observations, if they lie below the
    sample percentage AND they're the most recent still in the set, include.

    Otherwise return them and repeat.
    Each time, take no more than the remaining necessary to fill the count.
    '''
    count = int(len(df)*holdout_perc)
    sample = []
    while count >0:
        df['p'] = np.random.rand(len(df),1) #generate probabilities
        x = list(
            df.loc[~df.index.isin(sample)] # exclude already selected
            .sort_values(['unix_timestamp'], ascending=False)
            .groupby('user_id').head(1) # only allow the first in each group
            .query("p < @holdout_perc").index # grab the indices
        )
        rnd.shuffle(x) # ensure our previous sorting doesn't bias the users subset
        sample += x[:count] # add observations up to the remaining needed
        count -= len(x[:count]) # decrement the remaining needed

    df.drop(columns=['p'], inplace=True)

    test = df.iloc[sample]
    train = df[~df.index.isin(test.index)]
    return train, test
```

This is an effective and important validation scheme for inherently sequential datasets.

WSABIE

Let's focus again on optimizations and modifications. Another optimization is to treat the MF problem as a single optimization.

The paper "WSABIE: Scaling Up to Large Vocabulary Image Annotation" (*https://oreil.ly/1GB3x*) by Jason Weston et al. also contains a factorization for just the item matrix. In this scheme, we replace the user matrix with a weighted sum of the items a user has affinity to. We cover web scale annotation by image embedding (WSABIE) and Warp loss in "WARP" on page 233. Representing a user as the average of items they like is a way of saving space and not needing a separate user matrix if there are large numbers of users.

> **Latent Space HPO**
>
> A completely alternative way to do HPO for RecSys is via the latent spaces themselves! "Hyper-Parameter Optimization for Latent Spaces in Dynamic Recommender Systems" (*https://oreil.ly/RLeEC*) by Bruno Veloso et al. attempts to modify the relative embeddings during each step to optimize the embedding model.

Dimension Reduction

Dimension-reduction techniques are frequently employed in recommendation systems to decrease computational complexity and enhance the accuracy of recommendation algorithms. In this context, the primary concepts of dimension reduction for recommendation systems include MF and SVD.

The *matrix factorization method* decomposes the user-item interaction matrix $\left(A \in \mathbb{R}^{(m \times n)}\right)$ into two lower-dimensional matrices, representing the user $\left(U \in \mathbb{R}^{(m \times r)}\right)$ and item $\left(V \in \mathbb{R}^{(n \times r)}\right)$ latent factors, respectively. This technique can reveal the underlying data structure and offer recommendations based on a user's previous interactions. Mathematically, MF can be represented as follows:

$$A \sim U \times V^{(T)}$$

SVD is a linear-algebra technique that decomposes a matrix (A) into three matrices—the left singular vectors (U), the singular values (Σ), and the right singular vectors (V). SVD can be utilized for MF in recommendation systems, where the user-item interaction matrix is decomposed into a smaller number of latent factors. The mathematical representation of SVD is as follows:

$$A = U \times \Sigma \times V^{(T)}$$

In practice, though, rather than using a mathematical library to find the eigenvectors, folks might use the power iteration method (*https://oreil.ly/DCsRs*) to discover the eigenvectors approximately. This method is far more scalable than a full dense SVD solution that is optimized for correctness and dense vectors:

```
import jax
import jax.numpy as jnp


def power_iteration(a: jnp.ndarray) -> jnp.ndarray:
    """Returns an eigenvector of the matrix a.
    Args:
      a: a n x m matrix
    """
    key = jax.random.PRNGKey(0)
    x = jax.random.normal(key, shape=(a.shape[1], 1))
    for i in range(100):
      x = a @ x
      x = x / jnp.linalg.norm(x)
    return x.T

key = jax.random.PRNGKey(123)
A = jax.random.normal(key, shape=[4, 4])
print(A)
[[ 0.52830553  0.3722206  -1.2219944  -0.10314374]
 [ 1.4722222   0.47889313 -1.2940298   1.0449569 ]
 [ 0.23724185  0.3545859  -0.172465   -1.8011322 ]
 [ 0.4864215   0.08039388 -1.2540827   0.72071517]]
S, _, _ = jnp.linalg.svd(A)
print(S)
[[-0.375782    0.40269807  0.44086716 -0.70870167]
 [-0.753597    0.0482972  -0.65527284  0.01940039]
 [ 0.2040088   0.91405433 -0.15798494  0.31293103]
 [-0.49925917 -0.00250015  0.5927009   0.6320123 ]]
x1 = power_iteration(A)
print(x1.T)
[[-0.35423845]
 [-0.8332922 ]
 [ 0.16189891]
 [-0.39233655]]
```

Notice that the eigenvector returned by the power iteration is close to the first column of S, but not quite. This is because the method is approximate. It relies on the fact that an eigenvector doesn't change in direction when multiplied by the matrix. So by repeatedly multiplying by the matrix, we eventually iterate onto an eigenvector. Also notice that we solved for column eigenvectors instead of the row eigenvectors. In this example, the columns are users, and the rows are items. It is important to play with transposed matrices because a lot of ML involves reshaping and transposing matrices, so getting used to them early is an important skill.

Eigenvector Examples

Here's a nice exercise for you: the second eigenvector is computed by subtracting out the first eigenvector after the matrix multiplication. This is telling the algorithm to ignore any component along the first eigenvector in order to compute the second eigenvector. As a fun exercise, hop over to Colab (*https://oreil.ly/0zmWq*) and try computing the second eigenvector. Extending this to sparse vector representations is another interesting exercise, as it allows you to start computing the eigenvectors of sparse matrices, which is usually the form of matrix that recommender systems use.

Next, we construct a recommendation for a user by creating a column and then taking the dot product with all the eigenvectors and finding the closest. We then find all the highest-scoring entries in the eigenvector that the user hasn't seen and return them as recommendations. So in the preceding example, if the eigenvector x_1 was the closest to the user column, then the best item to recommend would be item 3 because it is the largest component in the eigenvector and thus rated most highly if the user is closest to the eigenvector x_1. Here's what this looks like in code:

```
import jax
import jax.numpy as jnp

def recommend_items(eigenvectors: jnp.ndarray, user:jnp.ndarray) -> jnp.ndarray:
    """Returns an ordered list of recommend items for the user.
    Args:
      eigenvectors: a nxm eigenvector matrix
      user: a user vector of size m.
    """
    score_eigenvectors = jnp.matmul(eigenvectors.T, user)
    which_eigenvector = jnp.argmax(score_eigenvectors)
    closest_eigenvector = eigenvectors.T[which_eigenvector]
    scores, items = jax.lax.top_k(closest_eigenvector, 3)
    return scores, items

S = jnp.array(
[[-0.375782,    0.40269807],
 [-0.753597,    0.0482972],
 [ 0.2040088,   0.91405433],
 [-0.49925917, -0.00250015]])
u = jnp.array([-1, -1, 0, 0]).reshape(4, 1)
scores, items = recommend_items(S, u)
print(scores)
[ 0.2040088  -0.375782   -0.49925917]
print(items)
[2 0 3]
```

In this example, a user has downvoted item 0 and item 1. The closest column eigenvector is therefore column 0. We then select the closest eigenvector to the user, order the entries, and recommend item 2 to the user, which is the highest-scoring entry that the user has not seen.

Two techniques aim to extract the most relevant features from the user-item interaction matrix and reduce its dimensionality, which can improve performance:

Principal component analysis (PCA)
> This statistical technique transforms the original high-dimensional data into a lower-dimensional representation while retaining the most important information. PCA can be applied to the user-item interaction matrix to reduce the number of dimensions and improve the computational efficiency of the recommendation algorithm.

Nonnegative matrix factorization (NMF)
> This technique decomposes the nonnegative user-item interaction matrix $\left(A \in \mathbb{R}^{(m \times n)^{*} +} \right)$ into two nonnegative matrices $\left(W \in \mathbb{R}^{(m \times r)^{*} +} \right.$ and $\left. H \in \mathbb{R}^{(r \times n)+} \right)$. NMF can be utilized for dimension reduction in recommendation systems, where the latent factors are nonnegative and interpretable. The mathematical representation of NMF is $A \simeq W \times H$.

MF techniques can be further extended to incorporate additional information, such as item content or user demographic data, through the use of side information. Side information can be employed to augment the user-item interaction matrix, allowing for more accurate and personalized recommendations.

Furthermore, MF models can be extended to handle implicit feedback data, where the absence of interaction data is not equivalent to the lack of interest. By incorporating additional regularization terms into the objective function, MF models can learn a more robust representation of the user-item interaction matrix, leading to better recommendations for implicit feedback scenarios.

Consider a recommendation system that employs MF to model the user-item interaction matrix. If the system comprises many users and items, the resulting factor matrices can be high-dimensional and computationally expensive to process. However, by using dimension-reduction techniques like SVD or PCA, the algorithm can reduce the dimensionality of the factor matrices while preserving the most important information about the user-item interactions. This enables the algorithm to generate more efficient and accurate recommendations, even for new users or items with limited interaction data.

Isometric Embeddings

Isometric embeddings are a specific type of embedding that maintains distances between points in high-dimensional space when mapping them onto a lower-dimensional space. The term *isometric* signifies that the distances between points in the high-dimensional space are preserved precisely in the lower-dimensional space, up to a scaling factor.

In contrast to other types of embeddings, such as linear or nonlinear embeddings, which may distort the distances between points, isometric embeddings are preferable in numerous applications where distance preservation is essential. For example, in ML, isometric embeddings can be employed to visualize high-dimensional data in two or three dimensions while preserving the relative distances between the data points. In NLP, isometric embeddings can be utilized to represent the semantic similarities between words or documents while maintaining their relative distances in the embedding space.

One popular technique for generating isometric embeddings is *multidimensional scaling (MDS)*. MDS operates by computing pairwise distances between the data points in the high-dimensional space and then determining a lower-dimensional embedding that preserves these distances. The optimization problem is generally formulated as a constrained optimization problem, where the objective is to minimize the difference between the pairwise distances in the high-dimensional space and the corresponding distances in the lower-dimensional embedding. Mathematically, we write: $min_{(x)}\Sigma_{(i,j)}\left(d_{ij} - ||x_i - x_j||\right)^2$.

Here, d_{ij} denotes the pairwise distances in the high-dimensional space, and x_i and x_j represent points in the lower-dimensional embedding.

Another approach for generating isometric embeddings is through the use of kernel methods, such as kernel PCA or kernel MDS. Kernel methods work by implicitly mapping the data points into a higher-dimensional feature space, where the distances between the points are easier to compute. The isometric embedding is then calculated in the feature space, and the resulting embedding is mapped back to the original space.

Isometric embeddings have been employed in recommendation systems to represent the user-item interaction matrix in a lower-dimensional space where the distances between the items are preserved. By preserving the distances between items in the embedding space, the recommendation algorithm can better capture the underlying structure of the data and provide more accurate and diverse recommendations.

Isometric embeddings can also be employed to incorporate additional information into the recommendation algorithm, such as item content or user demographic data. By using isometric embeddings to represent the items and the additional information, the algorithm can capture the similarities between items based on both the user-item interaction data and the item content or user demographics, leading to more accurate and diverse recommendations.

Moreover, isometric embeddings can also be used to address the cold-start problem in recommendation systems. By using the isometric embeddings to represent the items, the algorithm can make recommendations for new items based on their similarities to the existing items in the embedding space, even in the absence of user interactions.

In summary, isometric embeddings are a valuable technique in recommendation systems for representing the user-item interaction matrix in a lower-dimensional space where the distances between the items are preserved. Isometric embeddings can be generated using MF techniques and can be employed to incorporate additional information, address the cold-start problem, and improve the accuracy and diversity of recommendations.

Nonlinear Locally Metrizable Embeddings

Nonlinear locally metrizable embeddings are yet another method to represent the user-item interaction matrix in a lower-dimensional space where the local distances between nearby items are preserved. By preserving the local distances between items in the embedding space, the recommendation algorithm can better capture the local structure of the data and provide more accurate and diverse recommendations.

Mathematically, let $X = x_1, x_2, \ldots, x_n$ be the set of items in the high-dimensional space, and $Y = y_1, y_2, \ldots, y_n$ be the set of items in the lower-dimensional space. The goal of nonlinear locally metrizable embeddings is to find a mapping $f: X \rightarrow Y$ that preserves the local distances, i.e., for any $x_i, x_j \in X$, we have this:

$$d_Y\big(f(x_i), f(x_j)\big) \simeq d_X\big(x_i, x_j\big)$$

One popular approach to generating nonlinear locally metrizable embeddings in recommendation systems is via autoencoder neural networks. Autoencoders work by mapping the high-dimensional user-item interaction matrix onto a lower-dimensional space through an encoder network, and then reconstructing the matrix back in the high-dimensional space through a decoder network. The encoder and decoder networks are trained jointly to minimize the difference between the input data and the reconstructed data, with the objective of capturing the underlying structure of the data in the embedding space:

$$min_{(\theta, \phi)} \sum_{(i\,=\,1)}^{n} \|x_i - g_\phi(f_\theta(x_i))\|^2$$

Here, f_θ denotes the encoder network with parameters θ, g_θ denotes the decoder network with parameters θ, and $|| \cdot ||$ represents the Euclidean norm.

Another approach for generating nonlinear locally metrizable embeddings in recommendation systems is through the use of t-distributed stochastic neighbor embedding (t-SNE). t-SNE works by modeling the pairwise similarities between the items in the high-dimensional space, and then finding a lower-dimensional embedding that preserves these similarities.

A more popular approach in modern times is UMAP, which instead attempts to fit a minimal manifold that preserves density in local neighborhoods. UMAP is an essential technique for finding low-dimensional representations in complex and high-dimensional latent spaces; find it's documentation at *https://oreil.ly/NLqDg*. The optimization problem is typically formulated as a cost function C that measures the difference between the pairwise similarities in the high-dimensional space and the corresponding similarities in the lower-dimensional embedding:

$$C(Y) = \Sigma_{(i,j)} p_{ij} * log\left(\frac{p_{ij}}{q_{ij}}\right)$$

Here, p_{ij} denotes the pairwise similarities in the high-dimensional space, q_{ij} denotes the pairwise similarities in the lower-dimensional space, and the sum is over all pairs of items (i, j).

Nonlinear locally metrizable embeddings can also be used to incorporate additional information into the recommendation algorithm, such as item content or user demographic data. By using nonlinear locally metrizable embeddings to represent the items and the additional information, the algorithm can capture the similarities between items based on both the user-item interaction data and the item content or user demographics, leading to more accurate and diverse recommendations.

Moreover, nonlinear locally metrizable embeddings can also be used to address the cold-start problem in recommendation systems. By using the nonlinear locally metrizable embeddings to represent the items, the algorithm can make recommendations for new items based on their similarities to the existing items in the embedding space, even in the absence of user interactions.

In summary, nonlinear locally metrizable embeddings are a useful technique in recommendation systems for representing the user-item interaction matrix in a lower-dimensional space where the local distances between nearby items are preserved. Nonlinear locally metrizable embeddings can be generated using techniques such as autoencoder neural networks or t-SNE and can be used to incorporate additional information, address the cold-start problem, and improve the accuracy and diversity of recommendations.

Centered Kernel Alignment

When training neural networks, the latent space representations at each layer are expected to express correlation structures between the incoming signals. Frequently, these interstitial representations comprise a sequence of states transitioning from the initial layer to the final layer. You may naturally wonder, "How do these representations change throughout the layers of the network" and "How similar are these layers?" Interestingly, for some architectures, this question may yield deep insight into the network's behavior.

This process of comparing layer representations is called *correlation analysis*. For an MLP with layers $1, ..., N$, the correlations may be represented by an $N \times N$ matrix of pairwise relationships. The idea is that each layer comprises a series of latent factors, and similar to correlation analysis for other features of a dataset, these latent features' relationships may be simply summarized by their covariance.

Affinity and p-sale

As you've seen, MF is a powerful dimension-reduction technique that can yield an estimator for the probability of a sale (often shorted to *p-sale*). In MF, the goal has been to decompose this historical data on user behavior and the product sales matrix into two lower-dimensional matrices: one that represents user preferences and another that represents product characteristics. Now, let's convert this MF model into a sale estimator.

Let $R \in \mathbb{R}^{(M \times N)}$ be the historical data matrix, where M is the number of users and N is the number of products. The MF aims to find two matrices $U \in \mathbb{R}^{(M \times d)}$ and $V \in \mathbb{R}^{(N \times d)}$, where d is the dimensionality of the latent space, such that:

$$R \simeq U * V^T$$

The *probability of a sale*, or equivalently a read, watch, eat, or click, can be predicted using MF by first decomposing the historical data matrix into user and product matrices, and then calculating a score that represents the likelihood of a user purchasing a given product. This score can be calculated using the dot product of the corresponding row in the user matrix and the column in the product matrix, followed by a logistic function to transform the dot product into a probability score.

Mathematically, the probability of a sale for a user u and a product p can be represented as follows:

$$P(u, p) = \text{sigmoid}(u * p^T)$$

Here, sigmoid is the logistic function that maps the dot product of the user and product vectors to a probability score between 0 and 1:

$$sigmoid(x) = 1/(1 + exp(-x))$$

The p^T represents the transpose of the product vector. The dot product of the user and product vectors is a measure of the similarity between the user's preferences and the product's characteristics, and the logistic function maps this similarity score to a probability score.

The user and product matrices can be trained on the historical data by using various MF algorithms, such as SVD, NMF, or ALS. Once the matrices are trained, the dot product and logistic function can be applied to new user-product pairs to predict the probability of a sale. The predicted probabilities can then be used to rank and recommend products to the user.

It's worth highlighting that, since the loss function for ALS is convex (meaning there is a single global minimum), the convergence can be fast when we fix either the user or item matrix. In this method, the user matrix is fixed and the item matrix is solved for. Then the item matrix is fixed and the user matrix is solved for. The method alternates between the two solutions, and because the loss is convex in this regime, the method converges quickly.

The dot product of the corresponding row in the user matrix and column in the product matrix represents the affinity score between the user and the product, or how well the user's preferences match the product's characteristics. However, this score alone may not be a sufficient predictor of whether the user will actually purchase the product.

The logistic function applied to the dot product in the MF model transforms the affinity score into a probability score, which represents the likelihood of a sale. This transformation takes into account additional factors beyond just the user's preferences and the product's characteristics, such as the overall popularity of the product, the user's purchasing behavior, and any other relevant external factors. By incorporating these additional factors, MF is able to better predict the probability of a sale, rather than just an affinity score.

A comparison library (however, not in JAX) for computing latent embeddings linearly is libFM (*http://libfm.org*). The formulation for a factorization machine is similar to a GloVe embedding in that it also models the interaction between two vectors, but the dot product can be used for regression or binary classification tasks. The method can also be extended to recommend more than two kinds of items beyond user and item.

In summary, MF produces probabilities of sale instead of just affinity scores by incorporating additional factors beyond the user's preferences and the product's characteristics, and transforming the affinity score into a probability score by using a logistic function.

Propensity Weighting for Recommendation System Evaluation

As you've seen, recommendation systems are evaluated based on user feedback, which is collected from the deployed recommendation system. However, this data is causally influenced by the deployed system, creating a feedback loop that may bias the evaluation of new models. This feedback loop can lead to confounding variables, making it difficult to distinguish between user preferences and the influence of the deployed system.

If this surprises you, let's consider for a moment what would have to be true for a recommendation system to *not* causally influence the actions users take and/or the outcomes that result from those actions. That would require assumptions like "the recommendations are completely ignored by the user" and "the system makes recommendations at random." Propensity weighting can mitigate some of the worst effects of this problem.

The performance of a recommender system depends on many factors, including user-item characteristics, contextual information, and trends, which can affect the quality of the recommendations and the user engagement. However, the influence can be mutual: the user interactions influence the recommender, and vice versa. Evaluating the causal effect of a recommender system on user behavior and satisfaction is therefore a challenging task, as it requires controlling for potential confounding factors—those that may affect both the treatment assignment (the recommendation strategy) and the outcome of interest (the user's response to the recommendations).

Causal inference provides a framework for addressing these challenges. In the context of recommender systems, causal inference can help answer questions such as these:

- How does the choice of recommendation strategy affect user engagement, such as CTRs, purchase rates, and satisfaction ratings?
- What is the optimal recommendation strategy for a given user segment, item category, or context?
- What are the long-term effects of a recommendation strategy on user retention, loyalty, and lifetime value?

We'll round out this chapter by introducing one aspect of causal inference important to recommender systems, based on the concept of propensity score. We'll introduce propensity to quantify the adjusted likelihood of some items being shown to the user. We'll then see how this interacts with the famous Simpson's paradox.

Propensity

In many data science problems, we are forced to contend with confounders and, notably, the correlation between those confounders and a target outcome. Depending on the setting, the confounder may be of a variety of forms. Interestingly, in recommendation systems, that confounder can be the system itself! Offline evaluation of recommendation systems is subject to confounders derived from the item selection behavior of users and the deployed recommendation system.

If this issue seems a bit circular, it kind of is. This is sometimes called *closed-loop feedback*. One approach to mitigation is propensity weighting, which aims to address this problem by considering each feedback in the corresponding stratum based on the estimated propensities. You may recall that *propensity* refers to the likelihood of a user seeing an item; by inversely weighting by this, we can offset the selection bias. Compared to the standard offline holdout evaluation, this method attempts to represent the actual utility of the examined recommendation models.

Utilizing Counterfactuals

One other approach to mitigating selection bias that we won't dive into is *counterfactual evaluation*, which estimates the actual utility of a recommendation model with propensity-weighting techniques more similar to off-policy evaluation approaches in reinforcement learning (RL). However, counterfactual evaluation often relies on accurate logging propensities in an open-loop setting where some random items are exposed to the user, which is not practical for most recommendation problems. If you have the option to include randomized recommendations to users for rating, this can help de-bias as well. One such setting where these methods may be combined is in RL-based recommenders that use explore-exploit methods like a multiarmed bandit or other structured randomization.

Inverse propensity scoring (IPS) is a propensity-based evaluation method that leverages importance sampling to account for the fact that the feedback collected from the deployed recommendation system is not uniformly random. The propensity score is a balancing factor that adjusts the observed feedback distribution conditioned on the propensity score. The IPS evaluation method is theoretically unbiased if open-loop feedback can be sampled from all possible items uniformly at random. In Chapter 3, we discussed the Matthew effect, or "the rich get richer" for recommendation systems; IPS is one way to combat this effect. Note the relationship here between the two ideas of the Matthew effect and Simpson's paradox, when within different strata, selection effects create significant biasing.

Propensity weighting is based on the idea that the probability of an item being exposed to a user by the deployed recommendation system (the propensity score) affects the feedback that is collected from that user. By reweighting the feedback based on the propensity scores, we can adjust for the bias introduced by the deployed system and obtain a more accurate evaluation of the new recommendation model.

To apply IPS, we need to estimate the propensity scores for each item-user interaction in the collected feedback dataset. This can be done by modeling the probability that the deployed system would have exposed the item to the user at the time of the interaction. One simple approach is to use the popularity of the item as a proxy for its propensity score. However, more sophisticated methods can be used to model the propensity scores based on user and item features, as well as the context of the interaction.

Once the propensity scores are estimated, we can reweight the feedback by using importance sampling. Specifically, each feedback is weighted by the inverse of its propensity score so that items that are more likely to be exposed by the deployed system are downweighted, while items that are less likely to be exposed are upweighted. This reweighting process approximates a counterfactual distribution of feedback expected from surfacing recommendations from a uniform distribution of popularity.

Finally, we can use the reweighted feedback to evaluate the new recommendation model via standard metrics for evaluation, as we've seen in this chapter. The effectiveness of the new model is then compared to that of the deployed system by using the reweighted feedback, providing a fairer and more accurate evaluation of the new model's performance.

Simpson's and Mitigating Confounding

Simpson's paradox is predicated on the idea of a confounding variable that establishes strata within which we see (potentially misleading) covariation. This paradox arises when the association between two variables is investigated but these variables are strongly influenced by a confounding variable.

In the case of recommendation systems, this confounding variable is the deployed model's characteristics and tendencies of selection. The propensity score is introduced as a measure of a system's deviation from an unbiased open-loop exposure scenario. This score allows for the design and analysis of offline evaluation of recommendation models based on the observed closed-loop feedback, mimicking some of the particular characteristics of the open-loop scenario.

Traditional descriptions of Simpson's paradox often suggest stratification, a well-known approach to identify and estimate causal effects by first identifying the underlying strata before investigating causal effects in each stratum. This approach enables the measurement of the potential outcome irrespective of the confounding variable. For recommendation systems, this involves stratifying the observed outcome based on the possible values of the confounding variable, which is the deployed model's characteristics.

The user-independent propensity score is estimated via a two-step generative process using the prior probability that an item is recommended by the deployed model and the conditional probability that the user interacts with the item, given that it is recommended. Based on a set of mild assumptions (but too mathematically technical to cover here), the user-independent propensity score can be estimated using maximum likelihood for each dataset.

We need to define the user-propensity score $p_{u,i}$, which indicates the tendency—or frequency—of the deployed model to expose item $i \in I$ to user $u \in U$. In practice, we marginalize over users to get the user-independent propensity score $p_{*,i}$. As described in "Unbiased Offline Recommender Evaluation for Missing-Not-at-Random Implicit Feedback" (*https://oreil.ly/mpM87*) by Longqi Yang et al., the equation is as follows:

$$p_{*,i} \alpha (n_i^*)^{\frac{\gamma + 1}{2}}$$

Here, n_i^* is the total number of times item i interacted with, and γ is a parameter that affects the propensity distributions over items with different observed popularity. The power-law parameter γ affects the propensity distributions over items and depends on the examined dataset; we estimate the γ parameter by using maximum likelihood for each dataset.

With these estimates for propensity, we can then apply a simple inverse weighting $w_i = \frac{1}{p_i}$ when calculating the effect of feedback. Finally, we can combine these weightings with propensity matching, to generate counterfactual recommendations; by collecting approximately equal propensity items into strata, we can then use these strata as our confounding variable.

Doubly Robust Estimation

Doubly robust estimation (DRE) is a method that combines two models: one that models the probability of receiving the treatment (being recommended an item by the deployed model) and one that models the outcome of interest (the user's feedback on the item). The weights used in DRE depend on the predicted probabilities from both models. This method has the advantage that it can still provide unbiased estimates even if one of the models is misspecified.

The structural equations for a doubly robust estimator with propensity score weighting and outcome model is as follows:

$$\Theta = \frac{\sum w_i (Y_i - f(X_i))}{\sum w_i (T_i - p_i) + \sum w_i \left(p_i (1 - p_i)^2 (f(X_i) - f^*(X_i)) \right)}$$

Here, Y_i is the outcome, X_i are covariates, T_i is the treatment, p_i is the propensity score, w_i is the weight, $f(X_i)$ is the outcome model, and $f^*(X_i)$ is the estimated outcome model.

For a great introduction to these considerations, check out "Give Me a Robust Estimator—and Make It a Double! (*https://oreil.ly/sNhvF*).

Summary

What a whirlwind! Latent spaces are one of the *most* important aspects of recommendation systems. They are the representations that we use to encode our users and items. Ultimately, latent spaces are about more than dimension reduction; they are about understanding a geometry in which measures of distance encode the meaning relevant to your ML task.

The world of embeddings and encoders runs deep. We haven't had time to discuss CLIP embeddings (image + text) or the Poincaré disk (naturally hierarchical distance measures). We didn't dive deep into UMAP (a nonlinear density-aware dimension-reduction technique) or HNSW (a method for retrieval in latent spaces that respects local geometry well). Instead, we point you to the (contemporaneously published) article by Vicki Boykis (*https://oreil.ly/Rpu23*) on embeddings, the essay and guide to constructing embeddings (*https://oreil.ly/UDZ1_*) by Karel Minařík, or the beautiful visual guide to text embeddings (*https://oreil.ly/t1N48*) by Meor Amer from Cohere.

We're now equipped with representations, but next we need to optimize. We're building *personalized* recommendation systems, so let's define the metrics that measure our performance on our task.

## CHAPTER 11

Personalized Recommendation Metrics

Having explored the powerful methodologies of MF and neural networks in the context of personalization, we are now equipped with potent tools to craft sophisticated recommendation systems. However, the order of recommendations in a list may have a profound impact on user engagement and satisfaction.

Our journey so far has primarily been focused on predicting what a user may like, using latent factors or deep learning architectures. However, the manner in which we present these predictions, or more formally, how we rank these recommendations, holds paramount significance. Therefore, this chapter will shift our gaze from the prediction problem and will unravel the complex landscape of ranking in recommendation systems.

This chapter is dedicated to understanding key ranking metrics including mean average precision (mAP), mean reciprocal rank (MRR), and normalized discounted cumulative gain (NDCG). Each of these metrics takes a unique approach toward quantifying the quality of our rankings, catering to different aspects of the user interaction.

We'll dive into the intricacies of these metrics, unveiling their computational details and discussing their interpretation, covering their strengths and weaknesses, and pointing out their specific relevance to various personalization scenarios.

This exploration forms an integral part of the evaluation process in recommendation systems. It not only gives us a robust framework to measure the performance of our system but also provides essential insights into understanding how different algorithms might perform in online settings. This will lay the foundation for future discussions on algorithmic bias, diversity in recommendations, and a multistakeholder approach to recommendation systems.

In essence, the knowledge garnered in this chapter will be instrumental in fine-tuning our recommendation system, ensuring that we don't just predict well but also recommend in a way that truly resonates with individual user preferences and behaviors.

Environments

Before we dig into defining the key metrics, we're going to spend a few moments discussing the kinds of evaluation we can do. Evaluation for recommendation systems, as you'll soon see, is frequently characterized by how *relevant* the recommendations are for a user. This is similar to search metrics, but we add in additional factors to account for *where* in the list the most relevant items are.

For an extremely comprehensive view on evaluation of recommender systems, the recent project RecList (*https://oreil.ly/b6mPy*) builds a useful checklist-based framework for organizing metrics and evaluations.

Often you'll hear about evaluating recommenders in a few setups:

- Online/offline
- User/item
- A/B

Each setup provides slightly different kinds of evaluations and tells you different things. Let's quickly break down the differences to set some assumptions about terminology.

Online and Offline

When we refer to online versus offline recommenders, we are referring to *when* you're running evals. In *offline evaluation*, you start with a test/evaluation dataset, outside your production system, and compute a set of metrics. This is often the simplest recommender to set up but has the highest expectation of existing data. Using historical data, you construct a set of relevant responses, which you can then use during simulated inference. This approach is the most similar to other kinds of traditional ML, although with slightly different computations for the error.

When we're training large models, these datasets are similar to an offline dataset. We previously saw prequential data, which is much more relevant in recommendation systems than in lots of other ML applications. Sometimes you'll hear people say that "all recommenders are sequential recommenders" because of the importance of historical exposure to the recommender problem.

Online evaluation takes place during inference, usually in production. The tricky part is that you essentially never know the counterfactual outcomes. You can compute specific metrics on the online rankings: frequency and distributions of covariates, CTR/success rate, or time on platform, but ultimately these are different from the offline metrics.

Bootstrapping from Historical Evaluation Data

One of the most common questions from people building a recommender from scratch is "Where do you get the initial training data?" This is a hard problem. Ultimately, you have to be clever to come up with a useful dataset. Consider our co-occurrence data in the Wikipedia recommender; we didn't require any user interactions to get to a set of data to build a recommender. Bootstrapping from item to item is the most popular strategy, but you can use other tricks as well. The simplest way to start moving into user-item recommenders is to simply ask the user questions. If you ask for preference information across a set of item features, you can build simple models that start to incorporate this.

User Versus Item Metrics

Because recommender systems are personalization machines, it can be easy to think that we always want to be making recommendations for the user and measuring the performance as such. Subtleties exist, though. We want to be sure individual items are getting a fair chance, and sometimes looking at the other side of the equation can help assess this. In other words, are the items getting recommended frequently enough to have a chance to find their niche? We should explicitly compute our metrics over user *and* item axes.

Another aspect of item-side metrics is for set-based recommenders. The other items that are recommended in context can have a significant effect on the performance of a recommendation. As a result, we should be careful to measure the pairwise item metrics in our large-scale evaluations.

A/B Testing

It's good to use randomized, controlled trials to evaluate how your new recommendation model is performing. For recommendations, this is quite tricky. At the end of this chapter, you'll see some of the nuance, but for now, let's consider a quick reminder of how to think about A/B testing in a closed-loop paradigm.

A/B tests ultimately attempt to estimate the effect size of swapping one model in for another; effect size estimation is the process of measuring the causal impact of an intervention on a target metric. First, we would need to deploy two recommender models. We'd also hope that there's a reasonable randomization of users into each of the recommenders. However, what's the randomization unit? It's easy to quickly assume it's the user, but what has changed about the recommender? Has the recommender changed in a way that covaries with some properties of the distribution—e.g., have you built a new recommender that is less friendly toward seasonal TV specials just as we enter into the second week of November?

Another consideration with this sort of testing for recommendation systems is the long-term compounding effects. A frequent rejoinder about a series of positive A/B test outcomes over several years is "Have you tested the first recommender against the last?" This is because populations change, both the users and the items. As you also vary the recommender system, you frequently find yourself in a double-blind situation where you've never seen this user or item population with any other recommender. If all the effect sizes of every A/B test were additive across the industry, the world GDP would likely be two to three times as large.

The way to guard against protests like this is via a *long-term holdout*, a random subset of users (continually being added to) who will not be upgraded to new models through time. By measuring the target metrics on this set versus the most cutting-edge model in production, you're always able to understand the long-term effects of your work. The downside of a long-term holdout? It's hard to maintain, and it's hard to sacrifice some of the effects of your work on a subset of the population.

Now let's finally get to the metrics already!

Recall and Precision

Let's begin by considering four recommender problems and how each may have different implications for the kind of results you want.

First, let's consider entering a bookstore and looking for a book by a popular author. We would say this is the recommender problem:

- Provides a lot of recommendations
- Offers few possible relevant results

Additionally, if the bookstore has a good selection, we'd expect that *all* the relevant results are contained in the recommendations because bookstores often carry most or all of an author's oeuvre once they've become popular. However, many of the recommendations—the books in the bookstore–are simply not relevant for this search.

Second, let's consider looking for a gas station nearby on a mapping app while in a large metro. We expect that a lot of gas stations are relatively close by, but you would probably consider only the first couple—or maybe even only one, the first one that you see. Thus a recommender for this problem has the following:

- Many relevant results
- Few useful recommendations

In the first scenario, the relevant results may be fully contained in the recommendations, and in the second scenario, the recommendations may be fully contained in the relevant results.

Let's now look at more common scenarios.

For our third example, consider that you're searching on a streaming video platform for something to watch tonight when you're feeling romantic. Streaming platforms tend to show a lot of recommendations—pages and pages from this one theme or another. But on this night, and on just this platform, only a couple of movies or TV shows might really fit what you're looking for. Our recommender, then, does the following:

- Provides many recommendations
- Offers only a few that are actually relevant

However, importantly, not all relevant results will be in the recommendations! As we know, different platforms have different media, so some of the relevant results won't appear in the recommendations no matter how many we look at.

Fourth, and finally, you're a high-end coffee lover with distinguished tastes headed into the local roaster for a third-wave, single-origin coffee. As an experienced coffee connoisseur, you love high-quality coffees from all over the world and enjoy most but not all origins. On any given day, your local cafe has only a few single-origin hand-brewed options. Despite your worldly palette, there are some popular terroirs that you just don't love. This little recommendation brew bar can be described as follows:

- Provides a few recommendations
- Offers many possible recommendations that are relevant

On any given day, only some of the few recommendations may be relevant to you.

So those are our matching four scenarios. For the latter two, the intersection between recommendation and relevance may be proportionally small or large—or even empty! The main idea is that the full size of the smaller sample is not always in use.

Now that we've worked through a few examples, let's see how they relate to the core metrics for a recommender: precision and recall @ *k* (Figure 11-1). Focusing on examples 3 and 4, we can see that only some of the recommendations intersect with the options that are relevant. And only some of the relevant options intersect with the recommendations. It's often overlooked, but in fact *these two ratios define our metrics*—let's go!

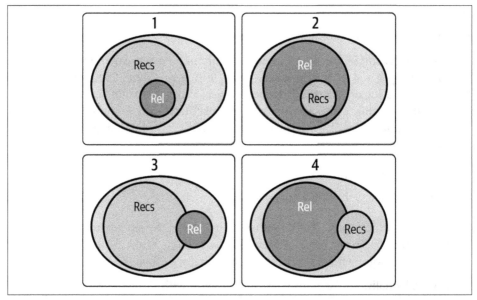

Figure 11-1. Recall and precision sets

@ k

In much of this chapter and RecSys metrics discussion, we say things like @ *k*. This means "at *k*," which should really be "in *k*" or "out of *k*." These are simply the size of the set of recommendations. We often anchor the customer experience on how many recommendations we can show the user without the experience suffering. We also need to know the cardinality of the set of relevant items, which we call @ *r*. Note that while it may not feel like it's possible to ever know this number, we assume this refers to "known relevant" options via our training or test data.

Precision at k

Precision is the ratio of the size of the set of relevant recommendations to k, the size of the set of recommendations.

$$Precision@k = \frac{num_{relevant}}{(k)}$$

Notice that the size of the relevant items doesn't appear in the formula. That's OK; the size of the intersection is still dependent on the size of the set of relevant items.

Looking at our examples, 2 technically has the highest precision, but it's a bit of a red herring because of the number of relevant results. This is one reason precision is not the most common metric for evaluating recommendation systems.

Recall at k

Recall is the ratio of the size of the set of relevant recommendations to r, the size of the set of relevant items.

But wait! If the ratio is the relevant recommendations over the relevant items, where is k? k is still important here because the size of the set of recommendations constrains the possible size of the intersection. Recall that these ratios are operating on that intersection that is always dependent on k. This means you often consider the max of r and k.

In scenario 3, we hope that some of the movies that fit our heart's desire will be on the right streaming platform. The number of these divided by the count of all the media anywhere is the *recall*. If all your relevant movies are on this platform, you might call that *total recall*.

Scenario 4's café experience shows that recall is sometimes the inverse probability of an avoid; because you like so many coffees, we might instead find it easier to talk about what you don't like. In this case, the number of avoids in the offering will have a large effect on the recall:

$$Recall@k = \frac{(k - Avoid@k)}{num_{relevant}}$$

This is the core mathematical definition for recall and is often one of the first measurements we'll consider because it's a pure estimate of how your retrieval is performing.

R-precision

If we also have a ranking on our recommendations, we can take the ratio of relevant recommendations to r in the *top-r* recommendations. This improves this metric in cases where r is very small, as in examples 1 and 3.

mAP, MMR, NDCG

Having delved into the reliable domains of precision@k and recall@k, we've gained valuable insights into the quality of our recommendation systems. However, these metrics, as crucial as they are, can sometimes fall short in capturing an important aspect of these systems: *the order of recommendations.*

In recommendation systems, the ordering in which we present suggestions carries significant weight and needs to be evaluated to ensure that it's effective.

That's why we'll now journey beyond precision@k and recall@k to explore some key ranking-sensitive metrics—namely, mean average precision (mAP), mean reciprocal rank (MRR), and normalized discounted cumulative gain (NDCG). These metrics consider not only whether our recommendations are relevant but also whether they are well-ordered.

The mAP metric lends importance to each relevant document and its position, and MRR concentrates on the rank of the first relevant item. NDCG gives more importance to relevant documents at higher ranks. By understanding these metrics, you'll have an even more robust set of tools to evaluate and refine your recommendation systems.

So, let's carry on with our exploration, striking a balance between precision and comprehensibility. By the end of this section, you will be well equipped to handle these essential evaluation methods in a confident and knowledgeable manner.

mAP

This vital metric in recommendation systems is particularly adept at accounting for the rank of relevant items. If, in a list of five items, the relevant ones are found at positions 2, 3, and 5, mAP would be calculated by computing precision@2, precision@3, and precision@5 and then taking an average of these values. The strength of mAP lies in its sensitivity to the ordering of relevant items, providing a higher score when these items are ranked higher.

Consider an example with two recommendation algorithms A and B:

- For algorithm A, we compute the mAP as follows:

  (precision@2 + precision@3 + precision@5) / 3 = (1/2 + 2/3 + 3/5) / 3 = 0.6

- For algorithm B, which perfectly ranks the items, we calculate mAP as follows:

mAP = (precision@1 + precision@2 + precision@3) / 3 = (1/1 + 2/2 + 3/3) / 3 = 1

The generalized formula for mAP across a set of queries Q is shown here:

$$mAP = \frac{1}{|Q|} \Sigma_{q=1}^{|Q|} \frac{1}{m_q} \Sigma_{k=1}^{n} P(k) * rel(k)$$

Here, $|Q|$ is the total number of queries, m_q is the number of relevant documents for a specific query q, $P(k)$ stands for the precision at the _k_th cutoff, and $rel(k)$ is an indicator function equating to 1 if the item at rank k is relevant, and 0 otherwise.

MRR

Another effective metric used in recommendation systems is MRR. Unlike MAP, which considers all relevant items, MRR primarily focuses on the position of the first relevant item in the recommendation list. It's computed as the reciprocal of the rank where the first relevant item appears.

Consequently, MRR can reach its maximum value of 1 if the first item in the list is relevant. If the first relevant item is found farther down the list, MRR takes a value less than 1. For instance, if the first relevant item is positioned at rank 2, the MRR would be 1/2.

Let's look at this in the context of the recommendation algorithms A and B that we used earlier:

- For algorithm A, the first relevant item is at rank 2, so the MRR equals 1/2 = 0.5.
- For algorithm B, which perfectly ranked the items, the first relevant item is at rank 1, so the MRR equals 1/1 = 1.

Extending this to multiple queries, the general formula for MRR is as follows:

$$MRR = \frac{1}{|Q|} \Sigma_{i=1}^{|Q|} \frac{1}{rank_i}$$

Here, $|Q|$ represents the total number of queries, and $rank_i$ is the position of the first relevant item in the list for the _i_th query. This metric provides valuable insight into how well a recommendation algorithm delivers a relevant recommendation right at the top of the list.

NDCG

To further refine our understanding of ranking metrics, let's step into the world of NDCG. Like mAP and MRR, NDCG also acknowledges the rank order of relevant items but introduces a twist. It discounts the relevance of items as we move down the list, signifying that items appearing earlier in the list are more valuable than those ranked lower.

NDCG begins with the concept of cumulative gain (CG), which is simply the sum of the relevance scores of the top k items in the list. Discounted cumulative gain (DCG) goes a step further, discounting the relevance of each item based on its position. NDCG, then, is the DCG value normalized by the ideal DCG (IDCG), the DCG that we would obtain if all relevant items appeared at the very top of the list.

Assuming we have five items in our list and a specific user for whom the relevant items are found at positions 2 and 3, the IDCG@k would be $(1/\log(1 + 1) + 1/\log(2 + 1)) = 1.5 + 0.63 = 2.13$.

Let's put this into the context of our example algorithms A and B.

For algorithm A
- DCG@5 = $1/\log(2 + 1) + 1/\log(3 + 1) + 1/\log(5 + 1) = 0.63 + 0.5 + 0.39 = 1.52$
- NDCG@5 = DCG@5 / IDCG@5 = 1.52 / 2.13 = 0.71

For algorithm B
- DCG@5 = $1/\log(1 + 1) + 1/\log(2 + 1) + 1/\log(3 + 1) = 1 + 0.63 + 0.5 = 2.13$
- NDCG@5 = DCG@5 / IDCG@5 = 2.13 / 2.13 = 1

The general formula for NDCG can be represented as

$$NDCG@k = \frac{DCG@k}{IDCG@k}$$

where

- $DCG@k = \Sigma_{i=1}^{k} \frac{rel_i}{log_2(i + 1)}$

- $IDCG@k = \Sigma_{i=1}^{|\mathcal{R}|} \frac{1}{log_2(i + 1)}$

and $\mathcal{R}$ is the set of relevant documents.

This metric gives us a normalized score for how well our recommendation algorithm ranks relevant items, discounting as we move further down the list.

mAP Versus NDCG?

Both mAP and NDCG are holistic metrics that offer a comprehensive perspective of ranking quality by incorporating all relevant items and their respective ranks. However, the interpretability and use cases of these metrics can vary based on the specifics of the recommendation context and the nature of relevance.

While MRR does not consider all relevant items, it does provide an interpretable insight into an algorithm's performance, highlighting the average rank of the first relevant item. This can be particularly useful when the topmost recommendations hold significant value.

mAP, on the other hand, is a rich evaluation measure that effectively represents the area under the precision-recall curve. Its average aspect confers an intuitive interpretation related to the trade-off between precision and recall across different rank cutoffs.

NDCG introduces a robust consideration of the relevance of each item and is sensitive to the rank order, employing a logarithmic discount factor to quantify the diminishing significance of items as we move down the list. This allows it to handle scenarios in which items can have varying degrees of relevance, extending beyond binary relevance often used in mAP and MRR. However, this versatility of NDCG can also limit its interpretability because of the complexity of the logarithmic discount.

Further, although NDCG is well equipped for use cases where items carry distinct relevance weights, procuring accurate ground-truth relevance scores can pose a significant challenge in practical applications. This imposes a limitation on the real-world usefulness of NDCG.

Cumulatively, these metrics form the backbone of offline evaluation methodologies for recommendation algorithms. As we advance in our exploration, we'll cover online evaluations, discuss strategies to assess and mitigate algorithmic bias, understand the importance of ensuring diversity in recommendations, and optimize recommendation systems to cater to various stakeholders in the ecosystem.

Correlation Coefficients

While correlation coefficients like Pearson's or Spearman's can be employed to evaluate the similarity between two rankings (for instance, between the predicted and the ground-truth rankings), they do not provide the exact same information as mAP, MRR, or NDCG.

Correlation coefficients are typically used to measure the degree of linear association between two continuous variables, and in the context of ranking, they can indicate the overall similarity between two ordered lists. However, they do not directly account for aspects such as the relevance of individual items, the position of relevant items, or varying degrees of relevance among items, which are integral to mAP, MRR, and NDCG.

For example, say a user has interacted with five items in the past. A recommender system might predict that the user will interact with these items again but rank them in the opposite order of importance. Even though the system has correctly identified the items of interest, the reversed ranking would lead to poor performance as measured by mAP, MRR, or NDCG, but a high negative correlation coefficient would be obtained because of the linear relationship.

As a result, while correlation coefficients can provide a high-level understanding of ranking performance, they are not sufficient substitutes for the more detailed information provided by metrics like mAP, MRR, and NDCG.

To utilize correlation coefficients in the context of ranking, it would be essential to pair them with other metrics that account for the specific nuances of the recommendation problem, such as the relevance of individual items and their positions in the ranking.

RMSE from Affinity

Root mean square error (RMSE) and ranking metrics like mAP, MRR, and NDCG offer fundamentally different perspectives when evaluating a recommendation system that outputs affinity scores.

RMSE is a popular metric for quantifying prediction error. It computes the square root of the average of squared differences between the predicted affinity scores and the true values. Lower RMSE signifies better predictive accuracy. However, RMSE treats the problem as a standard regression task and disregards the inherent ranking structure in recommendation systems.

Conversely, mAP, MRR, and NDCG are explicitly designed to evaluate the quality of rankings, which is essential in a recommendation system. In essence, while RMSE measures the closeness of predicted affinity scores to actual values, mAP, MRR, and NDCG assess the ranking quality by considering the positions of relevant items. Therefore, if your main concern is ranking items rather than predicting precise affinity scores, these ranking metrics are generally more appropriate.

Integral Forms: AUC and cAUC

When it comes to recommendation systems, we are producing a ranked list of items for each user. As you've seen, these rankings are based on affinity, the probability or level of preference that the user has for each item. Given this framework, several metrics have been developed to evaluate the quality of these ranked lists. One such metric is the AUC-ROC, which is complemented by mAP, MRR, and NDCG. Let's take a closer look at understanding these.

Recommendation Probabilities to AUC-ROC

In a binary classification setup, the area *under the receiver operating characteristic curve* (AUC-ROC) measures the ability of the recommendation model to distinguish between positive (relevant) and negative (irrelevant) instances. It is calculated by plotting the true positive rate (TPR) against the false positive rate (FPR) at various threshold settings and then computing the area under this curve.

In the context of recommendations, you can think of these "thresholds" as varying the number of top items recommended to a user. The AUC-ROC metric becomes an evaluation of how well your model ranks relevant items over irrelevant ones, irrespective of the actual rank position. In other words, AUC-ROC effectively quantifies the likelihood that a randomly chosen relevant item is ranked higher than a randomly chosen irrelevant one by the model. This, however, doesn't account for the actual position or order of items in the list, only the relative ranking of positive versus negative instances. The affinity of a calibrated item may be interpreted as a confidence measure by the model that an item is relevant, and when considering historical data, even uncalibrated affinity scores may make a great suggestion for the number of recommendations necessary to find something useful.

One serious implementation of these affinity scores might be to show users only items over a particular score and otherwise tell them to come back later or use exploration methods to improve the data. For example, if you sold hygiene products and were considering asking customers to add some Aesop soap during checkout, you may wish to evaluate the Aesop ROC and make this suggestion only when the observed affinity passed the learned threshold. You'll also see these concepts used later in "Inventory Health" on page 268.

Comparison to Other Metrics

Let's put these in context with the other metrics:

mAP

This metric expands on the idea of precision at a specific cutoff in the ranked list to provide an overall measure of model performance. It does this by averaging the precision values computed at the ranks where each relevant item is found. Unlike AUC-ROC, mAP puts emphasis on the higher-ranked items and is more sensitive to changes at the top of the ranking.

MRR

Unlike AUC-ROC and mAP, which consider all relevant items in the list, MRR focuses only on the rank of the first relevant item in the list. It is a measure of how quickly the model can find a relevant item. If the model consistently places a relevant item at the top of the list, it will have a higher MRR.

NDCG

This metric evaluates the quality of the ranking by not only considering the order of recommendations but also taking into account the graded relevance of items (which the previous metrics don't). NDCG discounts items further down the list, rewarding relevant items that appear near the top of the list.

AUC-ROC provides a valuable aggregate measure of a model's ability to differentiate between relevant and irrelevant items; mAP, MRR, and NDCG offer a more nuanced evaluation of the model's ranking quality, considering factors like position bias and varying degrees of relevance.

Note that we sometimes compute the AUC per customer and then average. That's customer AUC (cAUC), which can often provide a good expectation for a user's experience.

BPR

Bayesian personalized ranking (BPR) presents a Bayesian approach to the task of item ranking in recommendation systems, effectively providing a probability framework to model the personalized ranking process. Instead of transforming the item recommendation problem into a binary classification problem (relevant or not), BPR focuses on pairwise preferences: given two items, which does the user prefer? This approach aligns better with the nature of implicit feedback that is common in recommendation systems.

The BPR model uses a pairwise loss function that takes into account the relative order of a positive item and a negative item for a specific user. It seeks to maximize the posterior probability of the observed rankings being correct. The model is typically optimized using stochastic gradient descent or a variant thereof. It's important to note that BPR (unlike other metrics we've discussed, including AUC-ROC, mAP, MRR, and NDCG) is a model training objective rather than an evaluation metric. Therefore, while the aforementioned metrics evaluate a model's performance post-training, BPR provides a mechanism to guide the model learning process in a way that directly optimizes for the ranking task. A much deeper discussion of these topics is in "BPR: Bayesian Personalized Ranking from Implicit Feedback" (*https://oreil.ly/NwCYa*) by Steffen Rendle et al.

Summary

Now that you know how to evaluate the performance of the recommendation systems that you train, you may be wondering how to actually train them. You may have noticed that many of the metrics we introduced would not make very good loss functions; they involve a lot of simultaneous observations about sets and lists of items. This would unfortunately make the signal that the recommender would be learning from highly combinatorial. Additionally, the metrics we've presented really have two aspects to consider: the binary metric associated to recall, and the rank weighting.

In the next chapter, you're going to learn some loss functions that make excellent training objectives. The importance of these, we're sure, won't be lost on you.

## CHAPTER 12

Training for Ranking

Typical ML tasks usually predict a single outcome, such as the probability of being in a positive class for classification tasks, or an expected value for regression tasks. Ranking, on the other hand, provides a relative ordering of sets of items. This kind of task is typical of search results or recommendations, where the order of items presented is important. In these kinds of problems, the score of an item usually isn't shown to the user directly but rather is presented—maybe implicitly—with the ordinal rank of the item: the item at the top of the list is numbered lower than the next item.

This chapter presents various kinds of loss functions that ML algorithms can use during training. These scores should estimate list orderings such that when compared to one another, they result in sets that are ordered more closely to the relevance ordering observed in a training dataset. Here we will focus on introducing the concepts and computations, which you'll put to work in the next chapter.

Where Does Ranking Fit in Recommender Systems?

Before we dive into the details of loss functions for ranking, we should talk about where ranking fits into the larger scheme of recommender systems as a whole. Typical large-scale recommenders have a retrieval phase, in which a cheap function is used to gather a decent number of candidate items into a candidate set. Usually, this retrieval phase is only item based. For example, the candidate set might include items related to recently consumed or liked items by a user. Or if freshness is important, such as for news data, the set might include the newest popular and relevant items for the user. After items are gathered into a candidate set, we apply ranking to its items.

Also, since the candidate set is usually much smaller than the entire corpus of items, we can use more expensive models and auxiliary features to help the ranking.

These features could be user features or context features. User features could help in determining the items' usefulness to the user, such as the average embedding of recently consumed items. Context features could indicate details about the current session, such as time of day or recent queries that a user has typed—a feature that differentiates the current session from others and helps in determining relevant items. Finally, we have the representation of the items themselves, which can be anything from content features to learned embeddings that represent the item.

The user, context, and item features are then concatenated into one feature vector that we will use to represent the item; we then score all the candidates at once and order them. The rank ordered set might then have extra filtering applied to it for business logic, such as removing near duplicates or making the ranked set more diverse in the kinds of items displayed.

In the following examples, we will assume that the items can all be represented by a concatenated feature vector of user, context, and item features and that the model could be as simple as a linear model with a weight vector W that is dotted with the item vector to obtain a score for sorting the items. These models can be generalized to deep neural networks, but the final layer output is still going to be a scalar used to sort the items.

Now that we have set the context for ranking, let's consider ways we might rank a set of items represented by vectors.

Learning to Rank

Learning to rank (LTR) is the name for the kind of models that score an ordered list of items according to their relevancy or importance. This technique is how we go from the potentially raw output of retrieval to a sorted list of items based on their relevance.

LTR problems have three main types:

Pointwise
> The model treats individual documents in isolation and assigns them a score or rank. The task becomes a regression or classification problem.

Pairwise
> The model considers pairs of documents simultaneously in the loss function. The goal is to minimize the number of incorrectly ordered pairs.

Listwise
> The model considers the entire list of documents in the loss function. The goal is to find the optimal ordering of the entire list.

Training an LTR Model

The training data for an LTR model typically consists of a list of items, and each item has a set of features and a label (or ground truth). The features might include information about the item itself, and the label typically represents its relevance or importance. For instance, in our recommender systems, we have item features, and in the training dataset, the labels will show if the item is relevant to the user. Additionally, LTR models sometimes make use of the query or user features.

The training process is about learning a ranking function by using these features and labels. These ranking functions are then applied to the retrieved items before serving.

Let's see some examples of how these models are trained.

Classification for Ranking

One way to pose the ranking problem is as a multilabel task. Every item appearing in the training set that is associated to the user is a positive example, while those outside would be negative. This is, in effect, a multilabel approach at the scale of the set of items. The network could have an architecture with each item's features as input nodes, and then some user features as well. The output nodes would be in correspondence with the items you wish to label.

With a linear model, if X is the item vector and Y is the output, we learn W, where $sigmoid(WX) = 1$ if X is an item in the positive set; otherwise, $sigmoid(WX) = 0$. This corresponds to the binary cross-entropy loss (*https://oreil.ly/5Rd14*) in Optax.

Unfortunately, the relative ordering of items isn't taken into account in this setup, so this loss function consisting of sigmoid activation functions for each item won't optimize ranking metrics very well. Effectively, this ranking is merely a downstream *relevance model* that only helps to filter those options retrieved in a previous step.

Another problem with this approach is that we have labeled everything outside of the training set to be negative, but the user might never have seen a new item that could be relevant to a query—so it would be incorrect to label this new item as a negative when it is simply unobserved.

You may have realized that the ranking needs to consider the relative positions in the list. Let's consider this next.

Regression for Ranking

The most naive way to rank a set of items is simply to regress to the rank of a similar number like NDCG or our other personalization metrics that are rank respective.

In practice, this is achieved by conditioning the set of items against a query. For example, we could pose the problem as regression to the NDCG, given the query as the context of the ranking. Furthermore, we can supply the query as an embedding context vector to a feed-forward network that is concatenated with the features of the items in the set and regress toward the NDCG value.

The query is needed as a context because a set of item's ordering might be dependent upon the query. Consider, for example, typing into a search bar the query **flowers**. We would then expect a set of items most representative of flowers to be in the top results. This demonstrates that the query is an important consideration of the scoring function.

With a linear model, if X is the item vector and Y is the output, then we learn W, where $WX(i) = NDCG(i)$ and $NDCG(i)$ is the NDCG for item i. Regression can be learned using the L2 loss (*https://oreil.ly/IHw-Z*) in Optax.

Ultimately, this approach is about attempting to learn the underlying features of items that lead to higher-rank scores in your personalization metric. Unfortunately, this also fails to explicitly consider the relative ordering of items. This is a pretty serious limitation, which we'll consider shortly.

Another consideration: what do we do for items that aren't ranked outside of the top-k training items? The rank we would assign them would be essentially random, as we do not know what number to assign them. Therefore, this method needs improvement, which we'll explore in the next section.

Classification and Regression for Ranking

Suppose we have a web page such as an online bookstore, and users have to browse through and click items in order to purchase them. For such a funnel, we could break the ranking into two parts. The first model could predict the probability of a click on an item, given a set of items on display. The second model could be conditioned on a click-through and could be a regression model estimating the purchase price of the item.

Then, a full ranking model could be the product of two models. The first one computes the probability of clicking through an item, given a set of competing items. And the second one computes the expected value of a purchase, given that it had been clicked. Notice that the first and second model could have different features, depending on the stage of the funnel a user is in. The first model has access to features of competing items, while the second model might take into account shipping costs and discounts applied that might change the value of an item. Thus, in this setting, it would be advantageous to model both stages of the funnel with different models so as to make use of the most amount of information present at each stage of the funnel.

WARP

One possible way to generate a ranking loss stochastically is introduced in "WSABIE: Scaling Up to Large Vocabulary Image Annotation" (*https://oreil.ly/bagf-*) by Jason Weston et al. The loss is called *weighted approximate rank pairwise* (WARP). In this scheme, the loss function is broken into what looks like a pairwise loss. More precisely, if a higher-ranked item doesn't have a score that is greater than the margin (which is arbitrarily picked to be 1) for a lower-rank item, we apply the *hinge loss* to the pair of items. This looks like the following:

$$max(0, 1 - score(pos) + score(neg))$$

With a linear model, if X_pos is the positive item vector, and X_neg is the negative item vector, then we learn W, where $WX_pos - WX_neg > 1$. The loss for this is hinge loss (*https://oreil.ly/88zk3*), where the predictor output is $WX_pos - WX_neg$ and the target is 1.

However, to compensate for the fact that an unobserved item might not be a true negative, just something unobserved, we count the number of times we had to sample from the negative set to find something that violates the ordering of the chosen pair. That is, we count the number of times we had to look for something where:

$$score(neg) > score(pos) - 1$$

We then construct a monotonically decreasing function of the number of times we sample the universe of items (less the positives) for a violating negative and look up the weight for this number and multiply the loss with it. If it's very hard to find a violating negative, the gradient should therefore be lower because either we are close to a good solution already or the item was never seen before, so we should not be so confident as to assign it a low score just because it was never shown to the user as a result for a query.

Note that WARP loss was developed when CPUs were the dominant form of computation to train ML models. As such, an approximation to ranking was used to obtain the rank of a negative item. The *approximate rank* is defined as the number of samples with replacement in the universe of items (less the positive example) before we find a negative item whose score is larger than the positive by an arbitrary constant, called a *margin*, of 1.0.

To construct the WARP weight for the pairwise loss, we need a function to go from the approximate rank of the negative item to the WARP weight. A relatively simple bit of code to compute this is as follows:

```
import numpy as np

def get_warp_weights(n: int) -> np.ndarray:
    """Returns N weights to convert a rank to a loss weight."""

    # The alphas are defined as values that are monotonically decreasing.
    # We take the reciprocal of the natural numbers for the alphas.
    rank = np.arange(1.0, n + 1, 1)
    alpha = 1.0 / rank
    weights = alpha

    # This is the L in the paper, defined as the sum of all previous alphas.
    for i in range(1, n):
        weights[i] = weights[i] + weights[i -1]

    # Divide by the rank.
    weights = weights / rank
    return weights

print(get_warp_weights(5))
[1.         0.75       0.61111111 0.52083333 0.45666667]
```

As you can see, if we find a negative immediately, the WARP weight is 1.0, but if it is very difficult to find a negative that violates the margin, the WARP weight will be small.

This loss function is approximately optimizing precision@k, and thus a good step toward improving rank estimates in the retrieved set. Even better, WARP is computationally efficient via sampling and thus more memory efficient.

k-order Statistic

Is there a way to improve upon the WARP loss and straight-up pairwise hinge loss? Turns out there are a whole spectrum of ways. In "Learning to Rank Recommendations with the k-order Statistic Loss" (*https://oreil.ly/afphG*), Jason Weston et al. (including one of this book's coauthors) show how this can be done by exploring the variants of losses between hinge loss and WARP loss. The authors of the paper conducted experiments on various corpora and show how the trade-off between optimizing for a single pairwise versus selecting a harder negative like WARP affects metrics including mean rank and precision and recall at k.

The key generalization is that instead of a single positive item considered during the gradient step, the model uses all of them.

Recall again that picking a random positive and a random negative pair optimizes for the ROC, or AUC. This isn't great for ranking because it doesn't optimize for the top of the list. WARP loss, on the other hand, optimizes for the top of the ranking list for a single positive item but does not specify how to pick the positive item.

Several alternate strategies can be used for ordering the top of the list, including optimizing for mean maximum rank, which tries to group the positive items such that the lowest-scoring positive item is as near the top of the list as possible. To allow this ordering, we provide a probability distribution function over how we pick the positive sample. If the probability is skewed toward the top of the positive item list, we get a loss more like WARP loss. If the probability is uniform, we get AUC loss. If the probability is skewed toward the end of the positive item list, we then optimize for the worst case, like mean maximum rank. The NumPy function np.random.choice provides a mechanism from sampling from a distribution P.

We have one more optimization to consider: K, the number of positive samples to use to construct the positive set. If $K = 1$, we pick only a positive random item from the positive set; otherwise, we construct the positive set, order the samples by score, and sample from the positive list of size K by using the probability distribution P. This optimization made sense in the era of CPUs when compute was expensive but might not make that much sense these days in the era of GPUs and TPUs, which we will talk about in the following warning.

Stochastic Losses and GPUs

A word of caution about the preceding stochastic losses. They were developed for an earlier era of CPUs when it was cheap and easy to sample and exit if a negative sample was found. These days, with modern GPUs, making branching decisions like this is harder because all the threads on the GPU core have to run the same code over different data in parallel. That usually means both sides of a branch are taken in a batch, so less computational savings occur from these early exits. Consequently, branching code that approximates stochastic losses like WARP and k-order statistic loss appear less efficient.

What are we to do? We will show in Chapter 13 how to approximate these losses in code. Long story short, because of the way vector processors like GPUs tend to work by processing lots of data in parallel uniformly, we have to find a GPU-friendly way to compute these losses. In the next chapter, we approximate the negative sampling by generating a large batch of negatives and either scoring them all lower than the negative or looking for the most egregious violating negative or both together as a blend of loss functions.

BM25

While much of this book is targeted at recommending items to users, search ranking is a close sister study. In the space of information retrieval, or search ranking for documents, *best matching 25* (BM25) is an essential tool.

BM25 is an algorithm used in information-retrieval systems to rank documents based on their relevance to a given query. This relevance is determined by considering factors like TF-IDF. It's a bag-of-words retrieval function that ranks a set of documents based on the query terms appearing in each document. It's also a part of the probabilistic relevance framework and is derived from the probabilistic retrieval model.

The BM25 ranking function calculates a score for each document based on the query. The document with the highest score is considered the most relevant to the query.

Here is a simplified version of the BM25 formula:

$$\text{score}(D, Q) = \sum_{i=1}^{n} \text{IDF}(q_i) * \frac{f(q_i, D) * (k1 + 1)}{f(q_i, D) + k1 * \left(1 - b + b * \frac{|D|}{\text{avgdl}}\right)}$$

The elements of this formula are as follows:

- D represents a document.
- Q is the query that consists of words $\{q_1, q_2, \ldots, q_n\}$.
- $f(qi, D)$ is the frequency of query term q_i in document D.
- $|D|$ is the length of (the number of words in) the document D.
- avg_{dl} is the average document length in the collection.
- k_1 and b are hyperparameters. k_1 is a positive tuning parameter that calibrates the document term frequency scaling. b is a parameter that determines the scaling by document length: $b = 1$ corresponds to fully scaling the term weight by the document length, while $b = 0$ corresponds to no length normalization.
- $IDF(q_i)$ is the inverse document frequency of query term q_i, which measures the amount of information the word provides (whether it's common or rare across all documents). BM25 applies a variant of IDF that can be computed as follows:

$$\text{IDF}(q_i) = \log\left(\frac{N - n(q_i) + 0.5}{n(q_i) + 0.5}\right)$$

Here, N is the total number of documents in the collection, and $n(q_i)$ is the number of documents containing q_i.

Simply, BM25 combines both term frequency (how often a term appears in a document) and inverse document frequency (how much unique information a term provides) to calculate the relevance score. It also introduces the concept of document length normalization, penalizing too-long documents and preventing them from dominating shorter ones, which is a common issue in simple TF-IDF models. The free parameters k_1 and b allow the model to be tuned based on the specific characteristics of the document set.

In practice, BM25 provides a robust baseline for most information-retrieval tasks, including ad hoc keyword search and document similarity. BM25 is used in many open source search engines, such as Lucene and Elasticsearch, and is the de facto standard for what is often called *full-text search*.

So how might we integrate BM25 into the problems we discuss in this book? The output from BM25 is a list of documents ranked by relevance to the given query, and then LTR comes into play. You can use the BM25 score as one of the features in an LTR model, along with other features that you believe might influence the relevance of a document to a query.

The general steps to combine BM25 with LTR for ranking are as follows:

1. *Retrieve a list of candidate documents.* Given a query, use BM25 to retrieve a list of candidate documents.

2. *Compute features for each document.* Compute the BM25 score as one of the features, along with other potential features. This could include various document-specific features, query-document match features, user interaction features, etc.

3. *Train/evaluate the LTR model.* Use these feature vectors and their corresponding labels (relevance judgments) to train your LTR model. Or, if you already have a trained model, use it to evaluate and rank the retrieved documents.

4. *Rank.* The LTR model generates a score for each document. Rank the documents based on these scores.

This combination of retrieval (with BM25) and ranking (with LTR) allows you to first narrow the potential candidate documents from a possibly very large collection (where BM25 shines) and then fine-tune the ranking of these candidates with a model that can consider more complex features and interactions (where LTR shines).

It is worth mentioning that the BM25 score can provide a strong baseline in text document retrieval, and depending on the complexity of the problem and the amount of training data you have, LTR may or may not provide significant improvements.

Multimodal Retrieval

Let's take another look at this retrieval method, as we can find some powerful leverage. Think back to Chapter 8: we built a co-occurrence model, which illustrated how articles referenced jointly in other articles share meaning and mutual relevance. But how would you integrate search into this?

You may think, "Oh, I can search the names of the articles." But that doesn't quite utilize our co-occurrence model; it underleverages that joint meaning we discovered. A classic approach may be to use something like BM25 on article titles or articles. More modern approaches may do a vector embedding of the query and article titles (using something like BERT or other transformer models). However, neither of these really capture both sides of what we're looking for.

Consider instead the following approach:

1. Search with the initial query via BM25 to get an initial set of "anchors."
2. Search with each anchor as a query via your latent model(s).
3. Train an LTR model to aggregate and rank the union of the searches.

Now we're using a true multimodal retrieval, leveraging multiple latent spaces! One additional highlight in this approach is that queries are often out of distribution from documents with respect to encoder-based latent spaces. This means that when you type `Who's the leader of Mozambique?`, this question looks fairly dissimilar to the article title (Mozambique) or the relevant sentence as of summer 2023 ("The new government under President Samora Machel established a one-party state based on Marxist principles.")

When the embeddings are not text at all, this method becomes even more powerful: consider typing text to search for an item of clothing and hoping to see an entire outfit that goes with it.

Summary

Getting things in the right order is an important aspect of recommendation systems. By now, you know that ordering is not the whole story, but it's an essential step in the pipeline. We've collected our items and put them in the right order, and all that's left to do is send them off to the user.

We started with the most fundamental concept, learning to rank, and compared it with some traditional methods. We then got a big upgrade with WARP and WSABIE. That led us to the k-order statistic, which involves utilizing more careful probabilistic sampling. We finally wrapped up with BM25 as a powerful baseline in text settings.

Before we conquer serving, let's put these pieces together. In the next chapter, we're going to turn up the volume and build some playlists. This will be the most intensive chapter yet, so go grab a beverage and a stretch. We've got some work to do.

## CHAPTER 13

Putting It All Together: Experimenting and Ranking

In the last few chapters, we have covered many aspects of ranking, including various kinds of loss functions as well as metrics for measuring the performance of ranking systems. In this chapter, we will show an example of a ranking loss and ranking metric on the Spotify Million Playlist dataset (*https://oreil.ly/j3nvH*).

This chapter encourages a lot more experimentation and is more open-ended than the previous ones, whose goal was to introduce concepts and infrastructure. This chapter, on the other hand, is written to encourage you to roll up your sleeves and engage directly with loss functions and writing metrics.

Experimentation Tips

Before we begin digging into the data and modeling, let's cover some practices that will make your life easier when doing a lot of experimentation and rapid iteration. These are general guidelines that have made our experimentation faster. As a result, we're able to rapidly iterate toward solutions that help us reach our objectives.

Experimental code is different from engineering code in that the code is written to explore ideas, not for robustness. The goal is to achieve maximum velocity while not sacrificing too much in terms of code quality. So you should think about whether a piece of code should be thoroughly tested or whether this isn't necessary because the code is present only to test a hypothesis and then it will be thrown away. With that in mind, here are some tips. Keep in mind that these tips are the opinion of the authors, developed over time, and are not hard-and-fast rules, just some flavored opinions that some may disagree with.

Keep It Simple

In terms of the overall structure of research code, it's best to keep it as simple as possible. Try not to overthink too much in terms of inheritance and reusability during the early stages of the lifecycle of exploration. At the start of a project, we usually don't know what it needs yet, so the preference should be keeping the code easily readable and simple for debugging. That means you don't have to focus too much on code reuse because at the early stage of a project, many code changes will occur while the structure of the model, data ingestion, and interaction of various parts of a system are being worked out. When the uncertainties have been worked out, then you can rewrite the code into a more robust form, but refactoring too early actually slows velocity.

A general rule of thumb is that it is OK to copy code three times and then refactor out into a library the fourth time, because you'll have seen enough use cases to justify the reuse of code. If refactoring is done too early, you might not have seen enough use cases of a piece of code to cover the possible use cases that it might need to handle.

Debug Print Statements

If you've read a number of ML research papers, you may expect your data to be fairly clean and orderly at the start of a project. However, real-world data can be messy, with missing fields and unexpected values. Having lots of print functions allows you to print and visually inspect a sample of the data and also helps in crafting the input data pipelines and transformations to feed the model. Also, printing sample outputs of the model is useful in making sure the output is as expected.

The most important places to include logging are the input and output schema between components of your system; these help you understand where reality may be deviating from expectations. Later, you can make unit tests to ensure that refactoring of the model doesn't break anything, but the unit tests can wait for when the model architecture is stable. A good rule of thumb is to add unit tests when you want to refactor code or reuse or optimize the code to preserve functionality or when the code is stable and you want to ensure that it doesn't break a build. Another good use case of adding print statements is when you inevitably run into not-a-number (NaN) errors when running training code.

In JAX, you can enable NaN debugging by using the following lines:

```
from jax import config
config.update("jax_debug_nans", True)

@jax.jit
def f(x):
    jax.debug.print("Debugging {x}", x=x)
```

The debug NaNs configuration setting will rerun a jitted function if it finds any NaNs, and the debug print function will print the value of the tensors even inside a JIT. A regular print won't work inside a JIT because it is not a compilable command and is skipped over during the tracing, so you have to use the debug print function instead, which does work inside a JIT.

Defer Optimization

In research code, there is a lot of temptation to optimize early—in particular, focusing on the implementation of your models or system to ensure they're efficient computationally or the code is elegant. However, research code is written for higher velocity in experimentation, not execution speed.

Our suggestion is do not optimize too early unless it hinders research velocity. One reason for this is the system might not be complete, so optimizing one part might not make sense if another part of the system is even slower and is the actual bottleneck. Another reason is the part that you are optimizing might not make it to the final model, so all the optimization work might go to waste if the code is refactored away anyway.

Finally, optimization might actually hinder the ability to modify or inject newer design choices in terms of architecture or functionality. Optimized code tends to have certain choices that were made that fit the current structure of the data flow but might not be amenable to further changes. For example, in the code for this chapter, one possible optimization choice would have been to batch together playlists of the same size so that the code might be able to run in larger batches. However, at this point of the experimentation, that optimization would have been premature and distracting because it might make the metrics code more complicated. Our gentle advice is to defer optimization until after the bulk of experimentation has been done and the architecture, loss functions, and metrics have been chosen and settled upon.

Keep Track of Changes

In research code, too many variables are probably at play for you to change them one at a time to see their effects. This problem is particularly noticeable with larger datasets that require a lot of runs to determine which change causes which effects. So, in general, fixing a number of parameters and changing the code bit by bit is still a good idea so that you can keep track of the change that causes the most improvement. Parameters have to be tracked, but so do the code changes.

One way to keep track of changes is through services such as Weights & Biases that we discussed in Chapter 5. Keeping track of the exact code that led to a change and the parameters is a good idea so that experiments can be reproduced and analyzed. Especially with research code that changes so frequently and is sometimes not checked in, you have to be diligent in keeping a copy of the code that produced a run somewhere, and MLOps tools allow you to track code and hyperparameters.

Use Feature Engineering

Unlike in academic papers, most applied research is interested in a good outcome rather than a theoretically beautiful result. We're not shackled by purist views that the model has to learn everything about the data by itself. Instead, we're pragmatic and concerned about good outcomes.

We should not discard practices like feature engineering, especially when we have little data or are crunched for time and need decent results fast. Using feature engineering means that if you know whether a handcrafted feature is correlated positively or negatively with an outcome like the ranking of an item, then by all means add these engineered features to the data. An example in recommender systems is having an attribute of the item being scored that matches something in the user's profile. So, if an item has the same artist or album in the user's playlist, we can return a Boolean True; otherwise, we return False. This extra feature simply helps the model converge faster, and the model can still use other latent features such as embeddings to compensate if the hand-engineered features don't do so well.

It is generally a good practice to ablate the hand-engineered features once in a while. To do this, hold back an experiment without some features to see if those features have become obsolete over time or if they still benefit the business metrics.

Ablation

Ablation in ML applications is the practice of measuring the change in performance of a model when a particular feature is removed. In computer vision applications, ablation often refers to blocking part of the image or view field to see how it impacts the model's ability to identify or segment data. In other kinds of ML, it can mean strategically removing certain features.

One gotcha with ablation is what to replace the feature with. Simply *zeroing out* the feature can significantly skew the output of the model. This is called *zero-ablation*, and can force the model to treat that feature out of distribution, which yields less believable outcomes. Instead, some advocate for mean-ablation, or taking the average or most common value of that feature. This allows the model to see much more expected values, and reduce these risks.

However, this fails to consider the most important aspects of the kinds of models we've been working on—latent high-order interactions. One of the authors has investigated a deeper approach to ablation called *causal scrubbing*, in which you fix the ablation value to be sampled from the posterior distribution produced by other feature values, i.e., a value that "makes sense" with the rest of the values the model will see at that time.

Understand Metrics Versus Business Metrics

Sometimes, as ML practitioners, we obsess over the best possible metrics our models can achieve. However, we should temper that enthusiasm as the best ML metric might not totally represent the business interests at hand. Furthermore, other systems that contain business logic might sit on top of our models and modify the output. As a result, it is best not to obsess too heavily over ML metrics and to do proper A/B tests that contain business metrics instead since that's the main measure of a good outcome with ML.

The best possible circumstance is to find a loss function that aligns well or predicts the relevant business metric. This, unfortunately, is often not easy to find, especially when the business metrics are nuanced or have competing priorities.

Perform Rapid Iteration

Don't be afraid to look at results of runs that are rather short. There's no need to do a full pass over the data at the beginning, when you are figuring out the interaction between a model architecture and the data. It's OK to do some rapid runs with minor tweaks to see how they change the metrics over a short number of time steps. In the Spotify Million Playlist dataset, we tweaked the model architecture by using 100,000 playlists before doing longer runs. Sometimes the changes can be so dramatic that the effects can be seen immediately, even at the first test-set evaluation.

Now that we have the basics of experimental research coding covered, let's hop over to the data and code and play a bit with modeling music recommendations.

Spotify Million Playlist Dataset

The code for this section can be found in this book's GitHub repo (*https://git hub.com/BBischof/ESRecsys/tree/main/spotify*). The documentation for the data can be found at Spotify Million Playlist Dataset Challenge (*https://oreil.ly/eVA7f*).

The first thing we should do is take a look at the data:

```
less data/spotify_million_playlist_dataset/data/mpd.slice.0-999.json
```

That should produce the following output:

```
{
    "info": {
        "generated_on": "2017-12-03 08:41:42.057563",
        "slice": "0-999",
        "version": "v1"
    },
    "playlists": [
        {
            "name": "Throwbacks",
            "collaborative": "false",
            "pid": 0,
            "modified_at": 1493424000,
            "num_tracks": 52,
            "num_albums": 47,
            "num_followers": 1,
            "tracks": [
                {
                    "pos": 0,
                    "artist_name": "Missy Elliott",
                    "track_uri": "spotify:track:0UaMYEvWZi0ZqiDOoHU3YI",
                    "artist_uri": "spotify:artist:2wIVse2owClT7go1WT98tk",
                    "track_name": "Lose Control (feat. Ciara & Fat Man Scoop)",
                    "album_uri": "spotify:album:6vV5UrXcfyQD1wu4Qo2I9K",
                    "duration_ms": 226863,
                    "album_name": "The Cookbook"
                },
            }
    }
```

When encountering a new dataset, it is always important to look at it and plan which features to use to generate recommendations for the data. One possible goal of the Spotify Million Playlist Dataset Challenge is to see if the next tracks in a playlist can be predicted from the first five tracks in the playlist.

In this case, several features might be useful for the task. We have track, artist, and album universal resource identifiers (URIs), which are unique identifiers for tracks, artists, and albums, respectively. And we have artist and album names and names of playlists. The dataset also includes numerical features like duration of a track and the number of followers in a playlist. Intuitively, the number of followers of a playlist should not affect the ordering of tracks in a playlist, so you might want to look for better features before using these possibly uninformative ones. Looking at the overall statistics of features, you can also obtain a lot of insight:

```
less data/spotify_million_playlist_dataset/stats.txt
number of playlists 1000000
number of tracks 66346428
number of unique tracks 2262292
number of unique albums 734684
number of unique artists 295860
number of unique titles 92944
number of playlists with descriptions 18760
number of unique normalized titles 17381
avg playlist length 66.346428

top playlist titles
  10000 country
  10000 chill
   8493 rap
   8481 workout
   8146 oldies
   8015 christmas
   6848 rock
   6157 party
   5883 throwback
   5063 jams
   5052 worship
   4907 summer
   4677 feels
   4612 new
   4186 disney
   4124 lit
   4030 throwbacks
```

First of all, notice that the number of tracks is more than the number of playlists. This implies that quite a few tracks might have very little training data. So the track_uri might not be a feature that generalizes very well. On the other hand, the album_uri and artist_uri would generalize because they would occur multiple times in different playlists. For the sake of code clarity, we will mostly work with the album_uri and artist_uri as the features that represent a track.

In previous "Putting It All Together" chapters, we demonstrated the use of content-based features or text token-based features that may be used instead, but direct embedding features are the clearest for demonstrating ranking. In a real-world application, embedding features and content-based features may be concatenated together to form a feature that generalizes better for recommendation ranking. For the purposes of this chapter, we will represent a track as the tuple of (track_id, album_id, artist_id), where the ID is an integer representing the URI. We will build dictionaries that map from the URI to the integer ID in the next section.

Building URI Dictionaries

Similar to Chapter 8, we will first start by constructing a dictionary for all the URIs. This dictionary allows us to represent the text URI as an integer for faster processing on the JAX side, as we can easily look up embeddings from integers as opposed to arbitrary URI strings.

Here is the code for *make_dictionary.py*:

```python
import glob
import json
import os
from typing import Any, Dict, Tuple

from absl import app
from absl import flags
from absl import logging
import numpy as np
import tensorflow as tf

FLAGS = flags.FLAGS
_PLAYLISTS = flags.DEFINE_string("playlists", None, "Playlist json glob.")
_OUTPUT_PATH = flags.DEFINE_string("output", "data", "Output path.")

# Required flag.
flags.mark_flag_as_required("playlists")

def update_dict(dict: Dict[Any, int], item: Any):
    """Adds an item to a dictionary."""
    if item not in dict:
        index = len(dict)
        dict[item] = index

def dump_dict(dict: Dict[str, str], name: str):
    """Dumps a dictionary as json."""
    fname = os.path.join(_OUTPUT_PATH.value, name)
    with open(fname, "w") as f:
        json.dump(dict, f)

def main(argv):
    """Main function."""
    del argv  # Unused.

    tf.config.set_visible_devices([], 'GPU')
```

```
tf.compat.v1.enable_eager_execution()
playlist_files = glob.glob(_PLAYLISTS.value)
track_uri_dict = {}
artist_uri_dict = {}
album_uri_dict = {}

for playlist_file in playlist_files:
    print("Processing ", playlist_file)
    with open(playlist_file, "r") as file:
        data = json.load(file)
        playlists = data["playlists"]
        for playlist in playlists:
            tracks = playlist["tracks"]
            for track in tracks:
              update_dict(track_uri_dict, track["track_uri"])
              update_dict(artist_uri_dict, track["artist_uri"])
              update_dict(album_uri_dict, track["album_uri"])

    dump_dict(track_uri_dict, "track_uri_dict.json")
    dump_dict(artist_uri_dict, "artist_uri_dict.json")
    dump_dict(album_uri_dict, "album_uri_dict.json")

if __name__ == "__main__":
    app.run(main)
```

Whenever a new URI is encountered, we simply increment a counter and assign that unique identifier to the URI. We do this for tracks, artists, and albums and save it as a JSON file.

Although we could have used a data processing framework like PySpark for this, it is important to take note of the data size. If the data size is small, like a million playlists, it would just be faster to do it on a single machine. We should be wise about when to use a big data processing framework, and for small datasets it can sometimes be faster to simply run the code on one machine instead of writing code that runs on a cluster.

Building the Training Data

Now that we have the dictionaries, we can use them to convert the raw JSON playlist logs into a more usable form for ML training. The code for this is in *make_training.py*:

```
import glob
import json
import os
from typing import Any, Dict, Tuple

from absl import app
from absl import flags
from absl import logging
import numpy as np
import tensorflow as tf
```

```python
import input_pipeline

FLAGS = flags.FLAGS
_PLAYLISTS = flags.DEFINE_string("playlists", None, "Playlist json glob.")
_DICTIONARY_PATH = flags.DEFINE_string("dictionaries", "data/dictionaries",
                    "Dictionary path.")
_OUTPUT_PATH = flags.DEFINE_string("output", "data/training", "Output path.")
_TOP_K = flags.DEFINE_integer("topk", 5, "Top K tracks to use as context.")
_MIN_NEXT = flags.DEFINE_integer("min_next", 10, "Min number of tracks.")

# Required flag.
flags.mark_flag_as_required("playlists")

def main(argv):
    """Main function."""
    del argv  # Unused.

    tf.config.set_visible_devices([], 'GPU')
    tf.compat.v1.enable_eager_execution()
    playlist_files = glob.glob(_PLAYLISTS.value)

    track_uri_dict = input_pipeline.load_dict(
      _DICTIONARY_PATH.value, "track_uri_dict.json")

    print("%d tracks loaded" % len(track_uri_dict))
    artist_uri_dict = input_pipeline.load_dict(
      _DICTIONARY_PATH.value, "artist_uri_dict.json")
    print("%d artists loaded" % len(artist_uri_dict))
    album_uri_dict = input_pipeline.load_dict(
      _DICTIONARY_PATH.value, "album_uri_dict.json")
    print("%d albums loaded" % len(album_uri_dict))
    topk = _TOP_K.value
    min_next = _MIN_NEXT.value
    print("Filtering out playlists with less than %d tracks" % min_next)

    raw_tracks = {}

    for pidx, playlist_file in enumerate(playlist_files):
        print("Processing ", playlist_file)
        with open(playlist_file, "r") as file:
            data = json.load(file)
            playlists = data["playlists"]
            tfrecord_name = os.path.join(
              _OUTPUT_PATH.value, "%05d.tfrecord" % pidx)
            with tf.io.TFRecordWriter(tfrecord_name) as file_writer:
              for playlist in playlists:
                  if playlist["num_tracks"] < min_next:
                      continue
                  tracks = playlist["tracks"]
                  # The first topk tracks are all for the context.
                  track_context = []
```

```
            artist_context = []
            album_context = []
            # The rest are for predicting.
            next_track = []
            next_artist = []
            next_album = []
            for tidx, track in enumerate(tracks):
                track_uri_idx = track_uri_dict[track["track_uri"]]
                artist_uri_idx = artist_uri_dict[track["artist_uri"]]
                album_uri_idx = album_uri_dict[track["album_uri"]]
                if track_uri_idx not in raw_tracks:
                    raw_tracks[track_uri_idx] = track
                if tidx < topk:
                    track_context.append(track_uri_idx)
                    artist_context.append(artist_uri_idx)
                    album_context.append(album_uri_idx)
                else:
                    next_track.append(track_uri_idx)
                    next_artist.append(artist_uri_idx)
                    next_album.append(album_uri_idx)
            assert(len(next_track) > 0)
            assert(len(next_artist) > 0)
            assert(len(next_album) > 0)
            record = tf.train.Example(
              features=tf.train.Features(feature={
                "track_context": tf.train.Feature(
                int64_list=tf.train.Int64List(value=track_context)),
                "album_context": tf.train.Feature(
                int64_list=tf.train.Int64List(value=album_context)),
                "artist_context": tf.train.Feature(
                int64_list=tf.train.Int64List(value=artist_context)),
                "next_track": tf.train.Feature(
                int64_list=tf.train.Int64List(value=next_track)),
                "next_album": tf.train.Feature(
                int64_list=tf.train.Int64List(value=next_album)),
                "next_artist": tf.train.Feature(
                int64_list=tf.train.Int64List(value=next_artist)),
              }))
            record_bytes = record.SerializeToString()
            file_writer.write(record_bytes)

    filename = os.path.join(_OUTPUT_PATH.value, "all_tracks.json")
    with open(filename, "w") as f:
        json.dump(raw_tracks, f)

if __name__ == "__main__":
    app.run(main)
```

This code reads in a raw playlist JSON file, converts the URIs from textual identifiers to the index in the dictionary, and filters out playlists that are under a minimum size. In addition, we partition the playlist such that the first five elements are grouped into the context, or user that we are recommending items for, and the next items, which are the items we wish to predict for a given user. We call the first five elements the *context* because they represent a playlist and because there won't be a one-to-one mapping between a playlist and a user if a user has more than one playlist. We then write each playlist as a TensorFlow example in a TensorFlow record file for use with the TensorFlow data input pipeline. The records will always contain five tracks, albums, and artists for the context and at least five more next tracks for learning the inference tasks of predicting the next tracks.

 We use TensorFlow objects here because of their compatibility with JAX and to introduce some very convenient data formats.

We also store unique rows of tracks with all the features, which is mostly for debugging and display should we need to convert a track_uri into a human-readable form. This track data is stored in *all_tracks.json*.

Reading the Input

The input is then read via *input_pipeline.py*:

```python
import glob
import json
import os
from typing import Sequence, Tuple, Set

import tensorflow as tf
import jax.numpy as jnp

_schema = {
    "track_context": tf.io.FixedLenFeature([5], dtype=tf.int64),
    "album_context": tf.io.FixedLenFeature([5], dtype=tf.int64),
    "artist_context": tf.io.FixedLenFeature([5], dtype=tf.int64),
    "next_track": tf.io.VarLenFeature(dtype=tf.int64),
    "next_album": tf.io.VarLenFeature(dtype=tf.int64),
    "next_artist": tf.io.VarLenFeature(dtype=tf.int64),
}

def _decode_fn(record_bytes):
  result = tf.io.parse_single_example(record_bytes, _schema)
  for key in _schema.keys():
    if key.startswith("next"):
      result[key] = tf.sparse.to_dense(result[key])
  return result

def create_dataset(
    pattern: str):
    """Creates a spotify dataset.
```

```
    Args:
        pattern: glob pattern of tfrecords.
    """
    filenames = glob.glob(pattern)
    ds = tf.data.TFRecordDataset(filenames)
    ds = ds.map(_decode_fn)
    return ds
```

We use the TensorFlow data's functionality to read and decode the TensorFlow records and examples. For that to work, we need to supply a schema, or a dictionary, telling the decoder the names and types of features to expect. Since we have picked five tracks each for the context, we should expect five each of `track_context`, `album_context`, and `artist_context`. However, since the playlists themselves are of variable lengths, we tell the decoder to expect variable-length integers for the `next_track`, `next_album`, and `next_artist` features.

The second part of *input_pipeline.py* is for reusable input code to load the dictionaries and track metadata:

```
def load_dict(dictionary_path: str, name: str):
    """Loads a dictionary."""
    filename = os.path.join(dictionary_path, name)
    with open(filename, "r") as f:
        return json.load(f)

def load_all_tracks(all_tracks_file: str,
                    track_uri_dict, album_uri_dict, artist_uri_dict):
    """Loads all tracks.

    """
    with open(all_tracks_file, "r") as f:
        all_tracks_json = json.load(f)
    all_tracks_dict = {
        int(k): v for k, v in all_tracks_json.items()
    }
    all_tracks_features = {
        k: (track_uri_dict[v["track_uri"]],
            album_uri_dict[v["album_uri"]],
            artist_uri_dict[v["artist_uri"]])
        for k,v in all_tracks_dict.items()
    }
    return all_tracks_dict, all_tracks_features

def make_all_tracks_numpy(all_tracks_features):
    """Makes the entire corpus available for scoring."""
    all_tracks = []
    all_albums = []
    all_artists = []
    items = sorted(all_tracks_features.items())
    for row in items:
```

```
    k, v = row
    all_tracks.append(v[0])
    all_albums.append(v[1])
    all_artists.append(v[2])
all_tracks = jnp.array(all_tracks, dtype=jnp.int32)
all_albums = jnp.array(all_albums, dtype=jnp.int32)
all_artists = jnp.array(all_artists, dtype=jnp.int32)
return all_tracks, all_albums, all_artists
```

We also supply a utility function to convert the *all_tracks.json* file into the entire corpus of tracks for scoring in the final recommendations. After all, the goal is to rank the entire corpus, given the first five context tracks, and see how well they match the given next track data.

Modeling the Problem

Next, let's think of how we will model the problem. We have five context tracks, each with an associated artist and album. We know that we have more tracks than playlists, so for now we will simply ignore the track_id and just use the album_id and artist_id as features. One strategy could be to use one-hot encoding for the album and artist, and this would work well, but one-hot encoding tends to lead to models with high precision but less generalization.

An alternate way to represent identifiers is to embed them—that is, to make a lookup table to an embedding of a fixed size that is lower dimensional than the cardinality of the identifiers. This embedding can be thought of as a low-rank approximation to the full-rank matrix of identifiers. We covered low-rank embeddings in earlier chapters, and we use that concept here as features to represent the album and artists.

Take a look at *models.py*, which contains the code for SpotifyModel:

```
from functools import partial
from typing import Any, Callable, Sequence, Tuple

from flax import linen as nn
import jax.numpy as jnp

class SpotifyModel(nn.Module):
    """Spotify model that takes a context and predicts the next tracks."""
    feature_size : int

    def setup(self):
        # There are too many tracks and albums so limit by hashing.
        self.max_albums = 100000
        self.album_embed = nn.Embed(self.max_albums, self.feature_size)
        self.artist_embed = nn.Embed(295861, self.feature_size)

    def get_embeddings(self, album, artist):
        """
        Given track, album, artist indices return the embeddings.
```

```
Args:
    album: ints of shape nx1
    artist: ints of shape nx1
Returns:
    Embeddings representing the track.
"""
album_modded = jnp.mod(album, self.max_albums)
album_embed = self.album_embed(album_modded)
artist_embed = self.artist_embed(artist)
result = jnp.concatenate([album_embed, artist_embed], axis=-1)
return result
```

In the setup code, notice that we have two embeddings, for the albums and the artists. We have a lot of albums, so we show one way to reduce the memory footprint of album embeddings: take the mod of a smaller number than the number of embeddings so that multiple albums might share an embedding. If more memory is available, you can remove the mod, but this technique is demonstrated here as a way of getting some benefit of having an embedding for a feature with very large cardinality.

The artist is probably the most informative feature, and the data includes far fewer unique artists, so we have a one-to-one mapping between the artist_id and the embeddings. When we convert the tuple of (album_id, artist_id) to an embedding, we do separate lookups for each ID and then concatenate the embeddings and return one complete embedding to represent a track. If more playlist data becomes available, you might also want to embed the track_id. However, given that we have more unique tracks than playlists, the track_id feature will not generalize well until we have more playlist data and the track_id could occur more often as observations. A general rule of thumb is that a feature should occur at least 100 times to be useful; otherwise, the gradients for that feature will not be updated very often, and it might as well be a random number because it is initialized as such.

In the call section, we do the heavy lifting of computing the affinity of a context to other tracks:

```
def __call__(self,
             track_context, album_context, artist_context,
             next_track, next_album, next_artist,
             neg_track, neg_album, neg_artist):
    """Returns the affinity score to the context.
    Args:
        track_context: ints of shape n
        album_context: ints of shape n
        artist_context: ints of shape n
        next_track: int of shape m
        next_album: int of shape m
        next_artist: int of shape m
        neg_track: int of shape o
        neg_album: int of shape o
```

```
        neg_artist: int of shape o
    Returns:
        pos_affinity: affinity of context to the next track of shape m.
        neg_affinity: affinity of context to the neg tracks of shape o.
    """
    context_embed = self.get_embeddings(album_context, artist_context)
    next_embed = self.get_embeddings(next_album, next_artist)
    neg_embed = self.get_embeddings(neg_album, neg_artist)

    # The affinity of the context to the other track is simply the dot
    # product of each context embedding with the other track's embedding.
    # We also add a small boost if the album or artist match.
    pos_affinity = jnp.max(jnp.dot(next_embed, context_embed.T), axis=-1)
    pos_affinity = pos_affinity + 0.1 * jnp.isin(next_album, album_context)
    pos_affinity = pos_affinity + 0.1 * jnp.isin(next_artist, artist_context)

    neg_affinity = jnp.max(jnp.dot(neg_embed, context_embed.T), axis=-1)
    neg_affinity = neg_affinity + 0.1 * jnp.isin(neg_album, album_context)
    neg_affinity = neg_affinity + 0.1 * jnp.isin(neg_artist, artist_context)

    all_embeddings = jnp.concatenate(
    [context_embed, next_embed, neg_embed], axis=-2)
    all_embeddings_l2 = jnp.sqrt(
    jnp.sum(jnp.square(all_embeddings), axis=-1))

    context_self_affinity = jnp.dot(jnp.flip(
    context_embed, axis=-2), context_embed.T)
    next_self_affinity = jnp.dot(jnp.flip(
    next_embed, axis=-2), next_embed.T)
    neg_self_affinity = jnp.dot(jnp.flip(neg_embed, axis=-2), neg_embed.T)

    return (pos_affinity, neg_affinity,
            context_self_affinity, next_self_affinity, neg_self_affinity,
            all_embeddings_l2)
```

Let's dig into this a bit since this is the core of the model code. The first part is pretty straightforward: we convert the indices into embeddings by looking up the album and artist embedding and concatenating them as a single vector per track. It is in this location that you would add in other dense features by concatenation, or convert sparse features to embeddings as we have done.

The next part computes the affinity of the context to the next tracks. Recall that the context is composed of the first five tracks, and the next track is the rest of the playlist to be computed. We have several choices here for representing the context and computing the affinity.

For the affinity of the context, we have chosen the simplest form of affinity, that of a dot product. The other consideration is how we treat the context, since it is composed of five tracks. One possible way is to average all the context embeddings and use the average as the representation for the context. Another way is to find the track with the maximal affinity as the closest track in the context to that of the next track.

Details on various options can be found in "Affinity Weighted Embedding" (*https://oreil.ly/ig7Ch*) by Jason Weston et al. We have found that if a user has diverse interests, finding the max affinity doesn't update the context embeddings in the same direction as the next track, as using the mean embedding does. In the case of playlists, the mean context embedding vector should function just as well because playlists tend to be on a single theme.

Notice that we compute the affinity for the negative tracks as well. This is because we want the next tracks to have more affinity to the context than the negative tracks. In addition to the affinity of the context and next tracks to the context, we also compute the L2 norm of the vectors as a way to regularize the model so it does not overfit on the training data. We also reverse the embedding vectors and compute what we call *self-affinity*, or the affinity of the context, next, and negative embeddings to themselves, simply by reversing the list of vectors and taking the dot product. This does not exhaustively compute all the affinities of the set with itself; this again is left as an exercise for you as it builds intuition and skill in using JAX.

The results are then returned as a tuple to the caller.

Framing the Loss Function

Now, let's look at *train_spotify.py*. We will skip the boilerplate code and just look at the evaluation and training steps:

```
def eval_step(state, y, all_tracks, all_albums, all_artists):
    result = state.apply_fn(
            state.params,
            y["track_context"], y["album_context"], y["artist_context"],
            y["next_track"], y["next_album"], y["next_artist"],
            all_tracks, all_albums, all_artists)
    all_affinity = result[1]
    top_k_scores, top_k_indices = jax.lax.top_k(all_affinity, 500)
    top_tracks = all_tracks[top_k_indices]
    top_artists = all_artists[top_k_indices]
    top_tracks_count = jnp.sum(jnp.isin(
      top_tracks, y["next_track"])).astype(jnp.float32)
    top_artists_count = jnp.sum(jnp.isin(
      top_artists, y["next_artist"])).astype(jnp.float32)

    top_tracks_recall = top_tracks_count / y["next_track"].shape[0]
    top_artists_recall = top_artists_count / y["next_artist"].shape[0]

    metrics = jnp.stack([top_tracks_recall, top_artists_recall])

    return metrics
```

The first piece of code is the evaluation step. To compute the affinities of the entire corpus, we pass in the album and artist indices for every possible track in the corpus to the model and then sort them using jax.lax.top_k. The first two lines are the scoring code for recommending the next tracks from the context during recommendations. LAX is a utility library that comes with JAX that contains functions outside of the NumPy API that are handy to work with vector processors like GPUs and TPUs. In the Spotify Million Playlist Dataset Challenge, one of the metrics is the recall@k at the artist and track level. For the tracks, the isin function returns the correct metric of the intersection of the next tracks and the top 500 scoring tracks of the corpus divided by the size of the set of next tracks. This is because the tracks are unique in the corpus. However, JAX's isin doesn't support making the elements unique, so for the artist recall metric, we might count artists in the recall set more than once. For the sake of computational efficiency, we use the multiple counts instead so that the evaluation might be computed quickly on the GPU so as not to stall the training pipeline. On a final evaluation, we might want to move the dataset to a CPU for a more accurate metric.

We use Weights & Biases again to track all the metrics, as depicted in Figure 13-1. You can see how they fare with each other over several experiments:

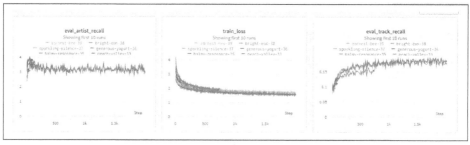

Figure 13-1. Weights & Biases experiment tracking

Next, we will look at the loss functions, another juicy part that you can experiment with in the exercises at the end of the chapter:

```python
def train_step(state, x, regularization):
    def loss_fn(params):
        result = state.apply_fn(
            params,
            x["track_context"], x["album_context"], x["artist_context"],
            x["next_track"], x["next_album"], x["next_artist"],
            x["neg_track"], x["neg_album"], x["neg_artist"])
        pos_affinity = result[0]
        neg_affinity = result[1]
        context_self_affinity = result[2]
        next_self_affinity = result[3]
        neg_self_affinity = result[4]
        all_embeddings_l2 = result[5]
```

```
mean_neg_affinity = jnp.mean(neg_affinity)
mean_pos_affinity = jnp.mean(pos_affinity)
mean_triplet_loss = nn.relu(1.0 + mean_neg_affinity - mean_pos_affinity)

max_neg_affinity = jnp.max(neg_affinity)
min_pos_affinity = jnp.min(pos_affinity)
extremal_triplet_loss = nn.relu(
                        1.0 + max_neg_affinity - min_pos_affinity
                        )

context_self_affinity_loss = jnp.mean(nn.relu(0.5 - context_self_affinity))
next_self_affinity_loss = jnp.mean(nn.relu(
                        0.5 - next_self_affinity)
                        )
neg_self_affinity_loss = jnp.mean(nn.relu(neg_self_affinity))

reg_loss = jnp.sum(nn.relu(all_embeddings_l2 - regularization))
loss = (extremal_triplet_loss + mean_triplet_loss + reg_loss +
        context_self_affinity_loss + next_self_affinity_loss +
        neg_self_affinity_loss)
return loss

grad_fn = jax.value_and_grad(loss_fn)
loss, grads = grad_fn(state.params)
new_state = state.apply_gradients(grads=grads)
return new_state, loss
```

We have several losses here, some directly related to the main task and others that help with regularization and generalization.

We initially started with the `mean_triplet_loss`, which is simply a loss that states that the positive affinity, or the affinity of the context tracks to the next tracks, should be one more than the negative affinity, or the affinity of the context tracks to the negative tracks. We will discuss how we experimented to obtain the other auxiliary loss functions.

Experiment tracking, depicted in Figure 13-2, is important in the process of improving the model, as is reproducibility. We have tried as much as possible to make the training process deterministic by using random-number generators from JAX that are reproducible by using the same starting random-number generator seed.

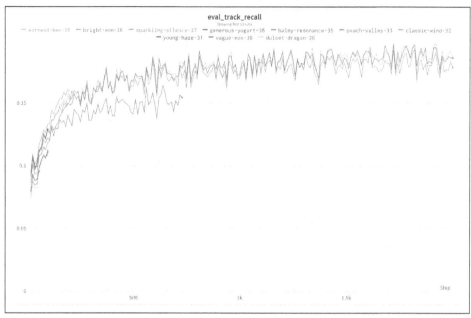

Figure 13-2. Track recall experiments

We started with the `mean_triplet_loss` and `reg_loss`, which is the regularization loss as a good baseline. These two losses simply make sure that the mean positive affinity of the context to the next track is one more than the negative affinity of the context to the negative tracks, and that the L2 norm of the embeddings does not exceed the regularization thresholds. These correspond to the metrics that did the worst. Notice that we do not run the experiment for the entire dataset. This is because for rapid iteration, it might be faster to just run on a smaller number of steps first and compare before interleaving occasionally with longer runs that use the entire dataset.

The next loss we added was the `max_neg_affinity` and the `min_pos_affinity`. This loss was inspired in part by "Efficient Coordinate Descent or Ranking with Domination Loss" (*https://oreil.ly/_aEF9*) by Mark A. Stevens and "Learning to Rank Recommendations with the *k*-Order Statistic Loss" (*https://oreil.ly/CPexf*) by Jason Weston et al. However, we do not use the entire negative set but merely a subsample. Why? Because the negative set is noisy. Just because a user hasn't added a particular track to a playlist doesn't mean that the track is not relevant to the playlist. Maybe the user hasn't heard the track yet, so the noise is due to lack of exposure. We also do not do the sampling step as discussed in the *k*-order statistic loss paper because sampling is CPU friendly but not GPU friendly. So we combine ideas from both papers and take the largest negative affinity and make it one less than the smallest positive affinity. The addition of this loss on the extremal tracks from both the next and negative sets gave us the next boost in performance in our experiments.

Finally, we added the self-affinity losses. These ensure that tracks from the context and next track sets have affinities of at least 0.5 and that the negative track affinities are at most 0. These are dot-product affinities and are more absolute as opposed to the relative positive and negative affinities that make the positive affinity one more than the negative affinities. In the long run, they didn't help much, but they did help the model converge faster in the beginning. We left them in because they still offer some improvement on the evaluation metrics on the last training step. This wraps up the explanatory part of this "Putting It All Together" chapter. Now comes the fun part, the exercises!

Exercises

We offer a lot of exercises because playing with the data and code is helpful in building out your intuition about different loss functions and ways of modeling the user. Also, thinking about how to write the code allows you to improve your proficiency with using JAX. So we have a list of helpful exercises to try out that are fun and will help you understand the material provided in this book.

To wrap up this chapter, here are some interesting exercises to experiment with. Doing them should give you lots of intuition about loss functions and the way JAX works, as well as a feel for the experimental process.

Here are some easy exercises to start with:

- Try out different optimizers (e.g., ADAM, RMSPROP).
- Try changing the feature sizes.
- Add in duration as a feature (take care on normalization!).
- What if you use cosine distance for inference and dot product for training?
- Add in a new metric, like NDCG.
- Play with distribution of positive versus negative affinities in the loss.
- Hinge loss with the lowest next track and the highest negative track.

Continue exploring with these more difficult exercises:

- Try using the track names as features and see if they help generalize.
- What happens if you use a two-layer network for affinity?
- What happens if you use an LSTM to compute affinity?
- Replace track embeddings with correlation.
- Compute all the self-affinities in a set.

Summary

What does it mean to replace an embedding with a feature? In our example of positive and negative affinity, we used the dot product to compute the affinity between two entities, such as two tracks, x and y. Rather than having the features as latent, represented by embeddings, an alternative is to manually construct features that represent the affinity between the two entities, x and y. As covered in Chapter 9, this can be log counts or Dice correlation coefficient or mutual information.

Some kind of counting feature can be made and then stored in a database. Upon training and inference, the database is looked up for each entity x and y, and the affinity scores are then used instead of or in conjunction with the dot product that is being learned. These features tend to be more precise but have less recall than an embedding representation. The embedding representation, being of low rank, has the ability to generalize better and improve recall. Having counting features is synergistic with embedding features because we can simultaneously improve precision with the use of precise counting features and, at the same time, improve recall with the help of low-rank features like embeddings.

For computing all n^2 affinities of tracks to other tracks in a set, consider using JAX's vmap function. vmap can be used to convert code that, for example, computes one track's affinity with all the other tracks and makes it run for all tracks versus all other tracks.

We hope that you have enjoyed playing with the data and code and that your skill in writing recommender systems in JAX has improved considerably after trying these exercises!

## PART IV

Serving

Well, you can't recommend that! Why sometimes the best recommendations aren't right.

One of the authors, Bryan, has a big question for the Amazon recommendation team: "Exactly how many vacuum cleaners do you think I need?" Just because Bryan bought the fancy Dyson to clean up after his dog doesn't mean he's soon going to buy a second one, and yet his Amazon home page seems hell-bent on recommending it. The reality is you'll always need to include business logic—or basic human logic—that you want to include in the flow of your recommendation system to prevent silliness. Whether you're facing contextually inappropriate recommendations, business infeasible recommendations, or simply the necessity to keep the set of recommendations a bit less monomaniacal, the last-step ordering can crucially improve recommendations.

But hold your horses! Don't think the ordering step is all switch cases and manually overriding your recommendation system. A synergy needs to exist between your ranking and your serving. Bryan also has a story about a certain query-based recommender he built for clothes: he wanted to implement a super-simple diversity filter on his recommendations—checking that the clothes recommended were of different merchandise classes. He made the output of his scoring model stack-rank the recommendations by merchandise class, so he could pick a few from each to serve. Lo and behold, the first week in production he was recommended 3, 4, even 5 backpacks out of 10 recommendations. Studious as users may be, this seemed erroneous and required a bit of QA. His error? Backpacks can be a member of up to three merch classes, so they were sneaking into several diversity classes!

Tricky problems where the theory meets production recommendations are the subject of this part of the book. We'll talk about diverse recommendations as in this example, but we'll also discuss other important business priorities that factor into the serving part of a recommendation pipeline.

CHAPTER 14
Business Logic

By now, you may be thinking, "Yes, our algorithmic ranking and recommendation has arrived! Personalization for every user with latent understanding is how we run our business." Unfortunately, the business is rarely this simple.

Let's take a really straightforward example, a recipe recommendation system. Consider a user who simply hates grapefruit (one of the authors of this book *really* does) but may love a set of other ingredients that go well with grapefruit: asparagus, avocado, banana, butter, cashews, champagne, chicken, coconut, crab, fish, ginger, hazelnut, honey, lemon, lime, melon, mint, olive oil, onion, orange, pecan, pineapple, raspberry, rum, salmon, seaweed, shrimp, star anise, strawberry, tarragon, tomato, vanilla, wine, and yogurt. These ingredients are the *most* popular to pair with grapefruit, and the user loves almost all of these.

What's the right way for the recommender to handle this case? It may seem like this is something that collaborative filtering (CF), latent features, or hybrid recommendations would catch. However, if the user likes all these shared flavors, the item-based CF model would not catch this well. Similarly, if the user truly *hates* grapefruit, latent features may not be sufficient to truly avoid it.

In this case, the simple approach is a great one: *hard avoids*. In this chapter, we'll talk about some of the intricacies of business logic intersecting the output of your recommendation system.

Instead of attempting to learn exceptions as part of the latent features that the model utilizes when making recommendations, it's more consistent and simple to integrate these business rules as an external step via deterministic logic. As an example: the model could remove all grapefruit cocktails that are retrieved instead of attempting to learn to rank them lower.

Hard Ranking

You can come up with a lot of examples of these phenomena when you start thinking of situations similar to our grapefruit scenario. *Hard ranking* usually refers to one of two kinds of special ranking rules:

- Explicitly removing some items from the list before ranking.
- Using a categorical feature to rank the results by category. (Note that this can even be done for multiple features to achieve a hierarchical hard ranking.)

Have you ever observed any of the following?

- A user bought a sofa. The system continues to recommend sofas to this user even though they won't need a sofa for the next five years.
- A user buys a birthday gift for a friend interested in gardening. Then the ecommerce site keeps recommending gardening tools despite the user having no interest in it.
- A parent wants to buy a toy for their child. But when the parent goes to the website where they usually buy toys, the site recommends several toys for a child a few years younger—the parent hasn't purchased from the site since the child was that age.
- A runner experiences serious knee pain and determines they can no longer go on long runs. They switch to cycling, which is lower impact. However, their local meetup recommendations are still all running oriented.

All of these cases can be relatively easy to deal with via deterministic logic. For these situations, we would prefer *not* to try to learn these rules via ML. We should assume that for these types of scenarios, we will get low signal about these preferences: negative implicit feedback is often lower in relevance, and many of the situations listed are represented by details that you want the system to learn once and for all. Additionally, in some of the previous examples, it can be upsetting or harmful to a relationship with a user to have the preferences not respected.

The name for these preferences is *avoids*—or sometimes constraints, overrides, or hard rules. You should think of them as explicit expectations of the system: "Don't show me recipes with grapefruit," "No more sofas," "I don't like gardening," "My child is older than 10 now," and "Don't show me trail runs."

Learned Avoids

Not all business rules are such obvious avoids that derive from explicit user feedback, and some derive from explicit feedback not directly related to specific items. It's important to include a wide variety of avoids when considering serving recommendations.

For the sake of simplicity, let's assume you're building a fashion recommender system. Examples of more subtle avoids include the following:

Already owned items
> These are items that users really need to purchase only once—for example, clothing users have bought through your platform or told you they already own. Creating a *virtual closet* might be a way to ask users to tell you what they have, to assist in these avoids.

Disliked features
> These are features of items that the user can indicate disinterest in. During an onboarding questionnaire, you may ask users if they like polka dots or if they have a favorite color palette. These are explicitly indicated pieces of feedback that can be used for avoids.

Ignored categories
> This is a category or group of items that doesn't resonate with the user. This can be implicit but learned outside the primary recommender model. Maybe the user has never clicked the Dresses category on your ecommerce website because they don't enjoy wearing them.

Low-quality items
> Over time, you'll learn that some items are simply low quality for most users. You can detect this via a high number of returns or low ratings from buyers. These items ultimately should be removed from inventory, but in the meantime, it's important to include them as avoids for all but the strongest signal of match.

These additional avoids can be implemented easily during the serving stage and can even include simple models. Training linear models to capture some of these rules and then applying them during serving can be a useful and reliable mechanism for improving ranking. Note that the small models perform very fast inference, so little negative impact usually results from including them in the pipeline. For larger-scale behavior trends or higher-order factors, we expect our core recommendation models to learn these ideas.

Hand-Tuned Weights

On the other side of the spectrum of avoids is *hand-tuned ranking*. This technique was popular in earlier days of search ranking, when humans would use analytics and observation to determine what they thought were the most important features in a ranking and then craft a multiobjective ranker. For example, flower stores may rank higher in early May as many users search for Mother's Day gifts. Since there could be many variable elements to track, these kinds of approaches don't scale well and have been largely deemphasized in modern recommendation ranking.

However, hand-tuned ranking can be incredibly useful as an *avoid*. While technically it's not an avoid, we sometimes still call it that. An example of this in practice is to know that new users like to start with a lower-priced item while they're learning whether your shipping is trustworthy. A useful technique is to then uprank lower-priced items before the first order.

While it may feel bad to consider building a hand-tuned ranking, it's important to not count this technique out. It has a place and is often a great place to start. One interesting human-in-the-loop application of this kind of technique is for hand-tuned ranking by experts. Back to our fashion recommender, a style expert may know that this summer's trending color is mauve, especially among the younger generation. Then can positively influence user satisfaction if the expert ranks these mauve items up for users in the right age persona.

Inventory Health

A unique and somewhat contentious side of hard ranking is inventory health. Notoriously hard to define, *inventory health* estimates how good the existing inventory is for satisfying user demand.

Let's take a quick look at one way to define inventory health, via affinity scores and forecasting. We can do this by leveraging a demand forecast, which is an incredibly powerful and popular way to optimize the business: what are the expected sales in each category over the next N time periods? Building these forecasting models is outside the scope of this book, but the core ideas are well captured in the famous book "Forecasting: Principles and Practice" (*https://otexts.com/fpp3/*) by Rob Hyndman and George Athanasopoulos (Otexts). For the sake of our discussion, assume that you're able to roughly approximate the number of socks you'll sell over the next month, broken down by size and usage type. This can be a really instructive estimate for the number of socks of various types you should have on hand.

However, it doesn't stop there; inventory may be finite, and in practice inventory is often a major constraint on businesses that sell physical goods. With that caveat, we have to turn to the other side of the market demand. If our demand outstrips our availability, we are ultimately disappointing users who don't have access to the item they desired.

Let's take an example of selling bagels; you've calculated average demand for poppy seed, onion, asiago cheese, and egg. On any given day, many customers will come to buy a bagel with a clear preference in mind, but will you have enough of that bagel? Every bagel you don't sell is wasted; people like fresh bagels. This means that the bagels you recommend to each person are dependent on good inventory. Some users are less picky; they can get one of two or three of the options and be just as happy. In that case, it's better to give them another bagel option and save the lowest inventory for the picky ones. This is a kind of model refinement called *optimization*, which has a huge number of techniques. We won't get into optimization techniques, but books on mathematical optimization or operations research will provide direction. *Algorithms for Optimization* by Mykel J. Kochenderfer and Tim A. Wheeler (MIT Press) is a good place to start.

Inventory health ties back to hard ranking, because actively managing inventory as part of your recommendations is an incredibly important and powerful tool. Ultimately, inventory optimization will degrade the perceived performance of your recommendations, but by including it as part of your business rules, the overall health of your business and recommender system improves. This is why it is sometimes called *global optimization*.

The reason that these methods stir up heated discussions is that not everyone agrees that the quality of recommendations for some users should be depressed to improve those for the "greater good." Health of the marketplace and average satisfaction are useful metrics to consider, but ensure that these are aligned with the north-star metrics for the recommendation system at large.

Implementing Avoids

The simplest approach to handling avoids is via downstream filtering. To do this, you'll want to apply the avoid rules for the user before the recommendations are passed along from the ranker to the user. Implementing this approach looks something like this:

```python
import pandas as pd

def filter_dataframe(df: pd.DataFrame, filter_dict: dict):
    """
    Filter a dataframe to exclude rows where columns have certain values.

    Args:
        df (pd.DataFrame): Input dataframe.
        filter_dict (dict): Dictionary where keys are column names
        and values are the values to exclude.

    Returns:
        pd.DataFrame: Filtered dataframe.
    """
    for col, val in filter_dict.items():
        df = df.loc[df[col] != val]
    return df

filter_dict = {'column1': 'value1', 'column2': 'value2', 'column3': 'value3'}
```

```
df = df.pipe(filter_dataframe, filter_dict)
```

Admittedly, this is a trivial but also relatively naive attempt at avoids. First, working purely in pandas will limit some of the scalability of your recommender, so let's convert this to JAX:

```
import jax
import jax.numpy as jnp

def filter_jax_array(arr: jnp.array, col_indices: list, values: list):
    """
    Filter a jax array to exclude rows where certain columns have certain values.

    Args:
        arr (jnp.array): Input array.
        col_indices (list): List of column indices to filter on.
        values (list): List of corresponding values to exclude.

    Returns:
        jnp.array: Filtered array.
    """
    assert len(col_indices) == len(values),

    masks = [arr[:, col] != val for col, val in zip(col_indices, values)]
    total_mask = jnp.logical_and(*masks)

    return arr[total_mask]
```

But there are deeper issues. The next issue you may face is where that collection of avoids is stored. An obvious place is somewhere like a NoSQL database keyed on users, and then you can get all of the avoids as a simple lookup. This is a natural use of feature stores, as you saw in "Feature Stores" on page 90. Some avoids may be applied in real time, while others are learned upon user onboarding. Feature stores are a great place to house avoids.

The next potential gotcha with our naive filter is that it doesn't naturally extend to covariate avoids, or more complicated avoid scenarios. Some avoids are actually dependent on context—a user who doesn't wear white after Labor Day, users who don't eat meat on Fridays, or coffee-processing methods that don't mesh well with certain brewers. All of these require conditional logic. You might think that your powerful and effective recommendation system model can certainly learn these details, but this is true only sometimes. The reality is that many of these kinds of considerations are lower signal than the large-scale concepts your recommendation system should be learning, and thus are hard to learn consistently. Additionally, these kinds of rules are often ones you should require, as opposed to remain optimistic about. For that reason, you often should explicitly specify such restrictions.

This specification can often be achieved by explicit deterministic algorithms that impose these requirements. For the coffee problem, one of the authors hand-built a decision stump to handle a few bad combinations of coffee roast features and brewers—*anaerobic espresso?! Yuck!*

Our other two examples (not wearing white after Labor Day and not eating meat on Fridays), however, are a bit more nuanced. An explicit algorithmic approach may be tricky to handle. How do we know that a user doesn't eat meat on Fridays during one period of the year?

For these use cases, model-based avoids can impose these requirements.

Model-Based Avoids

In our quest to include more complicated rules and potentially learn them, we may sound like we're back in the realm of retrieval. Unfortunately, even with models like wide-and-deep with lots of parameters doing both user modeling and item modeling, learning such high-level relationships can be tricky.

While most of this book has focused on working fairly large and deep, this part of recommendation systems is well suited for simple models. For feature-based binary predictions (should this be recommended), we certainly have a zoo of good options. The best approach would obviously depend heavily on the number of features involved in implementing the avoid you wish to capture. It's useful to remember that many avoids that we're considering in this section start out as assumptions or hypotheses: we think some users may not wear white after Labor Day, and then attempt to find features that model this outcome well. In this way, it can be more tractable using extremely simple regression models to find covarying features with the outcome in question.

Another related piece of this puzzle is latent representations. For our Friday vegetarians, we may be trying to infer a particular persona that we know has this rule. That persona is a latent feature that we hope to map from other attributes. It's important to be careful with this kind of modeling (in general, personas can be a bit nuanced and worthy of thoughtful decision making), but it can be quite helpful. It may seem like the user-modeling parts of your large recommender model should learn these—and they can! A useful trick is to pull forward personas learned from that model and regress them against hypothesized avoids to allow for more signal. However, the other model doesn't always learn these personas because our loss functions for retrieval relevance (and downstream for ranking) are attempting to parse out relevance for individual users from the latent persona features—which may predict these avoids only amid context features.

All in all, implementing the avoids is both very easy and very hard. When building production recommendation systems, the journey is not over when you get to serving; many models factor into the final step of the process.

Summary

Sometimes you need to rely on more classic approaches to ensuring that the recommendations you're sending downstream are satisfying essential rules of your business. Learning explicit or subtle lessons from your users can be turned into simple strategies to continue to delight them.

However, this is not the end of our serving challenge. Another kind of downstream consideration is related to the kind of filtering we've done here but derives from user preference and human behavior. Ensuring that recommendations are not repeated, rote, and redundant is the subject of the next chapter on diversity in recommendations. We will also discuss how to balance multiple priorities simultaneously when determining exactly what to serve.

## CHAPTER 15

Bias in Recommendation Systems

We've spent much time in this book dissecting how to improve our recommendations, making them more personalized and relevant to an individual user. Along the way, you've learned that latent relationships between users and user personas encode important information about shared preferences. Unfortunately, all of this has a serious downside: bias.

For the purposes of our discussion, we'll talk about the two most important kinds of bias for recommendation systems:

- Overly redundant or self-similar sets of recommendations
- Stereotypes learned by AI systems

First, we'll delve into the crucial element of diversity in recommendation outputs. As critical as it is for a recommendation system to offer relevant choices to users, ensuring a variety of recommendations is also essential. Diversity not only safeguards against overspecialization but also promotes novel and serendipitous discoveries, enriching the overall user experience.

The balance between relevance and diversity is delicate and can be tricky. This balance challenges the algorithm to go beyond merely echoing users' past behavior and encourages an exploration of new territories, hopefully providing a more holistically positive experience with the content.

This kind of bias is primarily a technical challenge; how do we satisfy the multiobjectives of diverse recommendations and highly relevant ones?

We'll consider the intrinsic and extrinsic biases in recommendation systems as an often unintended yet significant consequence of both the underlying algorithms and the data they learn from. Systemic biases in data collection or algorithmic design can result in prejudiced outputs, leading to ethical and fairness issues. Moreover, they may create echo chambers or filter bubbles, curtailing users' exposure to a broader range of content and inadvertently reinforcing preexisting beliefs.

At the end of this chapter, we will discuss the risks and provide resources to learn more about them. We are not experts in AI fairness and bias, but all ML practitioners should understand and seriously consider these topics. We aim to provide an introduction and signposts.

Diversification of Recommendations

Our first investment into fighting bias is to explicitly target more diversity in our recommendation outputs. We'll briefly cover two of the many goals you may pursue: intra-list diversity and serendipitous recommendations.

Intra-list diversity attempts to ensure that there are a variety of types of items within a single recommendation list. The idea is to minimize similarity between the recommended items to reduce overspecialization and encourage exploration. High intra-list diversity within a set of recommendations increases the user's exposure to many items they may like; however, the recommendations for any particular interest will be shallower, reducing the recall.

Serendipitous recommendations are both surprising and interesting to the user. These are often items that the user might not have discovered independently or that are generally far less popular in the system. Serendipity can be introduced into the recommendation process by injecting nonobvious or unexpected choices—even if those have a relatively lower affinity score with the user—to improve overall serendipity. In an ideal world, these serendipitous choices are high affinity relative to other items of their popularity, so they're the "best of the outside choices."

Improving Diversity

Now that we have our measures of diversity, we can explicitly attempt to improve them. Importantly, by adding diversity metrics as one of our objectives, we will potentially sacrifice performance on things like recall or NDCG. It can be useful to think of this as a Pareto problem, or to impose a lower bound on ranking metric performance that you'll accept in pursuit of diversity.

In a *Pareto problem*, you have two priorities that often trade off with each other. In many areas of ML, and more generally applied mathematics, certain outcomes have a natural tension. Diversity in recommendations is an important example of a Pareto problem in recommendation systems, but it's not the only one. In Chapter 14, you briefly saw global optimization, which is an extreme case of trade-offs.

One simple approach to improve diversity metrics is *reranking*: a post-processing step in which the initially retrieved recommendation list is reordered to enhance diversity. Various algorithms for re-ranking consider not just the relevance scores but also the dissimilarity among the items in the recommendation list. Re-ranking is a strategy that can operationalize any external loss function, so using it for diversity is a straightforward approach.

Another strategy is to break out of the closed loop of recommendation feedback that we discussed in the section "Propensity Weighting for Recommendation System Evaluation" on page 208. As in multiarmed bandit problems, *explore-exploit trade-offs* can choose between exploiting what the model knows the user will like and exploring less certain options that may yield higher rewards. This trade-off can be used in recommendation systems to ensure diversity by occasionally choosing to *explore* and recommend less obvious choices. To implement a system like this, we can use affinity as a reward estimate and propensity as an exploitation measure.

Instead of using these posterior strategies, an alternative is to *incorporate diversity as an objective in the learning process* or include a diversity regularization term in the loss function. Multiobjective loss including pairwise similarity as a regularizer can help train the model to learn diverse sets of recommendations. You previously saw that kinds of regularization can coach the training process to minimize certain behaviors. One regularization term that can be used explicitly is *similarity among recommendations*; the dot product of each embedding vector in the recommendations to each other can approximate this self-similarity. Let $\mathscr{R} = (R_1, R_2, ..., R_k)$ be the list of embeddings for the recommendations, and then consider $\mathscr{R}$ as a column matrix—with each row a recommendation. Calculating $\mathscr{R}$'s Gramian would yield all our dot-product similarity calculations, and thus we can regularize by this term with appropriate hyperparameter weighting. Note that this differs from our previous Gramian regularization because we're considering the recommendations for only an individual query in this case.

Finally, we can use rankings from multiple domains to boost recommendation diversity. By integrating various ranking measures, the recommendation system can suggest items from outside the user's "mode," thus broadening the range of recommendations. A vibrant discipline exists around multimodal recommendations, with the PinnerSage paper (*https://oreil.ly/KOQK2*) from Pinterest a particularly impressive implementation. In many of the works about multimodal recommendations, the retrieval step returns too many recommendations near to the user's query vector. This forces self-similarity among the retrieved list. Multimodality forces multiple query vectors to be used for each request, allowing a built-in diversity.

Let's look at another perspective on item self-similarity and think about how the pairwise relationships between items can be used to this end.

Applying Portfolio Optimization

Portfolio optimization, a concept borrowed from finance, can be an effective approach to enhance diversity in recommendation systems. The goal here is to create a "portfolio" of recommended items that balances the two key parameters: relevance and diversity.

At its heart, portfolio optimization is about risk (in our case, relevance) and return (diversity). Here's a basic approach for applying this optimization to recommendation systems:

1. Formulate an item representation such that the distance in the space is a good measure of similarity. This is in line with our previous discussions about what makes a good latent space.

2. Calculate pairwise distance between items. You can do this by using whatever distance metric that enriches your latent space. It is important to calculate these pairwise distances across all items retrieved and be ready for consideration to return. Note that how you aggregate these distributions of distances can be nuanced.

3. Evaluate affinity for the retrieved set. Note that calibrated affinity scores will perform better as they provide a more realistic estimate of return.

4. Solve the optimization problem. Solving the problem will yield a weight for each item that balances the trade-off between relevance and diversity. Items with higher weights are more valuable in terms of both diversity and relevance, and they should be prioritized in the recommendation list. Mathematically, the problem looks like this:

$$Maximize(w^T * r - \lambda * w^T * C * w)$$

Here, w is a vector representing the weights (i.e., the proportion of each item in the recommendation list), r is the relevance score vector, C is the covariance matrix (which captures the diversity), and λ is a parameter to balance relevance and diversity. The constraint here is that the sum of the weights equals 1.

Remember, the hyperparameter λ trades off between relevance and diversity. This makes it a critical part of this process and may require experimentation or tuning based on the specific needs of your system and its users. This would be straightforward via hyperparameter optimization in one of many packages such as Weights & Biases.

Multiobjective Functions

Another related approach to diversity is to rank based on a multiobjective loss. Instead of the ranking stage being purely personalization affinity, introducing a second (or more!) ranking term can dramatically improve diversity.

The simplest approach here is something similar to what you learned in Chapter 14: hard ranking. A business rule that may apply to diversity is limiting each item category to only one item. This is the simplest case of multiobjective ranking because sorting by a categorical column and selecting the max in each group will achieve explicit diversity with respect to that covariate. Let's move on to something more subtle.

In "Stitching Together Spaces for Query-Based Recommendations" (*https://oreil.ly/OREt2*), one of this book's authors worked with coauthor Ian Horn to implement a multiobjective recommendation system that balanced both personalization and relevance to an image-retrieval problem.

The goal was to provide personalized recommendations for clothing that were similar to clothes in an image the user uploaded. This means there are two latent spaces:

- The latent space of personalized clothes to a user
- The latent space of images of clothing

To solve this problem, we first had to make a decision: what was more important for relevance? Personalization or image similarity? Because the product was centered around a photo-upload experience, we chose image similarity. However, we had another fact to consider: each uploaded image contained several pieces of clothing. As is popular in computer vision, we first segmented the model into several items and then treated each item as its own query (which we called *anchor-items*). This meant our image-similarity retrieval was multimodal, as we searched with several different query vectors. After we gathered them all, we had to make one final ranking—a multiobjective ranking for image similarity and personalization. The loss function we optimized is shown here:

$$s_i = \alpha \times (1 - d_i) + (1 - \alpha) \times a_i$$

The α is a hyperparameter that represents the weighting, d_i is the image distance, and a_i is the personalization. We learn α experimentally. The last step was to impose some hard ranking to ensure that one recommendation came from each anchor.

So let's sum this up:

1. We used two latent spaces with distances to provide rankings.
2. We did multimodal retrieval via image segmentation.
3. We retrieved using only one of the rankings.
4. Our final ranking was multiobjective, with hard ranking utilizing all our latent spaces and business logic.

This allowed our recommendations to be *diverse* in the sense that they achieved relevance in several areas of the query that corresponded to different items.

Predicate Pushdown

You may be happy and comfortable applying these metrics during serving—after all, that's the title for this part of the book—but before we move on from this topic, we should talk about an edge case that can have quite disastrous consequences. When you impose the hard rules from Chapter 14 and the diversity expectations discussed earlier in this chapter, and do a little multiobjective ranking, sometimes you arrive at…no recommendations.

Say you start by retrieving k items, but after the sufficiently diverse combinations that also satisfy business rules, there's simply nothing left. You might say, "I'll just retrieve more items; let's crank up k!" But this has some serious issues: it can really increase latency, depress match quality, and throw off your ranking model that is more tuned to lower-cardinality sets.

A common experience, especially with diversity, is that different modes for the retrieval have vastly different match scores. To take an example from our fashion recommender world: all jeans might be a better match than any shirt we have, but if you're looking for diverse categories of clothes to recommend, no matter how big the k, you'll potentially be missing out on shirts.

One solution to this problem is *predicate pushdown*. This optimization technique is used in databases, specifically in the context of data retrieval. The main idea of predicate pushdown is to filter data as early as possible in the data-retrieval process, to reduce the amount of data that needs to be processed later in the query execution plan.

For traditional databases, you see predicate pushdown applied, for example, as "apply my query's where clause in the database to cut down on I/O." It may achieve this by explicitly pulling the relevant columns to check the where clause first, and then getting the row IDs from those that pass before executing the rest of the query.

How does this help us in our case? The simple idea is if your vector store also has features for the vectors, you can include the feature comparisons as part of retrieval. Let's take an overly simple example: assume your items have a categorical feature called color, and for good diverse recommendations you want a nice set of at least three colors in your five recommendations. To achieve this, you can do a top-k search across each of the colors in your store (the downside is that your retrieval is C times as large, where C is the number of colors that exist) and then do ranking and diversity on the union of these sets. This has a much higher likelihood of surviving your diversity rule in the eventual recommendations. This is great! We expect that latency is relatively low in retrieval, so this tax of extra retrievals isn't bad if we know where to look.

This optimization technique can be applied on quite complicated predicates if your vector store is set up well for the kinds of filters you wish to impose.

Fairness

Fairness in ML in general is a particularly nuanced subject that is ill-served by short summaries. The following topics are important, and we invite you to consider the robust references included here:

Nudging

Fairness does not need to be only "equal probabilities for all outcomes"; it can be fair with respect to a specific covariate. Nudging via a recommender—i.e., recommending items to emphasize certain behavior or buying patterns—can increase fairness. Consider the work by Karlijn Dinnissen and Christine Bauer from Spotify about using nudging to improve gender representation in music recommendations (*https://oreil.ly/fit3j*).

Filter bubbles

Filter bubbles are a downside of extreme collaborative filtering: a group of users begin liking similar recommendations, the system learns that they should receive similar recommendations, and the feedback loop perpetuates this. For a deep look into not only the concept but also mitigation strategies, consider "Mitigating the Filter Bubble While Maintaining Relevance" (*https://oreil.ly/2jyeJ*) by Zhaolin Gao et al.

High risk

Not all applications of AI are equal in risk. Some domains are particularly harmful when AI systems are poorly guardrailed. For a general overview of the most high-risk circumstances and mitigation, consult *Machine Learning for High-Risk Applications* by Patrick Hall et al. (O'Reilly).

Trustworthiness

Explainable models is a popular mitigation strategy for risky applications of AI. While explainability does not *solve* the problem, it frequently provides a path toward identification and resolution. For a deep dive on this, *Practicing Trustworthy Machine Learning* by Yada Pruksachatkun et al. (O'Reilly) provides tools and techniques.

Fairness in recommendations

Because recommendation systems are so obviously susceptible to issues of AI fairness, much has been written on the topic. Each of the major social media giants has employed teams working in AI safety. One particular highlight is the Twitter Responsible AI team led by Rumman Chowdhury. You can read about the team's work in "Can Auditing Eliminate Bias from Algorithms?" (*https://oreil.ly/uvFep*) by Alfred Ng.

Summary

While these techniques provide pathways to enhance diversity, it's important to remember to strike a balance between diversity and relevance. The exact method or combination of methods used may vary depending on the specific use case, the available data, the intricacies of the user base, and the kind of feedback you're collecting. As you implement recommendation systems, think about which aspects are the most key in your diversity problem.

## CHAPTER 16

Acceleration Structures

So what are acceleration structures? In computer science terminology, when you try to rank every item in a corpus one by one, the typical amount of time it would take if there are N items is proportional to N. This is called big O notation (*https://oreil.ly/9-ton*). So if you have a user vector and you have a corpus of N items, it would take typically $O(N)$ time to score all the items in the corpus for one user. This is usually tractable if N is small and can fit into GPU RAM, typically $N < 1$ million items or so. However, if we have a very large corpus of, say, a billion items, it might take a very long time if we also have to make recommendations for a billion users. Then in big O notation it would be $O(10^{18})$ dot products to score a billion items for each and every one of a billion users.

In this chapter, we will try to reduce the $O(N * M)$ time to something sublinear in the number of items N and the number of users M. We will discuss strategies including the following:

- Sharding
- Locality sensitive hashing
- k-d Trees
- Hierarchical k-means
- Cheaper retrieval methods

We'll also cover the trade-offs related to each strategy and what they could be used for. For all the following examples, we assume that the user and items are represented by embedding vectors of the same size and that the affinity between the user and items is a simple dot product, cosine distance, or Euclidean distance. If we were to use a neural network like a two-tower model to score the user and item, then possibly the only method that could be used to speed things up would be sharding or some kind of cheaper pre-filtering method.

Sharding

Sharding is probably the simplest strategy to divide and conquer (*https://oreil.ly/ul_IK*). Suppose you have k machines, N items, and M users. Using a sharding strategy, you can reduce the runtime to $O(N * M / k)$. You can do this by assigning each item a unique identifier, so you have tuples of ($unique\_id$, $item\_vector$). Then, by simply taking `machine_id = unique_id % K`, we can assign a subset of the corpus to a different machine.

When a user needs a recommendation, we can then compute the top-scoring recommendations either ahead of time or on demand by distributing the workload onto k machines, thus making the computation k times faster, except for the overhead in gathering the top results on the server and ordering them jointly. Note that if you want, say, 100 top-scoring items, you would still have to obtain the top 100 results from each shard, collate them together, and then sort all the results jointly if you want to have the same results as in a brute-force method of scoring the entire corpus.

Sharding is useful in the sense that it can be combined with any of the other acceleration methods and is not dependent on the representation having any specific form, such as being a single vector.

Locality Sensitive Hashing

Locality sensitive hashing (LSH) is an interesting technique that converts a vector into a token-based representation. This is powerful because if CPUs are readily available, we can use them to compute the similarity between vectors by using cheaper integer arithmetic operations such as XOR and bit counting with specialized assembly instructions rather than floating-point operations. Integer operations tend to be much faster on CPUs than floating-point operations, so we can compute similarity between items much faster than using vector operations.

The other benefit is that once items are represented as a series of tokens, a regular search engine database would be able to store and retrieve these items by using token matching. Regular hashing, on the other hand, tends to result in vastly different hash codes if a slight change occurs in the input. This is not a criticism of the hash functions; they just have different uses for different kinds of data.

Let's walk through a couple of ways to convert a vector into a hash. LSH is different from regular hashing in that small perturbations to a vector should result in the same hash bits as the hash of the original vector. This is an important property as it allows us to look up the neighborhood of a vector by using fast methods such as hash maps.

One simple hashing method is called the Power of Comparative Reasoning (*https:// oreil.ly/_1Bd8*), or Winner Take All hashing. In this hashing scheme, the vector is first permuted using a known, reproducible permutation. We can generate this known permutation by simply shuffling the indices of all the vector dimensions with a random-number generator that accepts a seed and reliably reproduces the same exact shuffle sequence. It is important that the permutation is stable over different versions of Python, as we want to reproduce the hashing operation when generating the hashes as well as during retrieval time. Since we are using JAX's random library and JAX is careful about the reproducibility of permutations, we just directly use the permutation function in JAX. The hash code computation after that is simply a comparison between adjacent dimensions of the permuted vector, as shown in Example 16-1.

Example 16-1. Winner take all

```
def compute_wta_hash(x):
  """Example code to compute some Winner take all hash vectors
  Args:
    x: a vector
  Result:
    hash: a hash code
  """
  key = jax.random.PRNGKey(1337)
  permuted = jax.random.permutation(key, x)

  hash1 = permuted[0] > permuted[1]
  hash2 = permuted[1] > permuted[2]

  return (hash1, hash2)

x1 = jnp.array([1, 2, 3])
x2 = jnp.array([1, 2.5, 3])
x3 = jnp.array([3, 2, 1])
x1_hash = compute_wta_hash(x1)
x2_hash = compute_wta_hash(x2)
x3_hash = compute_wta_hash(x3)
print(x1_hash)
print(x2_hash)
print(x3_hash)

(Array(False, dtype=bool), Array(True, dtype=bool))
(Array(False, dtype=bool), Array(True, dtype=bool))
(Array(True, dtype=bool), Array(False, dtype=bool))
```

As you can see, the vector x2 is slightly different from x1 and results in the same hash code of 01, whereas x3 is different and results in a hash code of 10. The Hamming distance (*https://oreil.ly/RF-x1*) of the hash code is then used to compute the distance between two vectors, as shown in Example 16-2. The distance is simply the XOR of the two hash codes, which results in 1 whenever the bits disagree, followed by bit counting.

Example 16-2. Hamming function

```
x = 16
y = 15
hamming_xy = int.bit_count(x ^ y)
print(hamming_xy)
5
```

Using the Hamming distance as shown here results in some speedup in the distance computation, but the major speedup will come from using the hash codes in a hash map. For example, we could break up the hash code into 8-bit chunks and store the corpus into shards keyed by each 8-bit chunk, which results in a 256× speedup because we have to look only in the hash map that has the same key as the query vector for nearest neighbors.

This has a drawback in terms of recall, though, because all 8 bits have to match in order for an item to be retrieved that matches the query vector. A tradeoff exists between the number of bits of the hash code used in hashing and the Hamming distance computation. The larger the number of bits, the faster the search, because the corpus is divided into smaller and smaller chunks. However, the drawback is that more and more bits have to match, and thus all the hash code bits in a nearby vector in the original space might not match and thus might not be retrieved.

The remedy is to have multiple hash codes with different random-number generators and repeat this process a few times with different random seeds. This extra step is left as an exercise for you.

Another common way to compute hash bits uses the Johnson-Lindenstrauss lemma (*https://oreil.ly/vbAGn*), which is a fancy way of saying that two vectors, when multiplied by the same random Gaussian matrix, tend to end up in a similar location. However, the L2 distances are preserved, which means this hash function works better when using Euclidean distance to train the embeddings rather than dot products. In this scheme, only the hash code computation differs; the Hamming distance treatment is exactly the same.

The speedup from LSH is directly proportional to the number of bits of the hash code that have to be an exact match. Suppose only 8 bits of the hash code are used in the hash map; then the speedup is 2^8, or 256 times the original. The trade-off for the speed is having to store the hash map in memory.

k-d Trees

A common strategy for speeding up computation in computer science is *divide and conquer*. In this scheme, the data is recursively partitioned into two halves, and only the half that is relevant to the search query is searched. In contrast to a linear $O(n)$ in the number of items in the corpus scheme, a divide-and-conquer algorithm would be able to query a corpus in $O(\log 2(n))$ time, which is a substantial speedup if n is large.

One such binary tree for vector spaces is called a *k*-d tree (*https://oreil.ly/z0vFO*). Typically, to build a *k*-d tree, we compute the bounding box of all the points in the collection, find the longest edge of the bounding box and split it down the middle of that edge in the splitting dimension, and then partition the collection into two halves. If the median is used, the collection is more or less divided into two equal-numbered items; we say *more or less* because there might be ties along that split dimension. The recursive process stops when a small number of items is left in the leaf node. Many implementations of *k*-d trees exist—for example, SciPy's *k*-d tree (*https://oreil.ly/iZZD9*).

Although the speedup is substantial, this method tends to work when the number of feature dimensions of the vector is low. Also, similar to other methods, *k*-d trees work best when the L2 distance is the metric used for the embedding. Losses in retrieval can occur if the dot product was used for the similarity metric, as the *k*-d tree makes more sense for Euclidean space partitioning.

Example 16-3 provides sample code for splitting a batch of points along the largest dimension.

Example 16-3. Partitioning via a k-d tree

```
import jax
import jax.numpy as jnp

def kdtree_partition(x: jnp.ndarray):
    """Finds the split plane and value for a batch of vectors x."""
    # First, find the bounding box.
    bbox_min = jnp.min(x, axis=0)
    bbox_max = jnp.max(x, axis=0)
    # Return the largest split dimension and value.
    diff = bbox_max - bbox_min
    split_dim = jnp.argmax(diff)
    split_value = 0.5 * (bbox_min[split_dim] + bbox_max[split_dim])
    return split_dim, split_value

key = jax.random.PRNGKey(42)
x = jax.random.normal(key, [256, 3]) * jnp.array([1, 3, 2])
split_dim, split_value = kdtree_partition(x)
print("Split dimension %d at value %f" % (split_dim, split_value))
```

```
# Partition the points into two groups, the left subtree
# has all the elements left of the splitting plane.
left = jnp.where(x[:, split_dim] < split_value)
right = jnp.where(x[:, split_dim] >= split_value)
```

```
Split dimension 1 at value -0.352623
```

As you can see from the code, the *k*-d tree partitioning code can be as simple as splitting along the middle longest dimension. Other possibilities are splitting along the median of the longest dimension or using a surface area heuristic (*https://oreil.ly/ BxAf7*).

A *k*-d tree is constructed by repeatedly partitioning the data along only one spatial dimension at a time (usually along the largest axis aligned to the spread of data); see Figure 16-1.

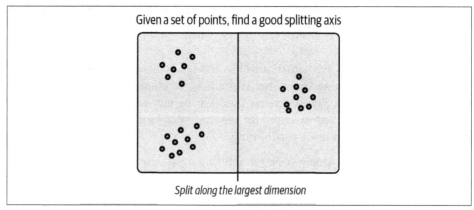

Figure 16-1. k-d tree construction's initial bounding box

Partitions are recursively subdivided again, usually along the longest axis, until the number of points in the partition is fewer than a chosen small number; see Figure 16-2.

The *k*-d tree lookup time is $O(\log2(n))$ in *n*, the number of items in the corpus. The tree also requires a small overhead of memory to store the tree itself, which is dominated by the number of leaf nodes, so it would be best to have a minimal number of items in a leaf to prevent splits that are too fine.

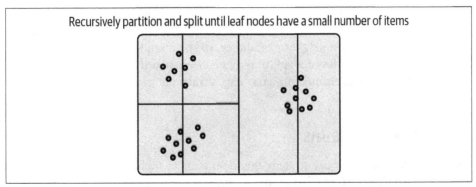

Recursively partition and split until leaf nodes have a small number of items

Figure 16-2. k-d tree construction recursively partitioned

From the root node, repeatedly check whether the query point (e.g., the item we are seeking nearest neighbors for) is in the left or right child of the root node, as shown in Figure 16-3. For example, use `go_left = x[split_dim] < value_split[dim]`. In binary tree convention, the left child contains all points whose value at the split dimension are less than the split value. Hence if the query point's value at the split dimension is less than the split value we go left, otherwise we go right. Recursively descend down the tree until reaching the leaf node; then exhaustively compute distances to all items in the leaf node.

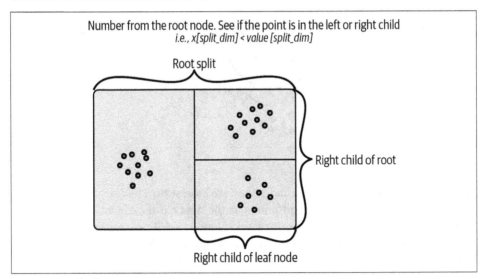

Number from the root node. See if the point is in the left or right child
i.e., x[split_dim] < value [split_dim]

Root split

Right child of root

Right child of leaf node

Figure 16-3. k-d tree query

A *k*-d tree has a potential drawback. If an item is close to a splitting plane, that item would be considered on the other side of the tree. As a result, the item would not be considered as a nearest neighbor candidate. In some implementations of *k*-d trees, called *spill trees*, both sides of a splitting plane are visited if the query point is close enough to the plane's decision boundary. This change increases runtime a little bit for the benefit of more recall.

Hierarchical k-means

Another divide-and-conquer strategy that does scale to higher feature dimensions is *k-means clustering*. In this scheme, the corpus is clustered into *k* clusters and then recursively clustered into *k* more clusters until each cluster is smaller than a defined limit.

An implementation of *k*-means can be found at scikit-learn's web page (*https://oreil.ly/E45Lo*).

To build the clustering, first create cluster centroids at random from existing points (Figure 16-4).

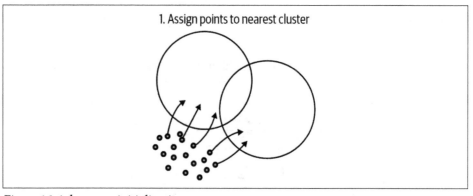

Figure 16-4. k-means initialization

Next, we assign all points to the cluster they are closest to. Then for each cluster, we take the average of all the assigned points as the new cluster center. We repeat until done, which can be a fixed number of steps. Figure 16-5 illustrates this process. The output is then *k* cluster centers of points. The process can be repeated again for each cluster center, splitting again into *k* more clusters.

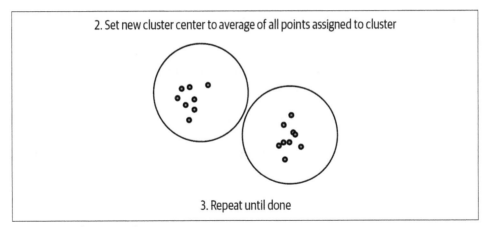

Figure 16-5. k-means clustering

Again, the speedup is $O(\log(n))$ in the number of items, but k-means is better adapted to clustering higher-dimensional data points than k-d trees.

The querying for a k-means cluster is rather straightforward. You can find the closest cluster to the query point and then repeat the process for all subclusters until a leaf node is found; then all the items in the leaf node are scored against the query point.

An alternative to k-means is to perform SVD and use the first k eigenvectors as the clustering criteria. The use of SVD is interesting in that there exists closed form and approximate methods like power iteration (*https://oreil.ly/ZgZ2-*) for computing the eigenvectors. Using the dot product to compute affinity might be better suited to vectors trained using the dot product as the affinity metric.

To learn more on this topic, you can consult "Label Partitioning for Sublinear Ranking" (*https://oreil.ly/rMg-3*) by Jason Weston et al. (including one of this book's authors). The paper compares LSH, SVD, and hierarchical k-means. You'll find a comparison of the speedup and the loss in retrieval, with the brute-force as a baseline.

Graph-Based ANN

An emerging trend in ANNs is using graph-based methods. Lately, *hierarchical navigable small worlds* is a particularly popular approach. This graph algorithm (*https://oreil.ly/Z2ohy*) encodes proximity in multilayer structures and then relies on the common maxim that "the number of connectivity steps from one node to another is often surprisingly small." In graph-based ANN methods, you often find one neighbor, and then traverse the edges connected to that neighbor to rapidly find others.

Cheaper Retrieval Methods

If your corpus has the ability to do an item-wise cheap retrieval method, one way to speed up searches is to use the cheap retrieval method to obtain a small subset of items and then use the more expensive vector-based methods to rank the subset. One such cheap retrieval method is to make a posting list of the top co-occurrences of one item with another. Then when it comes to generating the candidates for ranking, gather all the top co-occurring items together (from a user's preferred items, for example) and then score them together with the ML model. In this way, we do not have to score the entire corpus with the ML model but just a small subset.

Summary

In this chapter, we showed a few ways to speed up the retrieval and scoring of items in a corpus, given a query vector, without losing too much in terms of recall and while still maintaining precision. No ANN method is perfect, as the acceleration structures depend on the distribution of the data, and this varies from dataset to dataset. We hope that this chapter provides a launching pad for you to explore various ways to make retrieval faster and sublinear in the number of items in the corpus.

## PART V

The Future of Recs

I'm hungry for more. What are companies doing in Prod?

We've come so far, but there's so much more! RecSys moves fast, and it's worth knowing the concepts you'll see at next year's conferences. These ideas are already proven to some extent—none of them are pure science fiction—but they haven't settled into their final forms yet.

Before we get into these few very modern ideas, it's also worth noting all the topics we haven't covered in this book. Our most heinous omissions are probably reinforcement learning techniques and ideas related to conformal methods. Both are deeply important aspects of recommendation systems, but both also require a significantly different background and treatment, and thus are ill-suited to fit into the structure here. Additionally, neither is well introduced to the JAX ecosystem, and thus they are a much harder lift to scaffold.

When your scale is big enough, and the previous chapters are no longer buttering your toast, the following chapters will show you how to level up. At the time of writing, all these methods are in production at Fortune 500 companies valued at more than $10 billion. Learn these concepts and then go build the next TikTok.

## CHAPTER 17

Sequential Recommenders

In our journey so far, you've learned about a variety of features that appear as explicit or as latent components in the recommendation problem. One kind of feature, which has appeared implicitly, is the history of previous recommendations and interactions. You may wish to protest here: "All of the work we've done so far considers the previous recommendations and interactions! We've even learned about prequential training data."

That is true, but it fails to account for more explicit relationships between the *sequence of recommendations leading up to the inference request*. Let's look at an example to distinguish the two. Your video-streaming website knows that you've previously seen all of Darren Aronofsky's films, so when *The Whale* is released, the website is very likely to recommend it. But this type of recommendation is different from one you might receive after finishing episode 10 of *Succession*. You may have been watching Aronofsky films over a long time period—*Pi* many years ago and *Black Swan* earlier this year. But you have been watching an episode of *Succession* each night this week, and your entire recent history is made up of Logan Roy. This latter example is a sequential recommendation problem: using the most recent ordered list of interactions to predict what you'll enjoy next.

In terms of the modeling objective, the recommenders we've seen use pairwise relationships between potential recommendations and historical interactions. Sequential recommendation aims to predict users' next actions based on the sequential interactions in the past that may be of much higher *order*—i.e., combinations of interactions among three or more items. Most sequential recommendation models involve sequential data-mining techniques such as Markov chains, recurrent neural networks (RNNs), and self-attention. These models usually take into consideration short-term user behavior and are less sensitive, even oblivious, to the global user preferences that have stabilized over time.

Initial work in sequential recommendations focused on modeling the transitions between successive items. These used Markov chains and translation-based methods. As deep learning methods showed more and more promise in modeling sequential data—such as their biggest success in NLP—there have been many attempts to use neural network architectures to model sequential dynamics of a user's interaction history. Early successes in this direction include GRU4Rec using an RNN to model users' sequential interactions. Recently, transformer architectures have demonstrated superior performance for sequential data modeling. The transformer architecture lends itself to efficient parallelization and is effective at modeling long-range sequences.

Markov Chains

Despite mining for relationships to historical recommendations, the models we've been considering often fail to capture sequential patterns in user behavior, thereby disregarding the chronological order of user interactions. To address this shortcoming, sequential recommender systems were developed, incorporating techniques like Markov chains to model the temporal dependencies between items.

A *Markov chain* is a stochastic model that operates on the principle of *memorylessness*. It models the probability of transitioning from one state to another—given the current state—without considering the sequence of preceding events. Markov chains model the sequential behavior of users by considering each state as an item, and the transition probabilities as the likelihood of a user interacting with a certain item after the current one.

The first-order Markov chain, in which the future state depends solely on the current state, was a common strategy in early sequential recommenders. Despite its simplicity, the first-order Markov chain is effective in capturing short-term, item-to-item transition patterns, improving the quality of recommendations over nonsequential methods.

Take, for example, our preceding *Succession* example. If you're using only a first-order Markov chain, a really great heuristic would be "What is the next episode in the series, if it's a series; otherwise, fall back on a collaborative filtering (CF) model." You can see that for a huge percentage of watch hours, this naive first-order chain would simply tell the user to watch the next episode of a show. Not particularly enlightening, but a good sign. When you abstract this out further, you start to get more powerful methods.

The first-order assumption does not always hold in real-world applications, as user behavior is often influenced by a longer history of interactions. To overcome this limitation, higher-order Markov chains look further back: the next state is determined by a set of previous states, providing a richer model of user behavior. Nevertheless, it's crucial to select the appropriate order, as too high an order may lead to overfitting and sparsity of the transition matrix.

Order-Two Markov Chain

Let's consider an example of an *order-two Markov chain* model using the weather. Assume we have three states: sunny (S), cloudy (C), and rainy (R).

In an order-two Markov chain, the weather of today (t) would depend on the weather of yesterday ($t - 1$) and the day before yesterday ($t - 2$). The transition probability can be denoted as $P(S_t | S_{t-1}, S_{t-2})$.

The Markov chain can be defined by a transition matrix that provides the probabilities of transitioning from one state to another. However, because we're dealing with an order-two Markov chain, we would have a transition tensor instead. For simplicity, let's say we have the following transition probabilities:

$$P(S|S,S) = 0.7, P(C|S,S) = 0.2, P(R|S,S) = 0.1,$$
$$P(S|S,C) = 0.3, P(C|S,C) = 0.4, P(R|S,C) = 0.3,$$

$$\ldots$$

You can visualize these probabilities in a three-dimensional cube. The first two dimensions represent the state of today and yesterday, and the third dimension represents the possible states of tomorrow.

If the weather was sunny for the last two days and we want to predict the weather for tomorrow, we would look at the transition probabilities starting with (S, S), which are $P(S|S,S) = 0.7$, $P(C|S,S) = 0.2$, and $P(R|S,S) = 0.1$. Therefore, according to our model, there's a 70% chance that it will be sunny, a 20% chance that it will be cloudy, and a 10% chance that it will be rainy.

The probabilities in the transition matrix (or tensor) are typically estimated from data. If you have a historical record of the weather for several years, you can count the number of times each transition occurs and divide by the total number of transitions to estimate the probability.

This is only a basic demonstration of an order-two Markov chain. In real applications, the states might be much more numerous and the transition matrix much larger, but the principles remain the same.

Other Markov Models

A more advanced Markovian approach is the *Markov decision process* (*MDP*), which extends the Markov chain by introducing actions and rewards. In the context of recommender systems, each action could represent a recommendation, and the reward could be the user's response to the recommendation. By incorporating user feedback, the MDP can learn more personalized recommendation strategies.

MDPs are defined by a tuple (S, A, P, R), where S is the set of states, A is the set of actions, P is the state transition probability matrix, and R is the reward function.

Let's use a simplified MDP for a movie recommender system as an example:

States (S)
These could represent the genres of movies a user has watched in the past. For simplicity, let's say we have three states: Comedy (C), Drama (D), and Action (A).

Actions (A)
These could represent the movies that can be recommended. For this example, let's say we have five actions (movies): Movies 1, 2, 3, 4, and 5.

Transition probabilities (P)
This represents the likelihood of transitioning from one state to another, given a specific action. For instance, if the user just watched a Drama (D) and we recommend Movie 3 (which is an Action movie), the transition probability $P(A|D, Movie3)$ might be 0.6, indicating a 60% chance the user will watch another Action movie.

Rewards (R)
This is the feedback from the user after taking an action (recommendation). Let's assume for simplicity that a user's click on a recommended movie gives a reward of +1 and no click is a reward of 0.

The aim of the recommender system in this context is to learn a policy $\pi: S \rightarrow A$ that maximizes the expected cumulative reward. A policy dictates which action the agent (the recommender system) should take in each state.

This policy can be learned via reinforcement learning algorithms, such as Q-learning or policy iteration, which essentially learn the value of taking an action in a state (i.e., recommending a movie after the user has watched a certain genre), considering the immediate reward and the potential future rewards.

The main challenge in a real-world recommender system scenario is that both the state and action spaces are extremely large, and the transition dynamics and reward function can be complex and difficult to estimate accurately. But, the principles demonstrated in this simple example remain the same.

Despite the promising performance of Markov chain-based recommender systems, several challenges remain. The *memorylessness* assumption of the Markov chain may not hold in certain scenarios where long-term dependencies exist. Furthermore, most Markov chain models treat user-item interactions as binary events (either interaction or no interaction), which oversimplifies the variety of interactions users may have with items, such as browsing, clicking, and purchasing.

Next, we'll cover neural networks. We'll see how some architectures you're likely familiar with can be relevant to learning a sequential recommender task.

RNN and CNN Architectures

Recurrent neural networks (RNNs) are a type of neural network architecture designed to recognize patterns in sequences of data, such as text, speech, or time series data. These networks are *recurrent* in that the outputs from one step in the sequence are fed back into the network as inputs while processing the next step. This gives RNNs a form of memory, which is helpful for tasks like language modeling, where each word depends on the previous words.

At each time step, an RNN takes in an input (like a word in a sentence) and produces an output (like a prediction of the next word). It also updates its internal state, which is a representation of what it has "seen" last in the sequence. This internal state is passed back into the network when processing the next input. As a result, the network can use information from previous steps to influence its predictions for the current step. This is what allows RNNs to effectively process sequential data.

GRU4Rec (*https://oreil.ly/OwEFj*) used recurrent neural networks to model session-based recommendations in one of the first applications of neural network architectures to the recommendation problem. A *session* refers to a single contiguous period of user interaction, like time spent on a page without the user navigating away or turning off their computer.

Here we will see a dramatic advantage of sequential recommendation systems: most traditional recommendation methods rely on an explicit user ID to build a user-interest profile. However, session-based recommendations operate over anonymous user sessions that are often quite short to allow for a profile modeling. Moreover, a lot of variance can occur in user motivations in different sessions. A solution via user-agnostic recommendation that works for such recommendation situations is an item-based model in which an item-item similarity matrix is calculated based on items co-occurring within a single session. This precomputed similarity matrix is employed at runtime to recommend the most similar item to the one last clicked. This approach has obvious limitations such as relying only on the last clicked item. To this end, GRU4Rec uses all the items in the session and models the session as a sequence of items. The task of recommending items to be added translates to the prediction of the next item in the sequence.

Unlike the small fixed-size vocabulary of languages, recommendation systems are required to reason over a large number of items that grows over time as more items are added. To handle this concern, pairwise ranking losses (e.g., BPR) are considered. GRU4Rec is further extended in GRU4Rec+ (*https://oreil.ly/Y17DB*), which utilizes a new loss function specifically designed for gains in top-*k* recommendation. These loss functions blend deep learning and LTR to address neural recommendation settings.

A different approach to neural networks for recommendations adopted CNNs for sequential recommendation. We won't cover the basics of CNNs here, but you can consult "How Do Convolutional Neural Networks Work?" (*https://oreil.ly/-jEiE*) by Brandon Rohrer for the essentials.

Let's discuss one method that has shown a lot of success, CosRec (*https://oreil.ly/wlCdN*), as visualized in Figure 17-1. This method (and others) starts with a structure similar to that of our MF used throughout most of the book: a user-item matrix. We assume that there are two latent factor matrices, $E_{\mathcal{I}}$ and $E_{\mathcal{U}}$, but let's first focus on the item matrix.

Each vector in the item matrix is an embedding vector for a single item, but we wish to encode sequences: take sequences of length L and collect those embedding vectors. We now have an $L \times D$ matrix with a row per each item in the sequence. Take adjacent rows as pairs and concatenate them for each vector in a three-tensor; this effectively captures the sequence as a series of pairwise transitions. This three-tensor can be passed through a vectorized 2D CNN to yield a vector (of length L) that is concatenated with the original user vector and fed through a fully connected layer. Finally, binary cross-entropy is our loss function to attempt to predict the best recommendation.

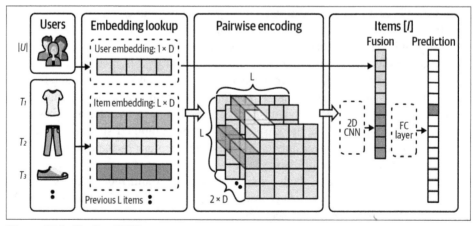

Figure 17-1. CosRec CNN

Attention Architectures

A term that is commonly associated with neural networks and that may ring a bell for you by now is *attention*. This is because transformers, in particular the kind that appear in large language models (LLMs) like the generalized pretrained transformer, have become a central focus among AI users.

We will give an extremely brief, and less technical, introduction to self-attention and the transformer here. For a more complete guide on transformers, consult the excellent overview in "Transformers from Scratch" (*https://oreil.ly/4PSx-*) by Brandon Rohrer.

First, let's state the key differentiating assumption about a transformer model: the embeddings are positional. We're hoping to learn not only one embedding for every item but also an embedding for every item-position pair. Therefore, when an article is the first in a session and the last in a session, those two instances are treated as *two separate items.*

Another important notion is stacking. When building transformers, we often think of the architecture as a layer cake, with sections stacked on top of one another. The key components are the embeddings, the self-attention layer, the skip-addition, and the feed-forward layer. The most complicated operations happen in self-attention, so let's focus on that first. We just discussed the positional embeddings, which are sent as a sequence of these embedding vectors; recall that a transformer is a sequence-to-sequence model! The skip-addition means that we push the embedding forward *around* the self-attention layer (and the feed-forward layer above) and add it to the positional output of the attention layer. The feed-forward layer is an unexciting multilayer perceptron that stays in the positional columns and uses a ReLU or GeLU activation.

ReLU Versus GeLU

ReLU (Rectified Linear Unit) is an activation function defined as $f(x) = \max(0, x)$. GeLU (Gaussian Error Linear Unit) is another activation function approximated as $f(x) = 0.5x\left(1 + \tanh\left(\sqrt{\frac{2}{\pi}}\left(x + 0.044715x^3\right)\right)\right)$, inspired by the Gaussian cumulative distribution function. The intuition behind GeLU is that it tends to allow small values of x to pass through while smoothly saturating extreme values, potentially enabling better gradient flow for deep models. Both functions introduce nonlinearity in neural networks, with GeLU often demonstrating improved learning dynamics over ReLU in certain contexts.

Here are some quick tips on self-attention:

- The idea behind self-attention is that everything in the sequence affects everything else, in some manner.

- The self-attention layer is learning four weight matrices per head.

- The heads are in 1-1 correspondence with the sequence length.

- We often call the weight matrices Q, K, O, V. Both Q and K get crossed with the positional embedding, but O and V are first crossed into an embedding-dimension-sized square matrix before dotting with the embedding. $Q\dot{E}$ and $K\dot{E}$ multiply to create the eponymous *attention* matrix, over which we take a row-wise softmax to get the attention vector.

- Some normalizations exist, but we'll disregard them as inessential for understanding.

When we want to speak accurately but briefly about attention, we usually say, "It takes a sequence of positional embeddings and mushes them all together to learn how they're related."

Self-Attentive Sequential Recommendation

SASRec (*https://oreil.ly/aKKzg*) is the first transformer model we'll consider. This autoregressive sequential model (similar to a causal language model) predicts the next user interaction from past user interactions. Inspired by the success of the transformer models in sequential mining tasks, the self-attention-based architecture is used for sequential recommendation.

When we say that the SASRec model is trained in an autoregressive manner, we mean that the self-attention is allowed to attend to only the earlier positions in the sequence; looking into the future is not permitted. In terms of the mushing we referenced earlier, think of this as only mushing forward the influence. Some people call this "causal" because it respects the causal arrow of time. The model also allows for a learnable positional encoding, which means that the updates carry down to the embedding layer. This model uses two transformer blocks.

BERT4Rec

Inspired by the BERT model in NLP, BERT4Rec (*https://oreil.ly/SH9ON*) improves upon SASRec by training a bidirectional masked sequential (language) model.

While BERT uses a masked language model for pretraining word embeddings, BERT4Rec uses this architecture to train end-to-end recommendation systems. It tries to predict the masked items in the user-interaction sequence. Similar to the original BERT model, the self-attention is bidirectional: it can look at both past and future interactions in the action sequence. To prevent leakage of future information and to emulate the realistic settings, only the last item in the sequence is masked during inference. Using item masking, BERT4Rec outperforms SASRec. However, a drawback of the BERT4Rec model is that it is quite compute intensive and requires much more training time.

Recency Sampling

Sequential recommendation and the adoption of transformer architecture in these tasks has seen a lot of interest recently. These deep neural network models like BERT4Rec and SASRec have shown improved performance over traditional approaches. However, these models suffer from slow training problems. A recently published paper—ha ha, get it—addresses the question of improving training efficiency while achieving state-of-the-art performance. See "Effective and Efficient Training for Sequential Recommendation Using Recency Sampling" (*https://oreil.ly/yV4ro*) by Aleksandr Petrov and Craig Macdonald for details.

The two training paradigms we've just described for sequential models are autoregressive, which tries to predict the next item in the user-interaction sequence, and masked, which tries to predict masked items in the interaction sequence. The autoregressive approach doesn't use the beginning of the sequence as labels in the training process, and thus valuable information is lost. The masked approach, on the other hand, is only weakly related to the end goal of the sequential recommendation.

The paper by Petrov and Macdonald proposes a recency-based sampling of positive examples from the sequences to build the training data. The sampling is designed to give more recent interactions higher chances of being sampled. However, because of the probabilistic nature of the sampling mechanism, even the oldest of the interactions have nonzero chances of being chosen. An exponential function is employed as a sampling routine that interpolates between the masking-based sampling, where each interaction has equal probability of being sampled, and autoregressive sampling, where items from the end of the sequence are sampled. This showed superior performance in sequential recommendation tasks while requiring much less training time. Compare this approach to some of the other examples where we saw sampling provide significant improvements in training recommender systems!

Merging Static and Sequential

Pinterest recently released "Rethinking Personalized Ranking at Pinterest: An End-to-End Approach" (*https://oreil.ly/r_kPN*) by Jiajing Xu et al. describing its personalized recommendation system, which is built to leverage raw user actions. The recommendation task is decomposed into modeling users' long-term and short-term intentions.

The process of comprehending long-term user interests is accomplished by training an end-to-end embedding model, referred to as PinnerFormer, to learn from a user's historical actions on the platform. These actions are subsequently transformed into user embeddings, which are designed for optimization based on anticipated long-term future user activities.

This procedure employs an adapted transformer model to operate on users' sequential actions with the intent to forecast their long-term future activities. Each user's activity is compiled into a sequence, encompassing their actions over a specific time window, such as one year. The graph neural network–based (GNN-based) PinnerSage embeddings, in conjunction with relevant metadata (for example, the type of action, the timestamp, and so forth), are used to add features to each action in the sequence.

Distinct from traditional sequential modeling tasks and sequential recommendation systems, PinnerFormer is designed to predict extended future user activities rather than the immediately subsequent action. This objective is achieved by training the model to foresee a user's positive future interactions over a window of 14 days following the embedding's generation. In comparison, traditional sequential models would anticipate only the subsequent action.

This alternate approach allows for the embedding generation to occur offline in a batch-processing mode, resulting in significant reductions in infrastructure needs. In contrast to most traditional sequential modeling systems, which operate in real time and incur substantial computational and infrastructure costs, these embeddings can be produced in batches (for instance, on a daily basis) rather than every time a user performs an action.

A dense all-action loss is introduced in this methodology to facilitate batch training of the model. The objective here is not to predict the immediate next action but rather all the actions the user will undertake over the subsequent k days. The aim is to predict all occurrences of a user's positive interactions at intervals such as $T + 3$, $T + 8$, and $T + 12$, thereby compelling the system to learn long-term intentions. While traditionally the last action's embedding is used to make the prediction, the dense all-action loss employs randomly selected positions in the action sequence, and the corresponding embedding is used to predict all actions for each of those positions.

Based on offline and online experimental results, the use of dense all-action loss to train for long-term user actions has significantly bridged the gap between batch generation and real-time generation of user embeddings. Moreover, to accommodate users' short-term interests, the transformer model retrieves the most recent actions for each user in real time, processing them along with the long-term user embeddings.

Summary

Transformers and sequential recommendation systems are really at the cutting edge of modern recommenders. These days, most research in recommendation systems is in the area of sequential datasets, and the hottest recommenders are using longer and longer sequences for prediction. Two important projects are worthy of attention:

Transformers4Rec
> This open source project is geared toward scalable transformer models by the NVIDIA Merlin team. For more details, see "Transformers4Rec: Bridging the Gap Between NLP and Sequential/Session-Based Recommendation" (*https://oreil.ly/jwWBq*) by Gabriel de Souza Pereira Moreira et al.

Monolith
> Also known as the TikTok For You page recommender, this is one of the most popular and exciting recommendation systems at this time. It is a fundamentally sequential recommender, with some elegant hybrid approaches. "Monolith: Real-Time Recommendation System with Collisionless Embedding Table" (*https://oreil.ly/EADgK*) by Zhuoran Liu et al. covers the architectural considerations.

Our final step before this book concludes is to consider a few approaches to recommendations. These don't build exactly on top of what we've done but will use some of what we've done and introduce a few new ideas. Let's sprint to the finish!

## CHAPTER 18

What's Next for Recs?

We find ourselves in a transitionary time for recommendation systems. However, this is quite normal for this field, as it is in many segments of the tech industry. One of the realities of a field that is so closely aligned with business objectives and with such strong capabilities for business value is that the field tends to be constantly searching for any and all opportunities to advance.

In this chapter, we'll briefly introduce some of the modern views of where recommendation systems are going. An important point to consider is that recommendation systems as a science spread both depth first and breadth first simultaneously. Looking at the most cutting-edge research in the field means that you're seeing deep optimization in areas that have been under study for decades or areas that seem like pure fantasy for now.

We've chosen three areas to focus on in this final chapter. The first you've seen a bit of throughout this text: multimodal recommendations. This area is increasingly important as users turn to platforms to do more things. Recall that multimodal recommendations occur when a user is represented by several latent vectors simultaneously.

Next up is graph-based recommenders. We've discussed co-occurrence models, which are the simplest such models for graph-based recommendation systems. They go much deeper! GNNs are becoming an incredibly powerful mechanism for encoding relations between entities and utilizing these representations, making them useful for recommendations.

Finally, we'll turn our attention to large language models and generative AI. During the writing of this book, LLMs have gone from something that a small subset of ML experts understood to something mentioned on HBO comedy broadcasts. While a rush is occurring to find relevant applications of LLMs to recommendation systems, the industry already has confidence in applying these tools in certain ways. Also exciting, however, is the application of recommendation systems to LLM apps.

Let's see what's coming next!

Multimodal Recommendations

Multimodal recommenders allow for the concession that *users contain multitudes*: a single representation for a user's preferences may not capture the entire story. Someone shopping on a large everything-ecommerce website, for example, may be all of the following:

- A dog owner who frequently needs items for their dog
- A parent who is always updating the closet for the growing baby
- A hobbyist race-car driver who buys the pieces necessary to drive their car on a track
- A LEGO investor who keeps hundreds of sealed boxes of Star Wars sets hidden away in the closet

The methods you've learned throughout this book should do well at providing recommendations for all of these users. However, you may notice in this list a few areas that are conflicting:

- If your child is very young, why do you buy LEGO sets already? Also, doesn't your dog chew on them?
- If your garage is full of LEGO sets, where do you keep all these car parts?
- Where do you put your dog in that two-seater Mazdaspeed MX-5 Miata?

You can probably think of other cases where some aspects of what you buy just don't match up well with others. This leads to a problem of multimodality: several places in the latent space of your interests coalesce into modes or medoids, but not only one.

Let's return to some of our geometric discussions from before: if you are using nearest neighbors to a user vector, then which of the medoids will take on the most importance?

The way we approach this problem is by multimodality, or providing several vectors associated to a single user. While a naive approach to scaling to consider all the modes for a user would be to simply increase the dimensionality of the model on the item side (to create more areas in which different types of items can be embedded disjointly), this presents serious challenges at scale in terms of training and memory concerns.

One of the first significant works in this area is coauthored by one of this book's authors and introduces an extension to MF to deal with this; see "Nonlinear Latent Factorization by Embedding Multiple User Interests" (*https://oreil.ly/OkzmZ*) by Jason Weston et al. The goal is to build multiple latent factors simultaneously as we did in our other matrix factorization methods, each factor hopefully taking on representation for one of the user's interests.

This is achieved by constructing a tensor that has its third tensor dimension represent each of the latent factors for distinct interests rather than encoding a user item factorization matrix. The factorization is generalized to the tensor case, and the WSABIE loss you saw earlier is used to train.

Building on this work, several years later Pinterest released PinnerSage, as we mentioned in Chapter 15. This modifies some of the assumptions of the Weston et al. paper, by not assuming a known number of representations for each user. Additionally, this approach uses graph-based feature representations, which we'll talk more about in the next section. Finally, the last important modification that this method uses is clustering: it attempts to build the modes via clustering in item space.

The basic PinnerSage approach is to do the following:

1. Fix item embeddings (they call these *pins*).
2. Cluster user interactions (unsupervised and unspecified in cardinality).
3. Build cluster representations as the medoid of the cluster embeddings.
4. Retrieve using medoid-anchored ANN search.

PinnerSage is still considered to be near state of the art for large-scale multimodal recommenders. Some systems take another approach to allow users to more directly modify their "mode" by selecting the theme of what they're looking for, while others hope to learn it from a sequence of interactions.

Next up, we'll look at how higher-order relationships between items or users can be explicitly specified.

Graph-Based Recommenders

Graph neural networks (GNNs) are a class of neural networks that use the structural information of data to build deeper representations of your data. They've proven especially useful when dealing with relational or networked data, both of which have utility.

One moment of disambiguation before we continue: *graphs* in the sense that we will use them here refer to collections of *nodes* and *edges*. These are purely mathematical concepts, but generally we can think of nodes as the objects of interest and edges as the relationships between them. These mathematical objects are useful for distilling down the core of what is necessary for the kind of representation you wish to build. While the objects may seem very simple, we can add just the right amount of complexity in a variety of ways to capture more nuance.

In the simplest setups, each node on the graph represents an item or user, and each edge represents a relationship such as a user's interaction with an item. However, user-to-user and item-to-item networks are extremely powerful extensions as well. Our co-occurrence models are simple graph networks; however, we did not learn a representation from these and instead directly took these as our models.

Let's consider a few examples of adding more structure to a graph to encode ideas:

Directionality
This ordering on an edge's vertices can be added to indicate a strict relationship of one node acting on the other; e.g., a user *reads* a book but not the other way around.

Edge decorations
Descriptors such as edge labels can be added to communicate features about the relationships; e.g., two users share account credentials, *and one of the users is identified as a child*.

Multiedges
These can allow for relationships to have higher multiplicity, or allow for the same two entities to have multiple relationships. In a graph of outfits with clothing items as nodes, each edge can be another clothing item that makes the other two go well together.

Hyper-edges
A step further up the level of abstraction may add these edges, which connect multiple nodes simultaneously. For video scenes, you may detect objects of various classes, and your graph may have nodes for those classes, but understanding not only which pairs of object classes appear but which higher-order combinations appear can be identified with hyper-edges.

Let's explore the basics of GNNs and how their representations are a bit different.

Neural Message Passing

In GNNs our object of interest is assigned as the nodes in our graph. Usually, the main objective in GNNs is to build powerful representations of the nodes and edges, or both, via their relationships.

The fundamental difference between GNNs and traditional neural networks is that during the training, we're explicitly using operators that transfer data between node representations "along the edges." This is called *message passing*. Let's start with an example to prime the basic idea.

Let nodes represent users, and their features are persona details such as demographic, onboarding survey question, etc. Let edges be the social network graph: are they friends? And let's add decoration to the edges, such as the number of DMs exchanged between them on the platform. If we are the social media company that wants to introduce ad shopping to our platform, we may start with those persona features, but we'd ideally like to use something about this network of communication. In theory, people who communicate and share content with each other a lot may have similar tastes. Somewhat tellingly, we introduce a concept called a *message function*, which allows features to be sent from node to node. The message function uses features from each node and the edge between them, written mathematically as follows, for $h_i^{(k)}$ the features at node i and $h_j^{(k)}$ at node j, respectively:

$$m_{ij}^{(k)} = \mathcal{M}\left(h_i^{(k)}, h_j^{(k)}, e_{ij}\right)$$

The features of the edge are e_{ij} and $\mathcal{M}$ is some differentiable function. Note that the superscript (k) refers to the layer as is standard in back-prop notation. Here are two simple examples:

- $m_{ij}^{(k)} = h_i^{(k)}$ means "take the features from a neighbor node"
- $m_{ij}^{(k)} = \dfrac{h_i^{(k)}}{c_{ij}}$ means "average by the number of edges between i and j"

Many powerful message-passing schemes that use learning use approaches from other areas of ML—like adding an attention mechanism on node features—but this book doesn't dive deep into this theory.

The next function we'll introduce is the *aggregation function*, which takes as input the collection of messages and aggregates them. The most common types of aggregation functions do the following:

- Concatenate all the messages
- Sum all the messages
- Average all the messages
- Take the max of the messages

Finally, we will use the output of the aggregation as part of our update function, which takes node features and aggregated message functions and then applies additional transformations. If you've been wondering, "Where does this model learn anything?" the answer is in the update function. The update function usually has a weight matrix associated to it, so as you train this neural network, you are learning the weights in the update function. The simplest update functions multiply a weight matrix by the vectorized output of your aggregation and then apply an activation function per vector.

This chain of message passing, aggregating, and updating is the core of GNNs and encompasses a broad capability. They've been useful for ML tasks of every kind, including recommendations. Let's see some direct applications to recommendation systems.

Applications

Let's revisit some of the high-level ideas that GNNs may touch in the RecSys space.

Modeling user-item interactions

In other methods we've presented, such as matrix factorization, the interactions between users and items are considered, but the complex network among users or items is not exploited. In contrast, GNNs can capture the complex connections in the user-item interaction graph and then use the structure of this graph to make more accurate recommendations.

Thinking back to our message passing, it allowed us to "spread" the information of some nodes (in this case, user and items) to their neighbors. An analogy for this would be that as a user interacts more and more with items with specific features, some of those features are imbued onto the user. This may sound similar to latent features, because it is! These are ultimately helping the network build a latent representation from the messages that pass features from items to user. This can be even more powerful than other latent embedding methods, because you explicitly define the structural relationships and how they communicate these features.

Feature learning

GNNs can learn more expressive feature representations of nodes (users or items) in a graph by aggregating feature information from their neighbors, leveraging the connections between nodes. These learned features can provide rich information about users' preferences or items' characteristics, which can greatly enhance the performance of recommendation systems.

Previously, we talked about how a user's representations can learn from the items they interact with, but items can also learn from one another. Similar to the way item-item collaborative filtering (CF) allows items to pick up latent features from shared users, GNNs allow us to add potentially many other direct relationships between items.

Cold-start problem

Recall our cold-start problem: providing recommendations for new users or items is difficult because of the lack of historical interactions. By using the features of nodes and the structure of the graph, GNNs can learn the embeddings for new users or items, potentially alleviating the cold-start problem.

In some of our graphical representations of our user graph, the edges need not only exist between users with lots of prior recommendations. It's possible to use other user actions to *bootstrap* some early edges. Structural edges like "share a physical location" or "invited by the same user" or "answers onboarding questions similarly" can be enough to quickly bootstrap several user-user edges, which allow us to warm-start recommendations for them.

Context-aware recommendations

GNNs can incorporate contextual information into the recommendation process. For example, in a session-based recommendation, a GNN can model the sequence of items a user has interacted with in a session as a graph, where each item is a node and the sequential order forms edges. The GNN can then learn the dynamic and complex transitions among items to make context-aware recommendations.

These high-level ideas should point to the opportunity in graph encoding for recommender problems, but let's look at two specific applications next: random walks and metapaths.

Random Walks

Random walks in GNNs enable methods to use the user-item interaction graph to learn effective node (i.e., user or item) embeddings. The embeddings are then used to make recommendations. In the context of graphs, a random walk is an iterative process of starting on a particular node and then stochastically moving to another connected node via a randomized choice.

One popular random-walk-based algorithm for network embedding is DeepWalk, which has been adapted and extended in many ways for various tasks, including recommendation systems.

Here's how a random-walk GNN approach might work in a recommendation context:

1. Random walks generation: start by performing random walks on the interaction graph. Starting from each node, make a series of random steps to other connected nodes. This results in a set of paths, or "walks," that represent the relationships between different nodes.

2. Node embeddings: the sequences of nodes generated by the random walks are treated similar to sentences in a corpus of text, and each node is treated like a word. Word2vec or similar language-modeling techniques are then used to learn embeddings for the nodes (vector representations), such that nodes appearing in similar contexts (in the same walks) have similar embeddings.

3. Recommendations: once you have learned node embeddings, you can use them to make recommendations. For a given user, you might recommend items that are "close" to that user in the embedding space, according to a distance metric. This can use all the techniques we've previously developed for recommendations from latent space representations.

This approach has some nice properties:

- It can capture the high-order connections in the graph. Each random walk can explore a part of the graph that's not directly connected to the starting node.

- It can help with the sparsity problem in recommender systems because it uses the graph's structure to learn representations, which requires less interaction data.

- It naturally attempts to handle cold-start issues. For new users or items with few interactions, their embeddings can be learned from connected nodes.

Nevertheless, this approach has some challenges. Random walks can be computationally expensive on large graphs, and it might be difficult to choose appropriate hyperparameters, such as the length of the random walks. Also, this approach may not work as well for dynamic graphs, where interactions change over time, since it doesn't inherently consider temporal information.

This method implicitly assumes that the nodes are heterogeneous, and so co-embedding them via connections is natural. While it was not an explicit requirement, the type of sequence embeddings DeepWalk builds tends to structurally assume this. Let's break this rule to accommodate learning between heterogeneous types in our next architecture example, metapaths.

Metapath and Heterogeneity

Metapath (*https://oreil.ly/pZIkC*) was introduced to improve explainable recommendations and integrate the ideas of knowledge graphs with GNNs.

A *metapath* is a path in a heterogeneous network (or graph) that connects different types of nodes via different types of relationships. Heterogeneous networks contain various types of nodes and edges, representing multiple types of objects and interactions. Beyond simply users and items, the node types can be "carts of items" or "viewing sessions" or "channel used for purchase."

Metapaths can be used in GNNs for handling heterogeneous information networks (HINs). These networks provide a more comprehensive representation of the real world. When used in a GNN, a metapath provides a scheme for the way information should be aggregated and propagated through the network. It defines the type of paths to be considered when pooling information from a node's neighborhood.

For example, in a recommender system, you might have a heterogeneous network with users, movies, and genres as node types, and "watches" and "belongs to" as edge types. A metapath could be defined as "User - watches → Movie - belongs to → Genre - belongs to → Movie - watches → User." This metapath represents a way of connecting two users through the movies they watch and the genres of those movies.

A popular method that utilizes metapaths is the heterogeneous GNN (Hetero-GNN) and its variants. These models leverage the metapath concept to capture the rich semantics in HINs, enhancing the learning of node representations.

Metapath-based models have shown promising results in various applications, as they allow you to explicitly encode much more abstract relationships into the message-passing mechanisms we've mentioned.

If higher-order modeling is your thing, buckle up for the last concept we'll cover in this book. This topic is state of the art and full of high-level abstractions. Language-model-backed agents are at the absolute cutting edge of ML modeling.

LLM Applications

All of the superlatives for LLMs have been used up. For that reason, we'll just say this: LLMs are powerful and have a surprisingly large number of applications.

LLMs are general models that allow users to interact with them via natural language. Fundamentally, these models are generative (they write text) and auto-regressive (what they write is determined by what came before). Because LLMs can speak conversationally, they've been branded as general artificial *agents*. It's natural to then ask, "Can an agent recommend things for me?" Let's start by examining how to use an LLM to make recommendations.

LLM Recommenders

Natural language is a wonderful interface to ask for recommendations. If you want a coworker's recommendation for lunch, maybe you'll show up at their desk and say nothing—hoping they'll remember their latent knowledge of your preferences, identify the time-of-day context, recall the availability of restaurants based on day-of-week, and keep in mind that yesterday you had a pastrami sandwich.

More effectively, you could simply ask, "Any suggestions for lunch?"

Like your astute coworker, models may be more effective at providing recommendations if you simply ask them to. This approach also adds the capability of defining more precisely the kind of recommendation you want. A popular application of LLMs is to ask them for recipes that use a set of ingredients. Thinking through this in the context of the kind of recommenders we've built, building a recommender of this kind has some hurdles. It probably needs some user modeling, but it's very dependent on the items specified. This means that there's a very low signal for each combination of specified items.

An LLM, on the other hand, is quite effective at the autoregressive nature of this task: given a few ingredients, what's most likely to be included next in the context of a recipe. By generating several items like this, a ranking model can augment this to provide a realistic recommender.

LLM Training

Large generative language models of the type that have exploded in popularity are trained in three stages:

1. Pretraining for completion
2. Supervised fine-tuning for dialogue
3. Reinforcement learning from human feedback

Sometimes the latter two steps are combined into what is called *Instruct*. For an exceptionally deep dive into this topic, see the original InstructGPT paper "Training Language Models to Follow Instructions with Human Feedback" (*https://oreil.ly/e-T2J*) by Long Ouyang et al.

Let's recall that text-completion tasks are equivalent to training the model to predict the correct word in a sequence after seeing k previous ones. This may remind you of GloVe from Chapter 8, or our discussion about sequential recommenders.

Next up is fine-tuning for dialogue; this step is necessary to teach the model that the "next word or phrase" should sometimes be a response instead of an extension of the original statement.

During this stage, the data used for this training is in the form of *demonstration data*, i.e., pairs of statements and responses. Examples include the following:

- A request and then a response to that request
- A statement and then a translation of that statement
- A long text and then a summarization of that text

For recommendations, you can imagine that the first is highly relevant to the task we hope the model to demonstrate.

Finally, we move to the reinforcement learning from human feedback (RLHF) stage; the goal here is to learn a reward function that we can later use to further optimize our LLM. However, the reward model *itself* needs to be trained. Interestingly for recommendation systems enthusiasts like yourself, AI engineers do this via a ranking dataset.

A large number of tuples—similar to the demonstration data we've seen—provide statements and responses, although instead of only one response, there are multiple responses. They are ranked (via a human labeler), and then for each pair of superior-inferior responses (x, sup, inf), we evaluate the loss:

- $r_{sup} = \Theta(x, sup)$ is the reward model's score for the superior response.
- $r_{inf} = \Theta(x, inf)$ is the reward model's score for the inferior response.

The final loss is computed: $-log(\sigma(sup - inf))$.

This reward function is then used to fine-tune the model.

OpenAI summarizes this approach via the diagram in Figure 18-1.

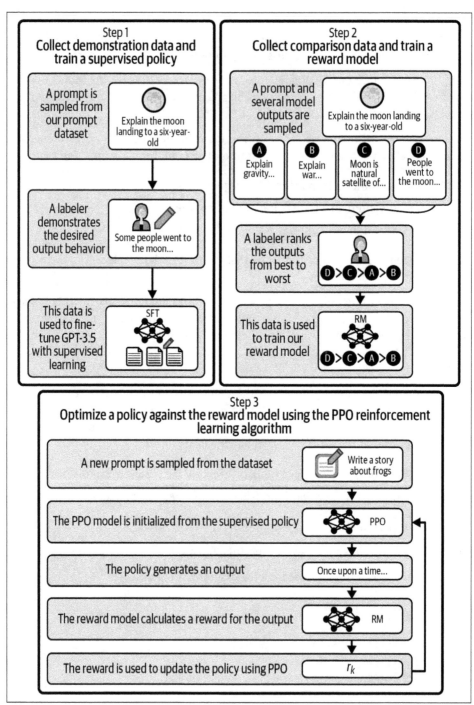

Figure 18-1. Instruct methodology for model fine-tuning

From this brief overview, you can see that these LLMs are trained to respond to requests—something well suited for a recommender. Let's see how to augment this training.

Instruct Tuning for Recommendations

In the previous discussion of instruct pairs, we saw that ultimately the aim of the training was to learn a rank comparison between two responses. This kind of training should feel quite familiar. In "TALLRec: An Effective and Efficient Tuning Framework to Align Large Language Model with Recommendation" (*https://oreil.ly/ViZCT*) by Keqin Bao et al., the authors use a similar setup to teach user preferences to the model.

As the paper mentions, historical interaction items are collected into two groups based on their ratings: user likes and user dislikes. They collect this information into natural language prompts to format a final "Rec Input":

1. User preference: $[item_1, \ldots, item_n]$
2. User preference: $[item_1, \ldots, item_n]$
3. Will the user enjoy the User preference, $[item_{n+1}]$?

These follow the same training pattern as InstructGPT noted previously. The authors achieve dramatically improved performance on recommender problems as compared to an untrained LLM for recommendations; however, those should be considered baselines as it's not their target task.

LLM Rankers

So far in this chapter, we've thought of the LLM as a recommender in totality, but instead, the LLM can be used as simply the ranker. The most trivial approach to this is to simply prompt the LLM with the relevant features of a user and a list of items and ask it to suggest the best options.

While naive, variants on this approach have seen somewhat surprising results in very generic settings: "The user wants to watch a scary movie tonight and isn't sure which will be the best if he doesn't like gore: movie-1, movie-2, etc." But we can do better.

Ultimately, as with LTR approaches, we can think of pointwise, pairwise, and listwise. If we wish to use an LLM for a pointwise ranking, we should constrain our prompting and responses to a setting in which these models may be useful. Take, for example, a recommender for scientific papers; a user may wish to write what they're working on and have the LLM helpfully suggest papers of relevance. While a traditional search problem, this is a setting in which our modern tools can bring a lot of utility: LLMs are effective at summarizing and semantic matching, which means that semantically similar results may be found from a large corpus, and then the agent can synthesize the output of those results into a cogent response. The biggest challenge here is hallucination, or suggesting papers that may not exist.

You can think of pairwise and listwise similarly: distilling the reference data into a shape that the unique capabilities of these LLMs can use to make significant assists.

While we're near the topic of search and retrieval, it's important to mention one of the ways in which recommendation can help LLM applications: retrieval augmentation.

Recommendations for AI

We've seen how LLMs can be used to generate recommendations, but how do recommenders improve LLM applications? LLM agents are extremely general in their capabilities but lack specificity on many tasks. If you ask an agent, "Which of the books I read this year were written by nonwestern authors?" the agent has no chance of success. Fundamentally, this is because the general pretrained models have no idea what books you've read this year.

To solve for this, you'll want to leverage *retrieval augmentation*, i.e., providing relevant information to the model from an existing data store. The data store may be an SQL database, a lookup table, or a vector database, but ultimately the important component here is that somehow from your request, you're able to find relevant information and then provide it to an agent.

One assumption we've made here is that your request is interpretable by your retrieval system. In the preceding example, you'd like the system to automatically understand the "which of the books I read this year" phrase as an information-retrieval task equivalent to something like this:

```
SELECT * FROM read_books
WHERE CAST(finished_date, YEAR) = CAST(today(), YEAR)
```

Here we've just made up an SQL database, but you can imagine schema to satisfy this request. Converting from the request to this SQL is now yet another task you need to model—maybe it's the job of another agent request.

In other contexts, you want a full-scale recommender to help with the retrieval: if you want users to ask an agent for a movie tonight, but also to continue to use your deep understanding of each user's tastes, you could first filter the potential movies by the user's preference and then send only movies your recommender model thinks are great for them. The agent can then service the text request from a subset of movies that are already determined to be great.

The intersection of LLMs and recommendation systems is going to dominate much of the conversation in recommendation systems for a while. There's a lot of low-hanging fruit in bringing the knowledge of recommender systems to this new industry. As Eugene Yan recently said:

> I think the key challenge, and solution, is getting them [LLMs] the right information at the right time. Having a well-organized document store can help. And by using a hybrid of keyword and semantic search, we can accurately retrieve the context that LLMs need.

Summary

The future of recommendation systems is bright, but the technology will continue to get more complicated. One of the major changes over the last five years has been an incredible shift to GPU-based training and the architectures that can use these GPUs. This is the primary motivation for why this book favors JAX over TensorFlow or Torch.

The methods in this chapter embrace bigger models, more interconnections, and potentially inference on a scale that's hard to house in most organizations. Ultimately, recommendation problems will always be solved via the following:

- Careful problem framing
- Deeply relevant representations of users and items
- Thoughtful loss functions that encode the nuances of the task
- Great data collection

Index

About the Authors

Bryan Bischof leads AI at Hex and is an adjunct professor in the Rutgers University Business Analytics master's program, where he teaches data science. Previously, he was the head of data science at Weights & Biases and built the DS, ML, and data engineering teams. He has built recommendation systems for clothing (at Stitch Fix), recommendation systems for technical blog posts (at Weights & Biases), and the world's first recommendation system for coffee (at Blue Bottle Coffee); currently, he is building recommendation systems for AI agents. His research interests are in geometric methods for ML, including higher-order graph methods and topological methods. His data visualization work appears in the popular book *The Day It Finally Happens* by Mike Pearl. His Ph.D. is in pure mathematics. You can find Bryan on LinkedIn at bryan-bischof (*https://www.linkedin.com/in/bryan-bischof/*) and on Twitter at @bebischof (*https://twitter.com/bebischof*).

Hector Yee is a staff software engineer at Google, where he has worked on multiple projects including creating the first content-based ranker on Image Search and self driving car perception. He also worked on the YouTube recommender system and was part of the team that won a technical Emmy Award for their work on personalized video ranking technology. He has an M.S. in computer graphics. You can find Hector on LinkedIn at yeehector (*https://www.linkedin.com/in/yeehector/*) and on Twitter at @eigenhector (*https://twitter.com/eigenhector*).

Colophon

The animal on the cover of *Building Recommendation Systems in Python and JAX* is a European goldfinch (*Carduelis carduelis*). Known for its colorful feathers, this passerine bird (or perching bird) can be found in the open, wooded lowlands of Europe, North Africa, and western and central Asia. It has been introduced to many other countries over the years, including the United States, Canada, Mexico, Peru, Argentina, Australia, and New Zealand. In particular, within the United States, they have established their homes in the western Great Lakes region.

The average European goldfinch is about 4.7–5.1 inches (12–13 centimeters) long, with a wingspan of 8.3–9.8 inches (21–25 centimeters); it weighs roughly 0.5–0.67 ounces. Male and female European goldfinches are similar in appearance, with a red face, black and white head, black and yellow wings, white underparts, and medium-brown upper parts. However, on closer inspection, male European goldfinches can be distinguished by a larger, darker patch of red on their face, and black feathers on their shoulders (whereas the feathers on a female are brown). After breeding season, European goldfinches shed their old feathers to make way for new growth; molt birds appear less colorful at first, but they regain their colors once their feathers regrow.

In terms of diet, European goldfinches prefer small seeds from thistles, cornflowers, and teasels; insects are mostly given to their young. These birds are also known to regularly visit residential gardens in Europe and North America, attracted by the bird feeders that contain seeds. Because of their pleasant songs, European goldfinches are commonly trapped and bred in captivity; there have been wildlife conversation attempts to limit bird trapping and the destruction of open space habitats to protect European goldfinches.

Many of the animals on O'Reilly covers are endangered; all of them are important to the world.

The cover illustration is by Karen Montgomery, based on an antique line engraving from *British Birds*. The cover fonts are Gilroy Semibold and Guardian Sans. The text font is Adobe Minion Pro; the heading font is Adobe Myriad Condensed; and the code font is Dalton Maag's Ubuntu Mono.

Printed in the USA
CPSIA information can be obtained
at www.ICGtesting.com
JSHW051312301223
54574JS00012B/4

9 781492 097990